CHICKEN SOUP FOR THE TEACHER'S SOUL

Stories to Open the Hearts and Rekindle the Spirits of Educators

Jack Canfield
Mark Victor Hansen

Health Communications, Inc.
Deerfield Beach, Florida

www.hci-online.com
www.chickensoup.com

We would like to acknowledge the following publishers and individuals for permission to reprint the following material. (Note: The stories that were penned anonymously, that are public domain, or that were written by Jack Canfield and Mark Victor Hansen are not included in this listing.)

Once Upon a Time . . . ©The Education Center, Inc. Reprinted by permission.

A Random Harvest. Reprinted by permission of James Elwood Conner. ©1998 James Elwood Conner.

Any Kid Can Be a Superstar! Reprinted by permission of Maureen G. Mulvaney. ©1999 Maureen G. Mulvaney.

Encouraging Kelly. Reprinted by permission of Seema Renee Gersten. ©1999 Seema Renee Gersten.

Am I Close? Reprinted by permission of Alice Stolper Peppler. ©2000 Alice Stolper Peppler.

(Continued on page 381)

Library of Congress Cataloging-in-Publication Data

Chicken soup for the teacher's soul : stories to open the hearts and rekindle the spirits of educators / [compiled by] Jack Canfield, Mark Victor Hansen.

p. cm.

ISBN 1-55874-978-0 (TP) —ISBN 1-55874-979-9 (HC)

1. Teachers—Conduct of life. 2. Teaching—Moral and ethical aspects. I. Canfield, Jack, date. II. Hansen, Mark Victor.

LB1775 .C5927 2002
371.1—dc21

2002020893

ISBN 1-55874-978-0 (trade paper) — ISBN 1-55874-979-9 (hardcover)

Publisher: Health Communications, Inc.
3201 S.W. 15th Street
Deerfield Beach, FL 33442-8190

R-06-02

Cover design by Lisa Camp
Inside formatting by Dawn Grove

We dedicate this book to those teachers everywhere who have committed their lives to educating, encouraging and empowering the students of our world.

I also dedicate this book to my teachers—Douglas Haywood, who taught me discipline and self-respect; Katherine Metzner, who challenged me to believe I was smart; David Judy, who believed in and nurtured my ability to write; Gerald Weinstein and Sid Simon, who taught me about the science of the self; Martha Crampton, Marti Glenn and Armand Bytton, who taught me about my internal world; Jack Gibb, who taught me about trust; Robert Resnick, who taught me to take 100 percent responsibility for my life; Bob Reasoner, who taught me to think globally about self-esteem; Dan Sullivan, who taught me to think strategically; and to Lacy Hall, Jim Nugent and Billy Sharp, who taught me that anything is possible.

—Jack

I dedicate this book to John Rhinehart, my sophomore English teacher, who taught me the love of reading; Dr. Buckminster Fuller, who taught me to think comprehensively and the love of making the world work for 100 percent of humanity; Jack Canfield, who taught me to keep on track to get everything done and the love of an ever-expanding book market; and Robert G. Allen, who exposed me to the idea that we can create one million millionaires and change the economic history of the world.

—Mark

"We know you're in there, Mrs. May—we can see you. Open the door."

Contents

Acknowledgments xv
Introduction xix
Share with Us xxi

1. A DAY IN THE LIFE

Once Upon a Time . . . *Joan Gozzi Campbell* 2
A Random Harvest *James Elwood Conner, Ed.D.* 7
Any Kid Can Be a Superstar! *Maureen G. Mulvaney (M.G.M.)* 10
Encouraging Kelly *Seema Renee Gersten* 16
Am I Close? *Alice Stolper Peppler* 20
The Girl in the Fifth Row *Leo Buscaglia* 22
The Teacher *Marion Bond West* 28
Roses in December *Herb Appenzeller, Ed.D.* 34
Danny's Gift *Karen Wasmer* 37
A Great Way to Make a Living *Lee Saye* 39
You Never Picked Me Last *Tee Carr, Ed.D.* 43

2. ANSWERING THE CALL

Why Choose Teaching? *Bonnie Block* 48
Teacher at Last *Eugene Edwards as told to Gloria Cassity Stargel* 51
Full Circle *Erin Kelley* 57

Anna *Isabel Bearman Bucher*.....60
Born a Teacher *Robin Lee Shope*.....64
Begin at the Beginning *Lola De Julio De Maci*.....67
Once a Teacher, Always . . . *Kay Conner Pliszka*.....71

3. LOVE IN THE CLASSROOM

Let's Go, Daddy *Marty Appelbaum*.....75
A Friday Night in May *Carolyn M. Mason*.....78
Love First, Teach Second *Joan Clayton*.....81
All Things Grow . . . with Love *Joan Bramsch*.....85
Sarah *Michele Wallace Campanelli*.....88
A Bear and a Rock *Sharon Wilkins*.....91
I Will Always Love You *Suzanne M. Perry, Ph.D.*.....95
A Couple of Teachers *Marsha Arons*.....98
Coo-Coo-Ca-Choo *Joseph Walker*.....102
The Bad Word Box *Julie Wassom*.....106
Need a Hand? *Suzanne Boyce*.....109

4. DEFINING MOMENTS

That's Just Roscoe *Sue L. Vaughn*.....114
Great Answer *Bonnie Block*.....117
Mother and Child *Patricia A. Habada*.....119
Promises to Keep *Kris Hamm Ross*.....122
Goals and Dreams—A Winning Team *Jodi O'Meara*.....126

5. MAKING A DIFFERENCE

You Elevated My Spirit *Adela Anne Bradlee*.....133
We Never Know *Larry L. Leathers*.....138
The Reader *Leon Lewandowski*.....143
Sergei *Molly Bernard*.....147

A Tribute to Many Uncrowned Kings and Queens
Daniel Eckstein, Ph.D. 150
The Sunday School Teacher *Robin Lee Shope* 153
Every Student Can Learn *Meladee McCarty* 156
Awakening *Beatrice O'Brien* 161
Easter in Jackson *Allison C. Miller* 163
Changing the World—One Clip at a Time *Steve Goodier* 166

6. THE CLASSICS

All the Good Things *Helen P. Mrosla* 170
Miss Hardy *H. Stephen Glenn, Ph.D.* 174
To Beth's First-Grade Teacher *Richard F. Abrahamson, Ph.D.* 178
The Magic Pebbles *John Wayne Schlatter* 182
Mr. Washington *Les Brown* 185
The Royal Knights of Harlem *Gloria Steinem* 189
How Could I Miss? I'm a Teacher *Hanoch McCarty, Ed.D.* 195
A Gift from Brandon *Myrna Flood* 199
I Am a Teacher *John Wayne Schlatter* 202

7. OVERCOMING OBSTACLES

Standing by Mr. Donato *Dennis McCarthy* 207
One of My Early Teaching Jobs *Angela K. Nelson* 210
The Big Kid *Joyce Belle Edelbrock* 215
Only a Shadow in His Past *Melinda Stiles* 219
Let a Miracle Happen *Aletha Jane Lindstrom* 222
Special Needs *Frankie Germany* 227
Moment in the Sun *Joe Edwards* 230
The Substitute's Surprise *Linda L. Osmundson* 234
Miracle in the Gym *Kimberly Ripley* 239
Benjamin *Dori Courtney* 242
The Virtue of Excellence *Linda Kavelin-Popov* 247

8. BEYOND THE CLASSROOM

In Case of Darkness *W. W. Meade* 250
Perils of a Preschool Husband *Roy Freeman* 255
Excellence Is Love in Action *Bettie B. Youngs, Ph.D., Ed.D.* 259
The Poems *Jeff Savage* 266
Positive Reinforcement *Rich Kornoelje* 270
So Little Meant So Much *Beth Teolis* 273
An Ordinary Woman *Marsha Arons* 275

9. LEARNING BY TEACHING

Master Teacher *Marikay Tillett* 280
Brush Strokes *Gail Davis Hopson* 283
A Letter to My Preschoolers *Jennifer L. DePaull* 285
You Can't Judge a William by Its Cover *Mary Chavoustie* 287
Eric *Willanne Ackerman* 292

10. INSIGHTS AND LESSONS

Chuck *Gerard T. Brooker, Ed.D.* 296
The Greatest Lesson *Carol Toussie Weingarten, Ph.D., R.N.* 298
Annie Lee's Gift *Glenda Smithers* 300
Old Miss Mac *Bettie B. Youngs, Ph.D., Ed.D.* 304
The Problem Class *Donald Arney* 312
Permission to Fail *Aletha Jane Lindstrom* 316
Lasting Lessons from a Fifth-Grade Teacher *Terry Miller Shannon* 319
I Touch the Future *Kathy A. Megyeri* 323

11. THANKS

Meeting Josiah *Denaé Adams Bowen* 328
Gifts of Love on Valentine's Day *Jodi O'Meara* 333
A Note in My Mailbox *Ron Wenn and Nancy J. Cavanaugh* 336
A Humble Gift *Amanda Krug* 340

Hall of Fame *Debra Peppers, Ph.D.* 342
A Typical Day *Brian Totzke* 346
Start Your Engine *Christina Cheakalos and Kenneth Baker* 349
A Very Special Delivery *Pauline Moller* 352
What I Learned in Spite of Myself *MaryJanice Davidson* 355
Yours Are the Hands . . . *Julie Sykes* 360

More Chicken Soup? 363
Supporting Teachers Around the World 364
Who Is Jack Canfield? 365
Who Is Mark Victor Hansen? 366
Jack Canfield's Teacher Resources 367
Contributors 368
Permissions *(continued)* 381

Acknowledgments

Chicken Soup for the Teacher's Soul was a joy to produce. It has been a labor of love for all of us. Without the love and support of our families, friends and publisher, this book would never have happened. We would like to acknowledge all of you who continue to love and support us, and allow us the time and space to create such wonderful books.

Our families, who have been chicken soup for our souls!

Inga, Travis, Riley, Christopher, Oran and Kyle, for all their love and support.

Patty, Elisabeth and Melanie Hansen, for once again sharing and lovingly supporting us in creating yet another book.

Patty Aubery, for making sure the daily business at Chicken Soup for the Soul Enterprises continued with ease.

Our publisher, Peter Vegso, for all of his love, support, vision and commitment to everyone at Chicken Soup for the Soul. He continues to amaze us at every level. To everyone at Health Communications, especially Terry Burke, Susan Tobias, Lisa Drucker, Christine Belleris, Allison Janse and Kathy Grant, for their complete support on this project. To Larissa Hise Henoch, Lisa Camp, Dawn

Grove and Anthony Clausi, a big thank-you. You guys went way above and beyond for this one. Many thanks.

Heather McNamara and D'ette Corona, for producing a final manuscript with magnificent ease, finesse and care.

Leslie Riskin, for her care and determination to secure our permissions and get everything just right under tremendous time pressures.

Nancy Mitchell-Autio and LeAnn Theiman, for nourishing us with truly wonderful stories and cartoons and helping us take this book to completion.

Maria Nickless, for her enthusiastic marketing and public-relations support and a brilliant sense of direction.

Patty Hansen, for her thorough and competent handling of the legal and licensing aspects of the *Chicken Soup for the Soul* books. You are magnificent at the challenge!

Laurie Hartman, for being a precious guardian of the *Chicken Soup* brand.

Veronica Romero, Robin Yerian, Teresa Esparza, Vince Wong, Cindy Holland, Stephanie Thatcher, Kathy Brennan-Thompson, Dana Drobny, Michelle Adams, Dave Coleman, Irene Dunlap, Jody Emme, Dee Dee Romanello, Gina Romanello, Brittany Shaw, Shanna Vieyra and Lisa Williams, for your commitment, dedication, professionalism and making sure Jack's and Mark's offices run smoothly.

Everyone at Chicken Soup for the Soul and HCI who has been mentioned, for your continued commitment to each and every project that comes your way.

All the *Chicken Soup for the Soul* coauthors, who make it such a joy to be part of this *Chicken Soup* family: Raymond Aaron, Patty and Jeff Aubery, Nancy Mitchell-Autio, Marty Becker, John Boal, Cynthia Brian, Cindy Buck, Ron Camacho, Barbara Russell Chesser, Dan Clark, Tim Clauss, Barbara De Angelis, Mark and Chrissy Donnelly, Irene

Dunlap, Bud Gardner, Patty Hansen, Jennifer Read Hawthorne, Kimberly Kirberger, Tom and Laura Lagana, Hanoch and Meladee McCarty, Heather McNamara, Paul J. Meyer, Arline Oberst, Marion Owen, Maida Rogerson, Martin Rutte, Amy Seeger, Barry Spilchuk, Pat Stone, Carol Sturgulewski, Jim Tunney and Diana von Welanetz Wentworth.

Our glorious panel of readers who helped us make the final selections and made invaluable suggestions on how to improve the book: Willanne Ackerman, Becky L. Alexander-Conrad, Fred Angelis, Paige Baek, Cheri Briggs, Sharon Castiglione, Heather Cook, Tara Coombo, Christine Dahl, Catherine Davis, Teri Detwiler, M. Dobbin, Tracy Donavan, Jamie Hickey, Kitty Howe, Melanie Johnson, Heidi Keller, Renee King, June Kolf, Ed Kostro, Terry LePine, Barbara LoMonaco, Susan Mason, Linda Mitchell, Swannee Rivers, Crystal Ruzicka, Shari Shields, Andrea Spears, Donna Thompson, Carla Thurber, Denene VanHecker, Sue Wade, Bill Welty and Charolette Willenborg. Your feedback was a gift!

And, most of all, everyone who submitted their heartfelt stories, poems, quotes and cartoons for possible inclusion in this book. While we were not able to use everything you sent in, we know that each word came from a magical moment in your life.

Because of the size of this project, we may have left out the names of some people who contributed along the way. If so, we are sorry, but please know that we really do appreciate you very much.

We are truly grateful and love you all!

Introduction

Having sat in the classrooms of many great teachers, having taught in the public schools, and having spent over twenty years training teachers, it is with great satisfaction and joy that we bring you this newest volume in the *Chicken Soup for the Soul* series.

Every day, along with a hundred million other parents, we entrust our children to you—the teachers. This book is our way of saying we appreciate your sacrifices, acknowledge your challenges and appreciate your contribution to our children. Faced with often overcrowded classrooms, ever-tightening budgets and increased expectations, you nevertheless continue to work your special magic with your students. You instruct them, discipline them, guide them, coach them and inspire them to fulfill their potential. You teach social skills as well as social studies, self-esteem as well as spelling, citizenship as well as science, tolerance as well as typing, and enthusiasm for learning as well as content mastery.

You have to be a counselor, mentor, friend, surrogate parent, disciplinarian, classroom control expert, group dynamics facilitator, learning disabilities specialist, motivational speaker, cultural torchbearer and coach, as well as a master of your subject matter. You are asked to package your lessons in creative and dynamic ways to hold the attention of a large group, as well as tailor your teaching to individual students with a myriad of different learning styles and learning disabilities.

You have chosen the most challenging and most rewarding profession there is or ever will be. While it doesn't pay a lot in dollars, the psychological and emotional rewards are enormous—the light in the eyes of a newly motivated student; the smile on a face when a seemingly unfathomable concept is finally grasped; the delighted laughter of an estranged child who is finally included; the joy of watching a challenging student walk across the stage at graduation; the appreciative smiles, hugs and thank-yous from a grateful parent; a thank-you card from a potential dropout who decides to stay in school and goes on to succeed; and the internal satisfaction of knowing that you have made a difference, done something that matters and left an undeniable mark on the future.

Once again, please consider this book a giant thank-you card for all you have done for so many for so long.

Share with Us

We would love to hear your reactions to the stories in this book. Please let us know what your favorite stories were and how they affected you.

We also invite you to send us stories you would like to see published in future editions of *Chicken Soup for the Soul,* including *A Second Bowl of Chicken Soup for the Teacher's Soul.* Please send us your favorite stories, anecdotes, cartoons and poems. They can be by you or by others. Please send your submissions to:

www.chickensoup.com
or
Chicken Soup for the Soul
P.O. Box 30880
Santa Barbara, CA 93130
fax: 805-563-2945

You can also access other information or find a current list of planned books at the *Chicken Soup for the Soul* site at *www.chickensoup.com.*

1

A DAY IN THE LIFE

People are just as wonderful as sunsets if I can let them be. I don't try to control a sunset. I watch it with awe as it unfolds, and I like myself best when appreciating the unfolding of a life.

Carl R. Rogers

Once Upon a Time . . .

The kids in our classroom are infinitely more significant than the subject matter we're teaching them.

Meladee McCarty

Some parents just don't want to hear any bad news about their children. Mr. Reardon* seemed to be one of them. Though I needed his help, I wasn't getting anywhere with him. I'd spent my entire lunch period trying to convince him that his ten-year-old daughter was in serious emotional pain. I didn't succeed; talking to him was like talking to a prosecutor.

After twelve years of teaching, I considered myself a "pro." Why was I doubting myself now, wondering if this father's accusations were true? Were Rachel's* problems my fault? Were my expectations unrealistic for this child described by her father as "supersensitive"? Was I putting more pressure on her than past teachers had? I honestly didn't think so.

---

*Names have been changed to ensure privacy.

Slender, blue-eyed Rachel was among my most capable students when the school year began. She grasped ideas quickly, managed math problems and social-studies reports with ease, and had a passion for creative writing. Though a bit shy, she was quick to laugh and chat with me and her classmates.

Midyear, however, I began to see disturbing changes. Rachel seemed distracted much of the time and found even the simplest tasks frustrating. Some days she couldn't put her name and date on a paper without tears or spurts of anger. She'd fold her arms across her chest, pinch her lips together and sit motionless for an hour or more. Except when I asked her to write a story, she rarely finished a single assignment by the end of the school day.

But what prompted me to make the call home was her antisocial behavior. At recess, she stood off by herself while classmates played Frisbee or kickball. In the cafeteria, she sat in the custodian's corner, often with no lunch or money to buy it. Even in the classroom, when I encouraged students to choose partners for informal projects, Rachel remained alone, staring out the window or sketching fantasy landscapes in her notebook.

Why had Rachel's father reacted so negatively to my call? Why wasn't he worried about the changes in his daughter's behavior? Obviously, Rachel was troubled about something. What about her mother? Would she have seen things differently had she answered the phone? Maybe a new baby was on the way. Or a relocation. I was sure Rachel's anxiety was home-related, but home was off-limits to me. Her father had made that very clear. I should concern myself only with Rachel's school environment, he'd said.

One morning, a few days after the phone call, Rachel came to school in a soiled, crumpled dress. Her hair was dirty and uncombed; her eyes were little more than slits in her pale face. She dropped into her chair, put a book on her desk as a pillow and fell asleep in minutes.

Three hours later, my class went to lunch, and I gently roused her, determined to find out what was going on. "Sometimes I stay awake at night so I don't have bad dreams," she said softly, rubbing her eyes.

"Want some fruit salad?" I asked, opening my lunch bag.

She looked away. "My mother used to make that for me," she said in almost a reverent whisper.

"Used to?" I knew I was in forbidden territory, but it was the first time in months Rachel had mentioned her mother.

She twisted her belt with one hand and tried to cover a quivering chin with the other. "Mom can't do anything now. She's . . . she's . . ."

"Away? Or sick, perhaps?" I probed.

"Yes. I mean, no!" she began to sob. "I can't tell you. I want to. But Dad made me promise never to tell anyone at school. I can't break my promise, can I?" Her eyes begged me to say "yes."

Forcing myself to stay calm, I handed Rachel a tissue and began spooning fruit onto a paper plate. I wondered how I could help lift her awful burdens of anxiety and isolation.

I leaned forward, facing Rachel squarely and, as I often did to start students writing, began a sentence, "Once upon a promise. . . ."

Instantly, Rachel's back straightened. She shot me a knowing look. "Once upon a promise . . ." she repeated, scrambling for her pencil.

Less than half an hour later, I held Rachel's creative-writing "assignment" in my hands.

Once upon a promise, in the Kingdom of Misery, a young princess lived alone with her father-the-king. Although their palace was beautiful and they had many riches, the king and princess were sad. This is because they missed (very very much) the queen who could not live with them. You see, she was terribly sick and the court doctor had put her in the hospital for a royal rest. But the queen's sickness was in her mind. Rest did not make her any better.

One day the doctor let her return to the palace for a visit. He thought she would feel better if she saw her daughter and husband. But this only made a royal mess because when the queen was home she swallowed too many pills (on purpose) and almost died!!!

The queen went back to the hospital (of course), and the king was sadder than ever. He was so sad that he stopped caring about the princess who was now SCARED OF EVERYTHING (even of going to the dungeons if she told anyone about her mother's sickness).

Mostly the princess was scared because she knew she would never live happily ever after. THE END!!!

Rachel's story didn't astonish me. But I was amazed at how easily she had unburdened herself now that she knew she could. Of course, I needed to verify the "facts," but I was sure I'd found the key to some very real dungeons in Rachel's world. Her mother's mental illness and suicide attempt were serious enough threats to Rachel's security and peace of mind. But her father's inability to support her emotionally and his insistence that she keep all the pain to herself were even more devastating.

Reluctantly, Rachel's father agreed to a private meeting with me and the school psychologist. When I handed him the lined yellow paper filled with his child's handwriting, he stiffened. As he read his daughter's story, he nodded with tears in his eyes.

He didn't have to insist anymore that their home situation wasn't affecting Rachel's behavior at school. And he didn't have to blame me, or anyone, for her academic and social problems. He was finally seeing his daughter's problems for what they really were: cries for help.

Rachel's mother remained hospitalized, with little hope for recovery. But her father now recognized that Rachel shouldn't have to cope with that reality on her own.

I couldn't help wondering: If Rachel had written a fairy tale just after that, how might she have begun? Perhaps with "Once upon a promise, in the Kingdom of Hope . . ."

Joan Gozzi Campbell

A Random Harvest

Setting: A school in rural Arkansas. The students consisted mainly of poor, underachieving African-American children. Thanks to a Rockefeller Foundation grant, "Chapter I" first-graders would participate in a different kind of reading program. The brainchild of Dr. Marie Carbo, it is based on the notion that the important thing about learning to read has far less to do with how smart students are than with how they are smart.

After children had successfully completed a book, they were rewarded by being allowed to take books, tapes and a Walkman home over the weekend.

The thinking was that this would provide additional reinforcement of learning. When Friday rolled around, Nicole left the school, clutching a book, tapes and Walkman. The understanding was that children would return on Monday with the items they took home.

On Monday, Nicole failed to bring the book and tapes back to school. Every day, she either said she forgot or didn't offer any excuse at all. The teacher knew this wasn't at all like Nicole. Something was wrong.

Three weeks passed. Still no book or tapes were returned!

Then one day, Nicole's astonishingly young mother—

dressed in a fast-food worker's uniform—came to the school. She told the school secretary she wanted to talk outside with the remedial reading teacher!

With understandable apprehension, the teacher walked out of the school to meet with Nicole's mother. The mother, clutching the book, tapes and Walkman, told the teacher that she wanted to explain why Nicole hadn't brought the books and tapes back as promised. Nicole was not to be blamed; she was.

It soon became clear to the teacher that Nicole's mother wasn't having an easy time telling her exactly why it had taken so long to bring the reading materials back.

In what seemed a long and uncomfortable silence, the teacher waited.

The mother's first words came haltingly. Then suddenly, the mother, seeming to have found her comfort zone, started to tell a remarkable story:

"When Nicole came home and told me she was learning to read, I didn't believe her. Nobody in my family can read. My daddy and momma can't read. My other brothers and sisters can't read. And I couldn't read!

"I was in sixth grade when I had Nicole. I had to quit school. I just gave up any hope of ever learning how to read.

"When Nicole brought this book home and read to me, I asked her, 'How'd you learn to do that?' Nicole said, 'It's easy, Momma. I just listened to the tape and followed along in the book with whatever the teacher reads. If I need to, I just keep listening to and reading along with the teacher until I can read all by myself. You can do it, too, Momma!'

"I didn't believe Nicole. But I just knew I had to try. . . . The reason Nicole didn't bring her reading stuff back to school was because I just couldn't let go of it! I had to find out if I could learn to read like my little girl."

There was a short pause, then, "Can I read to you?"

There on the steps of her child's school, this very young

mother, a child who herself had a child, began to read the book to the teacher. All the while, tears streamed down the mother's cheeks. In this intense moment, the teacher also began to cry. Anyone seeing the two would surely have thought something tragic had happened. How could anyone know that their tears were actually being shed over the birth of unrealized, God-given potentiality?

Nicole's mother went on to explain that with the help of this book—which she now clutched lovingly to her chest—*she* had learned to read!

There was no need for exclaiming hallelujahs. They abounded in the mother's every word. They were expressed through the transformed countenance of a newly acquired confidence.

For Nicole's teacher, this seemed a holy moment; no words could possibly express it. Awed, she sat enveloped by an unforeseen, unintended effect of the reading program. This served as a confirmation of what she had been taught about teaching, that so many wondrous things seemed to come about by accident. She couldn't help but reflect that, ironically, all the benefits that had accrued to this young mother were not part of her lesson plan. Was what had happened part of a cosmic joke, with the punch line being unintended consequences? Was what had happened to this mother really some kind of cosmic gift that she would never be able to understand, explain or control?

Shattering her reflections, the mother, who seemed to be sitting a bit taller, announced that she—who had come to accept, beyond all doubt, that she was just too dumb to learn to read—had actually done the impossible:

She had read to her mother!
From the Bible!
On Christmas morning!

James Elwood Conner, Ed.D.

Any Kid Can Be a Superstar!

Blessed is the influence of one true, loving human soul on another.

George Eliot

David was a fifth-grader, but his behavior was so aggressive they placed him in my special-education class. The first day of school, David arrived in an agitated and angry state. He hit every child in the class, screaming, "Get out of my way!" He then turned his wrath on me with a quick, "I hate you!" even though this was our first meeting. David flopped into his seat and began to disrupt the class by cussing and fussing. This behavior went on for the entire week.

At first, I suspected it was a reaction to being placed in the special-education class. Most kids would rather be labeled "class clown" or "bully" by peers than labeled stupid. After careful observation, I suspected there was more to the story. Every teacher who had previously taught David told me he was a handful. I heard, "It's a good thing you have no sense of smell because David literally stinks. The other children complain about sitting next to David so he has his own cubicle. Almost every child calls him Stinky David."

Knowing that the first experience of the day is the most significant, I decided to observe what David experienced each day as he came to school. As the buses arrived, I heard the bus driver screaming at David before he got off the bus. Then the two teachers on bus duty yelled, "Slow down, David. Walk, young man!"

Next, David raced to the lunchroom for his "free" breakfast. As David went down the line, he gobbled up everything in his path. The lunchroom staff hollered at him, "Don't eat like a little pig; wait until you sit down!" David had the breakfast gone before he sat down and started begging the other kids for their leftovers.

David had three more unpleasant encounters with administrators and teachers before he finally arrived in our wing. As if on cue, all the children began to taunt him. "Here comes Stinky David!" "I smell something; it must be Stinky David."

From all my observations, I concluded David's anger was a way to lash out because of the treatment he received every day at school. College Psychology 101 explained that children cannot learn when they are hungry, smelly or teased. I figured the reason for David's school problems were his parents, of course. If they only fed him and sent him to school clean, he wouldn't be tormented. I further concluded that his parents obviously did not care about him, and I should enlighten them immediately.

In the faculty lounge, I told the other teachers of my concerns and asked how to contact his parents. "Good luck. They've never once come to school even though they've had eight children go here. We have sent note after note, and they will not come in." It seemed my only recourse was to make a "home visit." The other teachers exclaimed, "Are you crazy? You can't do that. Let the social-services people take care of the problem." Nothing could dissuade me from going. David needed help, and his parents seemed to be the problem.

In class, I informed David I would be out to visit his family that afternoon. Because they had no phone, I asked if he would please tell his father I was coming. David said, "You come out to my house, Ms. Mulvaney, and our dogs will eat your chicken legs right off."

I replied, "Please tell your daddy I'll be out there, and I'll bring my chicken legs with me."

David lived in a very rural part of town. After many wrong turns, I was finally instructed to keep going until I heard the dogs. When I spotted David's house, my mouth fell open. It was about to tip over, or so it appeared. I'd heard there was neither running water nor bathroom facilities. Yet there stood David and all his siblings lined up on the porch, quiet and well-behaved. A grandmotherly woman was standing in the doorway, and David's father stood at the bottom of the stairs waiting for me.

Instantly, I was humbled. I had come ready to do battle with David's family, yet somehow I knew this man was trying to do the best he could. Immediately, I changed my attitude and asked permission to bring my chicken legs on his property. The speech I had prepared for this man suddenly didn't seem to fit. I quickly revised my words and blurted out, "Sir, I would like to tell you about your son David. I believe he is one of the most unique students I have ever had." Now, that was not a lie—he was unique. I continued, "I believe your son is very smart, but it seems he is receiving very poor customer service at our school. I would like to help him if I may."

"Ms. Mulvaney," said the father, "you do anything you want to help my David. No teacher ever come out to tell me they wanted to help. They send me these papers, but I don't read so good. I tries, as best I can. I don't got any help 'cept my mother, and she ain't doin' too good herself."

"Sir, I understand you do not have running water. We do at the school. Would it be all right if I let your son David take a shower every day?"

"Yes, Ma'am, that be okay."

"We have a washing machine at school. Would it be all right if I let David wash his clothes every day?"

"Yes, Ma'am, that be okay. Whatever you want to do with my David, you do."

"Sir, I am proud and honored you took the time out of your busy schedule to talk to me today. I hope I did not keep you from your work. I will do everything I can to help your child."

"Nobody ever been that kind. My son David is a super kid. With a little help from you, I knows he can be a superstar!"

That meeting changed my life. A man with a third-grade education seemed to have more insight than all of us supposedly educated teachers. David had been in the school for five years, and not one person had ever dared to find out about him. He was passed from teacher to teacher and class to class like a bad rumor. No one ever got close enough to see the superstar under all the dirt, except his father, who I foolishly thought didn't care.

The next day, David bypassed the teachers at the bus. He even bypassed the free breakfast, which he so loved, and bypassed the children who taunted him. He came racing into my classroom, screaming, "You better watch out or Ms. Mulvaney will find your house. She'll find your house and tell your daddy you is a superstar. I ain't stinky no more. I am a superstar!"

From that moment on, David was a different child, and I became a different teacher. I taught him how to take a shower, wash his clothes and take care of his personal cleansing. Next, I taught the school staff to see David as a superstar. I went to the lunchroom and asked them to send home extra food for the children and to change the way they addressed him and the rest of my class. "From now on, when my students come to the cafeteria, I would like you to say, 'Here come the superstars!'" They agreed.

In a faculty meeting, I instructed the other staff members to please help me increase the self-esteem of my students by addressing them as superstars for one solid month. They balked at first, but I promised if they would help me, the behavior of my students would change dramatically in a positive way. Since they had noticed the change in David, they agreed to help.

David's father taught me to see all the parents as superstars, too. He was doing the best he could with the tools and skills he possessed. When I stopped blaming and started partnering to find solutions, everyone won—children, parents and teachers.

Maureen G. Mulvaney (M.G.M.)

"You must be Timmy's dad. I'm Timmy's teacher."

Reprinted by permission of James K. Warren.

Encouraging Kelly

One mark of a great educator is the ability to lead students out to new places where even the educator has never been.

Thomas Groome

It was my very first teaching job, and I was anxious to make an excellent first impression. I had been hired to lead a vibrant group of four-year-olds. As the parents escorted children into the room, I attempted to deal with crying kids, teary-eyed moms and tense dads. Finally, I managed to seat the kids on the carpet and we were ready to start our "morning circle time."

We were in the middle of a rousing rendition of "Old McDonald" when the door opened and a mysterious woman entered the room. She stood next to the door quietly observing the children and me. My voice and smile never faltered, but quite frankly I was very nervous. *Who is this woman? Why is she here? What exactly is she observing?* When I looked up again she was gone.

The day went relatively smoothly, but by the time the last child was picked up, I was physically and emotionally drained. I longed for a nonfat latte, some Chopin and a bubble bath. Then my director came in and asked to meet with me before I left for the day.

My heart raced. *Did this have anything to do with the woman who had observed my class? Did I choose the wrong songs? Was the circle time too long? Too short?* By the time I reached the office, I was an emotional wreck. I sat perched on the edge of my seat and waited for the axe to fall. My director told me the woman who had visited my room earlier was a potential parent to the school and was concerned about how her daughter would function in a regular classroom. Her little girl was born with a birth defect that required she wear leg braces from the knees down. The child was ambulatory but walked very slowly with a lopsided gait. She would need to be carried out to the yard and back to the classroom. Her balance was poor, and she had a tendency to topple over if she was jostled, even slightly. We would need to remind the other children to be careful when walking near her so they wouldn't accidentally cause her to fall.

The director asked me how I felt about her becoming a member of my group. I was speechless. Here I was wondering if I could possibly survive a school year with fifteen of the liveliest four-year-olds in North America, and now I was being asked to take on a child with special needs? I replied that I would accept the child on a trial basis.

That night I couldn't fall asleep. I tossed and turned until morning, then drove to work with my stomach in knots. We were all gathered on the carpet for our morning circle when the door opened and the woman walked in carrying her daughter. She introduced herself as Kelly's mommy and she gingerly sat her daughter down on the edge of the carpet. Most of the children knew Kelly from synagogue and greeted her with warm, affectionate hugs. I looked at Kelly and she looked at me. "Welcome to our room, Kelly. We are so excited that you will be a member of our group."

The first day went really well; Kelly only fell over twice. After several days of carrying her to and from the yard, I thought, *Why not encourage her to walk down the hallway a little by herself?* I asked Kelly if she would like to try it, and she became very excited. The next day I sent the class out to the yard with my two assistants, and Kelly began her first journey down the hallway. She walked all the way to the next classroom, a total of ten feet. We were both thrilled! But my assistants were aghast that I was encouraging this poor child to walk. They pleaded with me to carry her outside and seat her on the bench so she could watch the other children run and play. "It would be so much easier," they murmured. But Kelly was persistent and eager to give it her best shot.

And so we began the strenuous task of walking daily down the hall. I winced when Kelly teetered precariously too far to the right, but she just giggled and told me not to worry, she was perfectly fine. I began to cherish our quiet moments alone in the hallway, my arms outstretched to help her regain her balance. Kelly always grinned and told me she had never felt better.

Each day Kelly and I continued our slow walk down the corridor. I charted her progress with little pencil marks on the wall. Every few days the pencil marks got farther and farther apart. Kelly's classmates started to notice and began cheering for her as she plodded along. After several weeks, Kelly made it all the way to the yard! She positively glowed as the children congratulated her with gentle pats on the back and warm hugs. My assistants were astonished and prepared a special snack in honor of Kelly's tremendous accomplishment.

Weeks passed and Kelly continued to walk out to the yard every single day. We rarely carried her as she became more independent.

One week in mid-December, Kelly was absent for

several days. When I called her home I was told she was in Manhattan getting her annual checkup with her doctors. On Monday morning, when her mom brought her back to school, she inquired if I had been doing anything differently with Kelly. I wasn't quite sure what she meant. Then came the dreaded question: "Have you been forcing Kelly to walk?"

I was dumbfounded. Maybe I shouldn't have encouraged Kelly to walk to the yard every day. Maybe I had caused permanent damage to her weakened legs. Maybe Kelly would need to be in a wheelchair for the rest of her life.

I very softly told Kelly's mom that I had encouraged her to walk outside to the yard by herself. I explained that she seemed to enjoy walking independently. The mother gently lifted Kelly's dress to show me that Kelly's knee braces had been replaced with ankle braces.

"Her legs have gotten more exercise in the past few months than in the past four years of her life." She looked at me with tears in her eyes. "I don't know how to thank you for everything you have done for my daughter."

I hugged her. "Having Kelly as a member of my group has been a privilege."

Seventeen years later, I still think back to the first time Kelly made it down the long hallway. Whenever I have a bad day teaching and life seems too overwhelming, I think of Kelly and her exuberant smile as she painstakingly walked down that hallway. She taught me that no obstacle in life is too big to overcome. You just need to keep working at it—one step at a time.

Seema Renee Gersten

Am I Close?

She had followed me around all week, either literally or with her eyes. Melissa was one of the brightest children in my first grade. She always watched and listened very carefully to my teaching, but this was different. I felt like she was trying to catch me doing something secretive.

I had enough problems of my own without worrying over Melissa's atypical behavior. It was only early afternoon and already I felt really tired. And my lower back hurt. *I guess I should expect that,* I thought. *After all, I am seven months pregnant.*

I was surprised that none of my pupils had asked me about my pregnancy. It was May now, and most of the children had reached the age of six. Many six-year-olds knew the signs. Someone in a friend's first grade had asked her portly principal, "Are you pregnant?" and the poor man had been so shocked he went on a diet! But no one had asked me.

The bell rang. Good, it was recess and soon I'd have a few minutes to put my feet up and rest. But what was Melissa doing? She didn't leave the room with the others. She was at my "teacher closet," a very sacred place. All the children knew they could never open the doors to this closet unless specifically requested to do so by me. The only glimpse any of them ever got of the inside was when I asked someone to bring out the scissors or the crayons.

But now Melissa was rummaging around in my closet. She had opened the doors without permission and was actually moving things around, albeit carefully, to see what was behind them. I couldn't believe it! Not this child. This pupil never disobeyed the rules. What could be motivating such strange behavior?

"Melissa," I asked. "Why are you looking in my closet?"

Melissa turned and looked at me. Tears started to run down her cheeks.

Tears of guilt, I thought at first. But I was wrong. No apology ventured forth from the little girl's mouth. Instead I heard a tiny, frustrated voice.

"Mrs. Peppler, where do you hide it? I heard my mother tell my father that you were carrying a baby, and I watch you all the time, but I never see you carry it. I thought maybe you hid it in your closet."

I stood, dumbfounded, wondering if I should be the one to answer this child's first question about the birds and the bees. Melissa walked over to me, put her arms around my big tummy, and looked up at me.

"Where is it, Mrs. Peppler? Where's the baby? Am I close?"

Alice Stolper Peppler

The Girl in the Fifth Row

I've come to a frightening conclusion that I am the decisive element in the classroom. It's my personal approach that creates the climate. It's my daily mood that makes the weather. As a teacher, I possess a tremendous power to make a person's life miserable or joyous. I can be a tool of torture or an instrument of inspiration. I can humiliate or humor, hurt or heal. In all situations, it is my response that decides whether a crisis will be escalated or de-escalated and a person humanized or de-humanized.

Haim Ginott

On my first day as an assistant professor of education at the University of Southern California, I entered the classroom with a great deal of anxiety. My large class responded to my awkward smile and brief greeting with silence. For a few moments I fussed with my notes. Then I started my lecture, stammering; no one seemed to be listening. At that moment of panic I noticed in the fifth row a poised, attentive young woman in a summer dress. Her skin was tanned, her brown eyes were clear and alert, and her hair was golden. Her animated expression and warm smile were an invitation for me to go on. When I'd say something, she would nod, or say, "Oh, yes!" and write it down. She emanated the comforting feeling that she cared about what I was trying so haltingly to say.

I began to speak directly to her, and my confidence and enthusiasm returned. After a while I risked looking about. The other students had begun listening and taking notes. This stunning young woman had pulled me through.

After class, I scanned the roll to find her name: Liani.* Her papers, which I read over the subsequent weeks, were written with creativity, sensitivity and a delicate sense of humor.

I had asked all my students to visit my office during the semester, and I awaited Liani's visit with special interest: I wanted to tell her how she had saved my first day, and encourage her to develop her qualities of caring and awareness.

Liani never came. About five weeks into the semester, she missed two weeks of classes. I asked the students seated around her if they knew why. I was shocked to learn that they did not even know her name. I thought of Albert Schweitzer's poignant statement: "We are all so much together and yet we are all dying of loneliness."

I went to our dean of women. The moment I mentioned Liani's name, she winced. "Oh, I'm sorry, Leo," she said. "I thought you'd been told. . . ."

Liani had driven to Pacific Palisades, a lovely community near downtown Los Angeles where cliffs fall abruptly into the sea. There, shocked picnickers later reported, she jumped to her death.

---

*Name has been changed to ensure privacy.

Liani was twenty-two years old! And her God-given uniqueness was gone forever.

I called her parents. From the tenderness with which Liani's mother spoke of her, I knew that she had been loved. But it was obvious to me that Liani had not felt loved.

"What are we doing?" I asked a colleague. "We're so busy teaching things. What's the value of teaching Liani to read, write, do arithmetic, if we taught her nothing of what she truly needed to know: how to live in joy, how to have a sense of personal worth and dignity?"

I decided to do something to help others who needed to feel loved. I would teach a course on love.

I spent months in library research but found little help. Almost all the books on love dealt with sex or romantic love. There was virtually nothing on love in general. But perhaps if I offered myself only as a facilitator, the students and I could teach one another and learn together. I called the course Love Class.

It took only one announcement to fill this noncredit course. I gave each student a reading list, but there were no assigned texts, no attendance requirements, no exams. We just shared our reading, our ideas, our experiences.

My premise is that love is learned. Our "teachers" are the loving people we encounter. If we find no models of love, then we grow up love-starved and unloving. The happy possibility, I told my students, is that love can be learned at any moment of our lives if we are willing to put in the time, the energy and the practice.

Few missed even one session of Love Class. I had to crowd the students closer together as they brought mothers, fathers, sisters, brothers, friends, husbands, wives—even grandparents. Scheduled to start at 7 P.M. and end at 10, the class often continued until well past midnight.

One of the first things I tried to get across was the

importance of touching. "How many of you have hugged someone—other than a girlfriend, boyfriend or your spouse—within the past week?" Few hands went up. One student said, "I'm always afraid that my motives will be misinterpreted." From the nervous laughter, I could tell that many shared the young woman's feeling.

"Love has a need to be expressed physically," I responded. "I feel fortunate to have grown up in a passionate, hugging Italian family. I associate hugging with a more universal kind of love.

"But if you are afraid of being misunderstood, verbalize your feelings to the person you're hugging. And for people who are really uncomfortable about being embraced, a warm, two-handed handshake will satisfy the need to be touched."

We began to hug one another after each class. Eventually, hugging became a common greeting among class members on campus.

We never left Love Class without a plan to share love. One night we decided we should thank our parents. This produced unforgettable responses.

One student, a varsity football player, was especially uncomfortable with the assignment. He felt love strongly, but he had difficulty expressing it. It took a great deal of courage and determination for him to walk into the living room, raise his dad from the chair and hug him warmly. He said, "I love you, Dad," and kissed him. His father's eyes welled up with tears as he muttered, "I know. And I love you, too, son." His father called me the next morning to say this had been one of the happiest moments of his life.

For another Love Class assignment we agreed to share something of ourselves, without expectation of reward. Some students helped disabled children. Others assisted derelicts on Skid Row. Many volunteered to work on suicide hot lines, hoping to find the Lianis before it was too late.

I went with one of my students, Joel, to a nursing home not far from U.S.C. A number of aged people were lying in beds in old cotton gowns, staring at the ceiling. Joel looked around and then asked, "What'll I do?" I said, "You see that woman over there? Go say hello."

He went over and said, "Uh, hello."

She looked at him suspiciously for a minute. "Are you a relative?"

"No."

"Good! Sit down, young man."

Oh, the things she told him! This woman knew so much about love, pain, suffering. Even about approaching death, with which she had to make some kind of peace. But no one had cared about listening—until Joel. He started visiting her once a week. Soon, that day began to be known as "Joel's Day." He would come and all the old people would gather.

Then the elderly woman asked her daughter to bring her in a glamorous dressing gown. When Joel came for his visit, he found her sitting up in bed in a beautiful satin gown, her hair done up stylishly. She hadn't had her hair fixed in ages: Why have your hair done if nobody really sees you? Before long, others in the ward were dressing up for Joel.

The years since I began Love Class have been the most exciting of my life. While attempting to open doors to love for others, I found that the doors were opening for me.

I ate in a greasy spoon in Arizona not long ago. When I ordered pork chops, somebody said, "You're crazy. Nobody eats pork chops in a place like this." But the chops were magnificent.

"I'd like to meet the chef," I said to the waitress.

We walked back to the kitchen, and there he was, a big,

sweaty man. "What's the matter?" he demanded.

"Nothing. Those pork chops were just fantastic."

He looked at me as though I was out of my mind. Obviously it was hard for him to receive a compliment. Then he said warmly, "Would you like another?"

Isn't that beautiful? Had I not learned how to be loving, I would have thought nice things about the chef's pork chops, but probably wouldn't have told him—just as I had failed to tell Liani how much she had helped me that first day in class. That's one of the things love is: sharing joy with people.

The pursuit of love has made a wonder of my life. But what would my existence have been like had I never known Liani? Would I still be stammering out subject matter at students, year after year, with little concern about the vulnerable human beings behind the masks? Who can tell? Liani presented me with the challenge, and I took it up!

It has made all the difference.

I wish Liani were here today. I would hold her in my arms and say, "Many people have helped me learn about love, but you gave me the impetus. Thank you. I love you." But I believe my love for Liani has, in some mysterious way, already reached her.

Leo Buscaglia

The Teacher

A mother once asked Gandhi to get her son to stop eating sugar. Gandhi told the child to come back in two weeks. Two weeks later the mother brought the child before Gandhi. Gandhi said to the boy, "Stop eating sugar." Puzzled, the woman replied, "Thank you, but I must ask you why you didn't tell him that two weeks ago." Gandhi replied, "Two weeks ago I was eating sugar."

Source Unknown

I scrunched down in the church pew when I heard the announcement that a teacher was needed immediately for the six- and seven-year-olds. I pretended to study my bulletin intently. Decades ago, I'd taught children in Sunday school. But now my time was my own. I loved the adult world I lived in. I eagerly anticipated the Sunday Bible class my husband Gene and I attended together. *Please, God, don't ask me to teach these children.*

A week later they still needed the teacher to "step forward," and once again I glanced down hurriedly at my bulletin, praying, *God, please prompt someone!*

The rest of the announcements faded into the background. All I heard in my heart was, *You're someone, Marion.* I longed to ignore the gentle, silent voice, but deep in my heart, I knew it was God.

Monday morning I phoned the church office, hoping to learn that someone younger and more enthusiastic had taken the class. I'd planned to utter a soft, regretful, "Ohhhh," upon hearing the good news. When I asked the busy church secretary, she answered flatly, "No. No one."

"I'll take it then," I heard myself say.

The next Sunday I entered the small trailer classroom behind the church, lugging a ton of teaching material I'd been given. Squeezing into the child-sized chair at the small table, I suddenly felt like Alice in Wonderland—too tall, awkward, clumsy and inadequate. I spilled a box of colored chalk and dropped my glasses. The four children didn't even glance my way. I felt like bellowing, "I didn't exactly want to teach y'all, but here I am and I've gone to a lot of trouble, so give me your attention."

Of course I didn't. I struggled on with the lesson while they communicated with each other, moving constantly. They wouldn't even give me eye contact. We seemed terribly mismatched.

That week as I prepared for the next Sunday, I realized I hadn't asked for God's help. I stopped and said, "Lord, I really need to see this is what you mean for me to do. Could you give me some kind of a sign here? Anything?"

That Saturday in the mail I got a postcard addressed in an adult's handwriting. But the message was printed in large, fat, careful letters that slanted downhill. "Miss Marion, God will help you. Love, Ava Claire."

If a twelve-foot angel had set down in my yard and spoken in ethereal tones, I don't think I would have been more reassured. Thank you, Lord! Thank you, Avie.

As I prayed about the upcoming lesson, I recalled *Two of*

Everything but Me, the book I'd written back in the seventies—short episodes about the adventures or misadventures of dealing with my superactive twin sons, Jon and Jeremy. It was sort of a modern-day Bobbsey Twins series in which God showed up in the nick of time in real-life everyday situations.

The next Sunday I began class with the regular assigned material. As I rattled on, no one looked at me or listened, except Avie gave me a quick half-smile, as though she felt sorry for me. I pulled out the book with the cartoon cover. Trying not to sound desperate, I asked, "Would y'all like to hear some true adventures about my terrible twins when they were about your age?"

Suddenly, I had everyone's undivided attention. Stunned but delighted, I began reading the story "Second Chance," about when my sons set fire to wrapping paper underneath my bed and their sister told on them just in time. I got the fire put out and punished my sons, but they still smirked. So I turned them in to the fire marshall (after I'd made a call to him first). You could have heard a pin drop in the tiny classroom. When I finished, there were lots of questions and opinions. "Did they ever start another fire?" "Which one cried first?" "Did they really believe the fire marshall would put them in jail?" "How do you know God told you to turn them in?" "Will you read us another story, pleeeeease?"

After that, classes went pretty well even though we didn't stay with the assigned material too long each Sunday. I'd been teaching for about four months when Avie came in looking really troubled one day. When we had prayer request time, she said, "Can I whisper mine to you?"

"Sure," I smiled.

She looked even more concerned and leaned over, putting her arm around my neck and whispering with a lovely lisp since her front two teeth were newly missing. "Remember back when you first started teaching. We talked about things we'd done wrong and about asking forgiveness?"

I nodded.

"I told everyone I'd colored on my grandmother's wall and finally had to tell her and ask for forgiveness?"

Again I nodded.

"And then you told us that seven years ago you accidentally broke one of the plates from your husband's set of antique china and never told him because he loved those family dishes so much and would get really mad?"

Another nod. All eyes were on us.

"Well, I've been praying for you, and I know God wants you to confess what you did to Mr. Gene and ask for forgiveness. Will you, please?"

Avie sat back in her seat, looking grave *and* staring down at her tightly folded hands.

"Oh, Avie," "I said aloud, "thank you for caring about me. I was wrong. I just can't tell my husband. He'll . . ."

"What? What?" the others exclaimed.

So I had to explain the whole ugly thing. I'd planned to have the broken china plate glued back together when I found an expert. But that never happened and sometimes I forgot about it for years. Then so much time passed. I was ashamed to tell Gene and . . .

"Oh, Miss Marion, you have to tell your husband. Ask him to forgive you," Bethany said softly, wide-eyed.

That week Avie wrote in the card she mailed to me, "Please, Miss Marion. Tell him. Please. I'm praying hard. I love you. Avie."

Bethany called and whispered into the phone that she, too, was praying. Then the boys Emory and Aaron joined the cause. "Have you told him yet?"

"All right, all right, I'll do it. I promise. I'll ask Mr. Gene to stop by class next Sunday, and I'll bring the broken dish and show it to him and ask for forgiveness."

A spontaneous cheer went up from everyone.

Early Sunday morning, I took the china plate, broken into two nearly equal halves and wrapped in tissue paper all these years, and placed it in a sack. Gene didn't suspect anything. I was always taking things to Sunday school in sacks. As we drove into the parking lot, I managed, "Could you stop by our class a few minutes before it's over?"

"Sure," he smiled. I tried to hold onto his smile in my mind.

In class I announced first thing, "My husband will be coming to class shortly before it's over, and we'll deal with this thing." Wild cheers went up as my heart sank even more.

Bethany asked softly, almost reverently, "Can we see the dish now?" I unwrapped the two halves and carefully laid them on our table. The four children looked silently, intently for a long time.

"What if he won't forgive you?" Emory roared loudly.

"He will!" Avie and Bethany screamed in unison, like well-trained cheerleaders.

We'd just finishing discussing a story from *Two of Everything but Me* when Gene entered and finally managed to squeeze into one of the small chairs. As I reached beneath the table for the plate, I saw Avie's mouth moving ever so slightly in fervent prayer.

"I need to ask your forgiveness, Gene. Seven years ago, I . . . I . . ." Dry-mouthed, I explained the whole thing as I placed the two halves of the china plate on the table. Gene stared in open horror. "Can you ever forgive me? I'm so sorry."

In the silence that followed I saw Avie and Bethany reach for one another's hands, and Avie chewed on her bottom lip. I think I did, too.

Then Gene's eyes met mine and words weren't really necessary, but he said them. "Of course I forgive you." Then he was gone.

As I rewrapped the two halves of the plate in tissue paper, Avie volunteered, "Maybe you can find another plate just like it."

"Don't think so, Honey. I've been looking for years now."

Undaunted, she replied all aglow, "Well, I'm still going to ask God to show you one."

Three days later, I was killing time in an antique store and there sitting on an old dresser in the very back of the shop was—yep—the exact plate, a perfect match.

No more perfect a match, though, than me and the wonderful, unforgettable children God had allowed me to teach.

And be taught by.

Marion Bond West

Roses in December

Coaches more times than not use their hearts instead of their heads to make tough decisions. Unfortunately, this wasn't the case when I realized we had a baseball conference game scheduled when our seniors would be in Washington, D.C. for the annual senior field trip. We were a team dominated by seniors, and for the first time in many years, we were in the conference race for first place. I knew we couldn't win without our seniors, so I called the rival coach and asked to reschedule the game when everyone was available to play.

"No way," he replied. The seniors were crushed and offered to skip the much-awaited traditional trip. I assured them they needed to go on the trip as part of their educational experience, though I really wanted to accept their offer and win and go on to the conference championship. But I did not, and on that fateful Tuesday, I wished they were there to play.

I had nine underclass players eager and excited that they finally had a chance to play. The most excited player was a young mentally challenged boy we will call Billy. Billy was, I believe, overage, but because he loved sports so much, an understanding principal had given him permission to be on the football and baseball teams. Billy lived and breathed sports and now he would finally get his chance to play. I think his happiness captured the imagination of the eight other substitute players. Billy was very small in size, but he had a big heart and had earned the respect of his teammates with his effort and enthusiasm. He was a left-handed hitter and had good baseball skills. His favorite pastime, except for the time he practiced sports, was to sit with the men at a local rural store talking about sports. On this day, I began to feel that a loss might even be worth Billy's chance to play.

Our opponents jumped off to a four-run lead early in the game, just as expected. Somehow we came back to within one run, and that was the situation when we went to bat in the bottom of the ninth. I was pleased with our team's effort and the constant grin on Billy's face. *If only we could win . . . ,* I thought, *but that's asking too much. If we lose by one run, it will be a victory in itself.* The weakest part of our lineup was scheduled to hit, and the opposing coach put his ace pitcher in to seal the victory.

To our surprise, with two outs, a batter walked, and the tying run was on first base. Our next hitter was Billy. The crowd cheered as if this were the final inning of the conference championship, and Billy waved jubilantly. I knew he would be unable to hit this pitcher, but what a day it had been for all of us. Strike one. Strike two. A fastball. Billy hit it down the middle over the right fielder's head for a triple to tie the score. Billy was beside himself, and the crowd went wild.

Ben, our next hitter, however, hadn't hit the ball even once in batting practice or intrasquad games. I knew there was absolutely no way for the impossible dream to continue. Besides, our opponents had the top of their lineup if we went into overtime. It was a crazy situation and one that needed reckless strategy.

I called a time-out, and everyone seemed confused when I walked to third base and whispered something to Billy. As expected, Ben swung on the first two pitches, not coming close to either. When the catcher threw the ball back to the pitcher Billy broke from third base sprinting as hard as he could. The pitcher didn't see him break, and when he did he whirled around wildly and fired the ball home. Billy dove in head first, beat the throw, and scored the winning run. This was not the World Series, but don't tell that to anyone present that day. Tears were shed as Billy, the hero, was lifted on the shoulders of all eight team members.

If you go through town today, forty-two years later, you'll likely see Billy at that same country store relating to an admiring group the story of the day he won the game that no one expected to win. Of all the spectacular events in my sports career, this memory is the highlight. It exemplified what sports can do for people, and Billy's great day proved that to everyone who saw the game.

J. M. Barrie, the playwright, may have said it best when he wrote, "God gave us memories so that we might have roses in December." Billy gave all of us a rose garden.

Herb Appenzeller, Ed.D.

Danny's Gift

I taught in the same small town where I grew up, in the same fourth-grade classroom where I was once a student. The first day of school usually brought no surprises. We knew every student, their parents and grandparents.

But this year was different. Danny had moved from Kentucky. He was the oldest of five children. Danny's dad was a truck driver and not home much, and his mom worked odd jobs when she could to help make ends meet. In October, I put Danny's name on the mitten and hat list (a program that provides mittens and hats to underprivileged children). He was so proud when he received his hat and mittens. He wore them to recess and carefully put them in his desk when he came in. After school, I was straightening the desks and a mitten fell out of Danny's desk. I opened his desk and found the other mitten and his new hat. When I questioned him, he explained that stuff got easily misplaced at home and he didn't want to lose his new things.

Danny didn't have a lot to be proud of. He wasn't a very good student, but he tried hard. His best subject was art. I knew he didn't have access to any supplies so every time he asked for paper or markers I didn't hesitate to let him have them. He was really a remarkable artist, and I incorporated several art projects into the reading curriculum that year to boost his self-esteem.

When it came time for the Christmas gift exchange, I knew I would need to help with Danny's gift as I had done for other students. I showed him several items that I had bought for the exchange. He picked something out and was excited when I gave him wrapping paper.

The room mothers that year, bless their hearts, collected twenty-five cents from each child who could afford it and bought a present for me. I wasn't supposed to know, but not much gets by a teacher in her own classroom, especially at lunch-money time. The child would get back a quarter then giggle and put it in their pocket. Danny was on free lunch, so I was pretty sure he wouldn't be bringing a quarter. But that is the beauty of this kind of present. I would never know who contributed and who did not. The card would say it was from the whole class.

The day of the party was always exciting. We watched a Christmas movie in the afternoon. Danny asked if he could borrow some paper and markers. I didn't hesitate but I was a little surprised. He later came up and asked if he could borrow a piece of tape. I gave it to him gladly. We exchanged gifts, and then the students presented me with the object of all of their quarters. I am sorry to say I don't remember what they gave me because after they left for the day, I went back to straighten my desk. I found a folded piece of red construction paper. I opened it up and read it. Before I could finish, I was crying so hard I couldn't see. The note said, "To my favorite teacher. You have always been there for me, and I really appreciate it. I couldn't afford to get you anything so I am giving you everything I have. Merry Christmas. Love, Danny."

Inside was taped a dime—everything he had.

Karen Wasmer

A Great Way to Make a Living

Sometimes our light goes out but is blown into flame by another human being. Each of us owes deepest thanks to those who have rekindled this light.

Albert Schweitzer

"That's it! I'm through! There are other ways to earn a living," I told Ben, our assistant principal, as he walked with me to my car. That day I had broken up a fight between two students; it seemed more than I could bear that I had to be back at the high school by 5:00 P.M. for parent conference night.

"It's been a rough year," said Ben. "But what will you do if you don't teach?"

I took a deep breath. "Could you see if Brett still wants to hire me?"

Ben's brother Brett owned a used-car lot and had once suggested I should sell cars. He predicted my income would at least double if I worked for him.

Ben sighed. "I'll call him this afternoon, but the students need you more than Brett does. Pray about it."

"See you at five." I cranked my rattling old Dodge Omni. I had to pick up my blood-pressure pills before my evening appointments.

I'd always dreamed of being the best teacher who ever lived. I put myself through college and graduate school, working days and attending class at night. I taught English courses for every ability level, receiving a great deal of personal satisfaction.

Until recently. After twenty years in education, I found my frustrations mounting. Disciplinary problems and politics drove me crazy. Students were apathetic; parents anything but supportive. Even my most creative lesson plans were met with blank stares. Why should I work so hard for such a thankless bunch?

But Ben was right; it was time to pray. "Dear Father, from childhood I've asked you to guide me in my life's work. If I'm really supposed to be an English teacher, give me a hint. Otherwise I might be selling cars this time next month. Amen."

At the pharmacy, I approached the counter. "Dr. Saye!" bellowed the pharmacist, who teases me because I'm not the kind of doctor who writes prescriptions.

Suddenly, a face with the wispy beginnings of a mustache popped over the shelves in the paperback book section. "Who?" the man asked.

I searched my gray cells as the face moved in my direction. Within seconds a young man stood in front of me, mouth open. Without taking his eyes off mine he shouted, "Marge! Bring the baby and c'mere!"

A short pretty woman appeared, holding a baby who couldn't have been a month old. "He's the one," said the man, pointing at me.

I prepared to relive some misery I had caused.

"Which one?" asked Marge.

"The English teacher I told you about. He had such a

line about Edgar Allan Poe and those old dudes!" He gleefully pumped my hand while maintaining a cockeyed, open-mouthed smile. It was coming back. *Julian . . . Moon. Developmental English . . . when? Way back.*

"I never read anything before your class," said Julian. "Now I've got a book in the bathroom and one by the TV for during commercials."

"Not like schoolbooks," said Marge. "Be honest, Hon. Westerns. Car books. Stuff about space. I've picked up one or two myself." She smiled at me. "And Julian reads the Bible to my mama, who can't hardly see. We got us a Bible, too."

Julian said, "Man, I'd have quit after ninth. . . . Hey! Show him the baby."

Marge introduced me to Edgar Scott.

"Named for Edgar Allan Poe and F. Scott Fitzgerald," said Julian. "That's so he'll know he's going to stay in school through senior year. Maybe even college. What do you think of that?"

"I think it's great," I said, truly meaning it.

I got my pills and stood on the sidewalk watching the family climb into a muddy pickup. Julian, beaming, waved as they peeled out of the parking lot. Marge grinned and waved Edgar Scott's tiny fist.

I climbed into my rattletrap.

Julian Moon had barely made it through grade eleven. I thought he had slept through my course. But, something had seeped through. He did have a book in the bathroom, and hadn't he named his boy after literary greats?

I headed back to my classroom, where only two of my six scheduled conferences actually took place. Ben appeared in the doorway. "How's it going?"

"Two confused, desperate parents and four no-shows," I replied.

"By the way, Brett wants you Saturdays, effective

immediately, and full-time when the term is over."

"Uh, Ben," I began, "I've had second thoughts. Do you remember Julian Moon?"

After hearing my story, Ben whistled. "Brother, you were called to be a teacher."

I could take a hint. I now knew that even though my frustrations may multiply, God had pegged me for a schoolman. Quitting wouldn't be fair to him or me—or to people like Julian Moon.

Lee Saye

You Never Picked Me Last

The direction in which education starts a man will determine his future life.

Plato

"Dr. Carr! Is it you? Is it really you?"

I turned from where I had been browsing in the bookstore to see a six-foot-six-inch, muscular, good-looking, smiling, sandy-haired young man calling me. "It's me, Dr. Carr! Gibby!"

"Gibby, it can't be. You're all grown up!"

Looking closer, I would have known those eyes anywhere: serious, intense, penetrating blue eyes. Yes, it was my Gibby, all right.

He leaned down to hug his former elementary principal, and my thoughts went back to that shy, overweight little boy who transferred to our school as he began the fifth grade. He was quiet and withdrawn then.

Gibby had a difficult time the first few months, as do many children when they enter a new school. Some of the boys teased him about his lack of athletic ability when he attempted to play games on the playground. Gibby wasn't coordinated and had difficulty keeping up. He always appeared to be stumbling over his shoestrings. Most of the time, he was. I would remind him, "Better tie your shoestrings, Son," and he'd reply, "Yes, ma'am, Dr. Carr."

Often I would watch the students playing at recess. I noticed that when they began to choose up sides for a game, serious little Gibby would usually be left standing alone. Several times I went out on the playground and said, "I never get to choose a team. May I?" The boys and girls would laugh at their principal who wanted to play and say, "Okay, Dr. Carr, it's your turn!" I'd call out a few names and then, around the fourth or fifth spot, I'd call Gibby's name and a few others who never seemed to get selected by their peers. My team may not have been the best, but we were, by far, the happiest and definitely the most committed, determined and loyal.

In the early spring of Gibby's fifth-grade year, I held an exercise class on the playground during recess for anyone who wanted to tone up their winter-weary muscles. Girls flocked to this program, and so did a few boys. Gibby was one of those.

We began by walking briskly around the perimeter of the large playground. I led the pack and Gibby invariably brought up the rear, puffing and panting and tripping over his shoestrings. As my group circled, we would pass Gibby, who was giving it his all, but nevertheless, lagging far behind. I'd call to him, "Good going, Gibby. Keep it up. You're getting the hang of it. Uh . . . better tie your shoestrings, Son."

"Yes, ma'am, Dr. Carr," he said, breathing hard and trying to put on a happy face.

After a month, Gibby shed a few pounds and didn't huff and puff as much. He still tripped over his shoestrings, but he did keep up with the group much easier.

By the fifth week, we had as many boys in our exercise

class as girls. I don't believe the boys were suddenly all that interested in their health, for it was about this time the girls decided to dress in shorts. We added some floor exercises to our program and held this class in the gym. Gibby was right there, in the back row, stretching and bending, lifting and kicking, as intense as ever. Gibby never gave up or made excuses. The little fellow just wasn't a quitter. He tried harder than anyone, and I admired his spunk. Many of his classmates did, too. In time, he gained confidence and began to smile and talk more. He wasn't the new kid anymore, and he began to make some solid friends.

Now, after all those years, here we were standing in the bookstore. My little Gibby towered over me.

"What are you doing here, Gibby?" I asked. "I heard you had moved to Georgia."

"Yes, I live in Atlanta now, and I'm division manager of a computer software company. I'm visiting my mom here this weekend," he replied.

"Well, you look good and sound happy, Gibby."

"I am happy, and I think of you often. You know, it was kinda hard for me to change schools back then and move to a new town, but you were real nice to me."

"Why, thank you, Gibby."

"Yeah, you were always laughing, and you made it fun to come to school," he said. "I'll never forget your exercise classes. You really made us work."

Then a big smile lit up his face as he continued, "But, Dr. Carr, you know the thing that I remember most about you?"

"I have no idea. What was it?"

"Well," he said, as he stared at me with those deep blue eyes, "whenever you got a chance to choose up sides on the playground, you never picked me last."

"Of course not, Gibby. You were one of my most determined players."

We hugged again, and he said, "I'm married now. She's really nice and always laughing. Come to think of it, she's a lot like you. And the best thing about her is—from everyone in the world she could have married, she picked me. She picked me first!"

Tears flooded my eyes. I looked down to avoid his gaze and tried to regain my control.

It was then that I noticed his shoes.

"Better tie your shoestrings, " I mumbled, wiping away my tears with the back of my hand.

"Yes, ma'am, Dr. Carr," he replied, flashing that boyish grin.

Tee Carr, Ed.D.

2

ANSWERING THE CALL

Teaching is the choicest of professions because everybody who is anybody was taught how to be somebody by a teacher.

Source Unknown

Why Choose Teaching?

I touch the future. I teach.

Christa McAuliffe

My family was gathered for a leisurely summer barbecue when the discussion arose about a celebrity who earned an excessive amount of money. I've forgotten if it was a sports figure or an actor. In today's society, it doesn't seem to matter. The major criteria for receiving mega dollars seem to be determined by how much the audience will pay to watch the performer achieve.

Then why choose teaching for a career? I only half-listened to their conversation as I pondered the answer to that question.

I remembered my three children watching me spend many nights and weekends planning for my class. I remembered how they intently listened to my frustrations concerning materials, procedures and the amount of responsibility that seemed to endlessly be thrust into the laps of classroom teachers. I remembered how they eagerly awaited to hear stories of my classroom children: those funny ones; those when the children had successfully achieved; and those when I shared my grave concerns about my students.

I remembered when it came time for each of my own children to choose a profession. How I waited to hear if any had plans to follow Mom into teaching. Long deliberations held no mention of anyone becoming a teacher. I sadly realized it was not even going to be a consideration. Their body language seemed to say, "Why would I choose teaching?"

Dessert was being served, and everyone was still engrossed in the discussion of the enormous salary of one individual, when the phone rang. My husband handed the phone to me, saying, "They're looking for Bonnie Block." Then he resumed eating his favorite dessert.

"Hello, this is Bonnie Block," I said, debating whether I should have even answered the phone during the family meal.

"Is this the Bonnie Block who used to teach kindergarten?"

A nervous sensation swelled in me, and my mind raced with memories of those days so long ago.

"Yes!" I exclaimed with a lump in my throat. It seemed like forever as I waited anxiously to hear what the caller would say next.

"I am Danielle—Danielle Russ. I was in your kindergarten class."

Tears of surprise and joy rolled down my flushed cheeks.

"Yes," I uttered softly as I remembered that darling, wonderful child.

"Well, I am graduating from high school this year, and I have been trying to find you. I wanted you to know what a difference you made in my life."

She proceeded to give details of how I made that difference. My influence on her wasn't limited to kindergarten but remained a strong motivating force when she needed a coach to help her meet a challenge. "I pictured you praising and encouraging me all the way."

Why choose teaching?

The pay is great!

Bonnie Block

IN THE BLEACHERS By Steve Moore

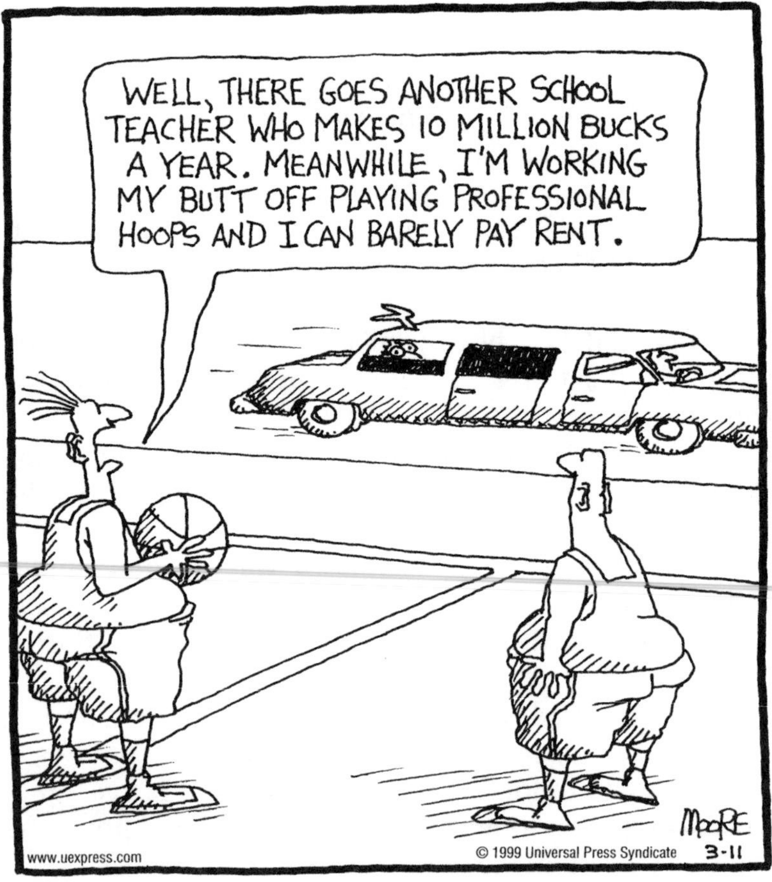

In another universe.

Teacher at Last

Teaching is not a profession; it's a passion.

Source Unknown

That January afternoon, I pulled on my black overcoat, stepped outside and paused. *Well, Atlas Plumbing Company, I've spent thirty years of my life turning you into a successful business. Now I must follow my heart.* I shut the door for the last time and hung the sign: "Gone Out of Business."

Climbing into my 1991 burgundy Explorer, at age fifty, I turned all thoughts toward my lifelong dream of being a schoolteacher. *Lord, you've brought me this far,* I pleaded, *please don't leave me now.*

While driving home, I wished Mr. Roy was still alive so we could discuss it. Mr. Roy was my mentor, my role model. Mr. Roy talked with me, asked me questions. Just like I was somebody instead of a scrawny little black kid.

I was about six when we found each other in Mayfield, South Carolina, where I was born. There was a little family-run store in our neighborhood. Out front, the American flag waved right next to the Coca-Cola sign above the screen door. Mr. Roy and some other old-timers usually were there, propped on upside-down nail kegs next to the pot-bellied stove, playing a round of checkers and swapping yarns.

Every day after school I sidled up by the checkerboard to "help out" Mr. Roy with his game. And it was there, at Mr. Roy's elbow, that many of my values were born. Not that my parents didn't teach me things. They did. But as there were seventeen of us children at home, individual attention was hard to come by.

"Eugene," Mr. Roy said one day, "whatta you want to be when you grow up?"

"A teacher," I fairly blurted out.

In a tone that left no room for doubt, Mr. Roy responded, "Then be one!"

Mr. Roy could see the pitfalls ahead. "Eugene," he said, dead serious as he wrapped one bony arm around my equally thin shoulders, "there will be times when folks will say, 'You can't do that.' Just take that in stride. Then set out to prove 'em wrong."

During my junior year of high school, Mom passed away and Dad needed me to help care for the younger children. As college now was out of the question, I put aside my teacher dream and took up a trade instead—plumbing.

I recalled another of Mr. Roy's admonitions. "One more thing, Eugene," he'd said. "Whatever you become, whether you're a ditch-digger or a schoolteacher, you be the best you can be. That's all the good Lord asks of us."

So I told myself, *If I can't be a teacher, I'll be the best plumber in the business.* I learned all I could about the trade. Practiced what I believed—do it right the first time, and you don't have to go back. Eventually I had my own business.

Meanwhile, Annette and I married and reared two fine children. Now Michael was completing his Ph.D., and Monique was a college senior, while Annette had gone back to school several years earlier and made a fine teacher.

Now that day had come when my dream no longer would be denied. Four days after I closed my shop, I started work at Hendrix Drive Elementary School. Not as a teacher, mind you, but as a custodian. I traded my wrenches and pipe fittings for brooms and paint brushes. And a 40 percent reduction in pay. I figured the job would be a good way to test the waters—to see if I could even relate to the youngsters of today.

I hit it off with the students. In the hallways while running the floor polisher, I'd throw them a big high five and each responded with wide grin and a "five back-at-you."

Often, I found a youngster propped up against the wall outside his classroom, having been banished there for misbehavior. "What'za matter, son?" I'd ask him, truly concerned. After he had related his current infraction of rules and I had emphasized his need to comply, I'd go in and talk with his teacher, smoothing the way for a return to the classroom.

Surprisingly, I made a very fine mediator. Maybe because I could put myself in the mind-set of these youngsters. So many—like my young friend Jeffrey—came from broken homes, being raised by their single moms or by a grandmother. They were hungry for a positive male role model, someone who would show genuine interest in them, show them they are loved. They desperately needed a Mr. Roy in their lives. I wanted to be that one.

Sometimes, too, that meant being strict. More than once I pulled a young man over to the side of the hallway and reprimanded him about his baggy pants with no belt, the waist dragging down around his knees and underwear showing. In fact, that's how I met Jeffrey.

"Wait right here," I told him. From my supply closet I brought a length of venetian-blind cord to run through his belt loops. The next day, Jeffrey came to school wearing a belt. So did the other boys when it came their turn for correction. Unorthodox behavior for a custodian? Maybe. But the kids respected my opinion because they knew I cared.

I did a lot of thinking and praying while I polished those floors. *I have a ministry right here as a custodian,* I rationalized. *Maybe I don't need to put myself through the rigors of college courses in order to help students.*

All the while, I could hear Mr. Roy saying, "Never settle for second best, Eugene. Whatever you become, you be the best you can be."

One night I ventured to the family, "Looks like I'm gonna have to go to college after all."

They said, "Go for it!"

So I did. In the fall, I registered for night and weekend courses at the Norcross branch of Brenau University. I plain had the jitters when I approached those first classes. Would I be the oldest student there? Was I too old, too tired to learn those tough subjects?

On top of those worries, working all day then studying until 2:00 A.M. only to get up at 5:30 was rough. While cleaning those floors, I carried on a running dialogue with God. *Lord, I'm bone weary. Remind me again that this is something you want me to do. 'Cause I tell you the truth, if it's just my wanting it, I'm about ready to quit.*

In answer, I believe God sent Jeffrey back to me. Jeffrey had graduated our school the year before; now he came to visit and found me about to replace a fluorescent bulb in a hallway. "Jeffrey, I am so glad to see you!" I said, while giving him a big bear hug. "How're you doing, Son?"

"Fine, Sir," he responded, his good manners impressing me beyond measure. "Mr. Edwards," he went on, "I want to thank you for the time you spent with me here, for caring about me. I never would have made it through sixth grade if it had not been for you."

"Jeffrey, I am so proud of you," I responded. "And

you're going to finish high school, aren't you?"

"Yes, Sir," he said, his face breaking into a huge smile. "I'm even going to college, Mr. Edwards! Like you!"

I almost cried. I determined to stick it out with my studies. Jeffrey was counting on me.

Now it is early morning—May 3, 1997—a day that will go down in history. Today is graduation day!

At Gainesville's Georgia Mountain Center, I am almost overcome with emotion. Standing outside in my black robe, mortarboard with tassel atop my head, I glance at the blue-stoned college class ring on my fifty-five-year-old plumber's work-worn hand. Tears threaten to run down my cheeks.

As the music swells, the processional begins with Brenau University's president and faculty in full academic regalia looking impressive indeed, along with trustees and guest speaker: the Honorable Edward E. Elson, United States ambassador to the kingdom of Denmark.

All those dignitaries remain standing to honor us as we file in—350 evening and weekend college undergraduates, candidates for degrees. When I hear my name echoing throughout the huge hall—EUGENE EDWARDS—somehow I get on the stage, never feeling my feet touch the floor!

I float back to my seat, beaming like a lit-up Christmas tree, clutching the tangible evidence of a long-cherished dream come true: a square of parchment with those all-important words, "Bachelor of Science Degree in Middle Grades Education."

Yessiree, my inner self is thinking, *just goes to show you. If you dream long enough—and work hard enough—the good Lord will help make your dream come true.*

A teacher at last!

Mr. Roy would be proud.

Eugene Edwards
As told to Gloria Cassity Stargel

Dunagin's People

"Aw, man! With school uniforms, we'd lose our individuality!"

Full Circle

The mediocre teacher tells. The good teacher explains. The superior teacher demonstrates. The great teacher inspires.

William Arthur Ward

When I was in the third grade I wanted to be just like Mrs. Abshere. She had a Dorothy Hamill haircut, wore high heels and always had a smile for her students. She took extra time to go over math concepts with me or praise my poetry. She rarely raised her voice and was respected by every one of her students. She made us feel both special and wanted. During recess, I would stay inside and play school, and Mrs. Abshere would lovingly let me use her special pens and worksheets. "You're a good teacher, Erin," she would say.

I was considered a "high-risk" child. My family had little money, and my mother's abusive boyfriend lived in our home. One of the reasons that I loved school was because it provided an escape, and I truly felt that Mrs. Abshere cared about me. Her patience and kindness helped me through many hard times. She used to carry a little tube of lip gloss and offer me some during story time. "Chapped lips hurt, and we must take care of them," she'd say. I thought of her somewhat like a surrogate mom and a model of the kind of person I hoped to be someday.

One day, after my mother had been involved in welfare fraud, the police came and arrested her. I was nine years old and scared to death! I held on to my brother and sister as we were driven to a children's home.

As my mother awaited her sentence, my brother, sister and I waited in the children's home. We went to a school provided by the home and slept in a room filled with other children whose parents were also in custody. Soon days turned into weeks, and I wondered if we would ever return to our parents. When I was told that my mother would be serving a six-month sentence, my hopes dwindled. The state was unable to locate my natural father, so in a few months, arrangements would be made for adoption.

As I walked back to my bunk, I felt numb. I was no longer nine years old writing poetry and playing school. I was now a prisoner and didn't understand why. I fell on my bed and sobbed for hours. I was mad at the world and no longer saw any future for myself. It was while I was in this state of mind that one of the girls came running up to me. "Hey, there's a lady here to see you. I think it's your mom." A flood of emotion came over me as I ran down the hall. Could it be true? Did they let her go?

When I got to the end of the hallway, there stood the pretty lady with the Dorothy Hamill haircut. It was Mrs. Abshere! She held her arms out to me. "I know no one is better than your mom, Honey, but I love you, too!" I hugged her and silently thanked God for bringing this angel thirty miles out of her way to see me.

After my hug, she reached in her pocket and took out the familiar lip gloss. "You still have chapped lips, I see." As

I walked Mrs. Abshere around the grounds, I began to feel hopeful again. I showed her my bunk and a few poems I had written. I was so excited to show her off to all my new friends. "This is my teacher, Mrs. Abshere!" I yelled. I wanted everyone to know her name.

When our visit came to an end, Mrs. Abshere made me promise to come to school to say good-bye so she would know that I was okay. I promised.

Two weeks later, my grandparents were awarded custody of us. We would be moving across the state. My grandma drove me to school so I could say good-bye to all my friends. When it came time to say good-bye to Mrs. Abshere, I just couldn't do it. I stood there and tried not to look at her. Sadness overwhelmed me; how could I leave this wonderful woman? As I stood there, tears streaming down my cheeks, she handed me a box and said, "This is a box filled with special teacher pens and worksheets so you can play school whenever you like. Every time you play, I hope you'll think of me because I will be thinking of you." I will never forget those words.

As my grandma and I drove off, I didn't know what would become of me. I only knew that I would survive—I would be okay—because a special teacher had shown that she cared. That knowledge was enough to get me through anything.

Sixteen years later, I searched for Mrs. Abshere so I could tell her how grateful I was. When I found her, we had the most wonderful conversation. I felt so much pride telling her that I was only a year away from becoming a teacher myself. "Oh!" she exclaimed. "You can student teach in my room!" So, perhaps I will be returning to Mrs. Abshere's classroom soon, only this time as a peer and a very grateful friend.

Erin Kelley

Anna

Benevolence alone will not make a teacher, nor will learning alone do it. The gift of teaching is a peculiar talent and implies a need and a craving in the teacher himself.

John Jay Chapman

Anna entered my life on a beautiful fall day in late August, behind her son, my new fifth-grader, William. Almost six feet tall, with striking green eyes, she had a freckled face framed in deep coppery hair. Reserved, as is the way with the northern New Mexico natives born in tiny mountainous towns, she introduced herself and her matching son with the musical Chicana accent. Both smiled shyly.

After a brief acquaintance period, I asked, "Would you like to help in the classroom? What helps the most is taking one day a month to grade a set of spelling and math papers."

"I wasn't so good in school," she almost whispered. "I only got to the eighth grade."

"Oh, that's okay," I said. "I'll help you."

She agreed, and I signed her up for the first Thursday of every month, beginning in September.

"Ms. Bucher?" Anna asked over the phone that first Thursday. "I don't know how to do this paper grading."

"I'll be right over," I stated.

I found her in her tiny, immaculate apartment, completely buried by the kids' work folders. Answer sheets were scattered everywhere. William was standing nervously over her back shoulder, obviously embarrassed that his mother couldn't help the teacher. It was clear that she was totally terrified at the task.

"You know, Anna," I began, "when I was in fifth grade, I didn't get math at all. My fear pulled the curtain down over the rest of my life for the next forty years. I thought that because I couldn't do multiplication right, or get the answers to story problems, I was dumb. It took teaching fifth grade, and having to learn my lessons each night, to cure my fear. "

They both smiled. Anna relaxed her hunched shoulders.

"Here is how you grade papers. . . ."

That began the first of many lessons with Anna. She was open, earnest and an intense listener. She breezed through paper grading and showed up at my classroom door after school asking if I needed help grading the "re-dos" in math. I almost kissed her! Anybody in our classroom who gets below a 75 percent must complete a "re-do," or sometimes "re-do-do-do." That means double, triple and quadruple paper grading to make sure the lesson is learned. Anna proved to be not only a dependable grader, but a tough one. She red-Xed every omitted decimal, dollar and operation sign, every word that was left out in a story problem, and marked those math papers with a vengeance and perfection. She calculated the appropriate grade mentally, never even needing the commercially bought sliding grader. Every kid knew that when Anna came, or the grading bag went home, they'd better mind their p's and q's, or suffer the low re-do grade.

Anna began to look more directly at the world, standing proud, speaking with her quiet reserve, but there was a determination, a purpose, stitching through her sentences.

In February of that year, I got a call.

"Mrs. Bucher," she began surely. "I want to help William with his colonial project. But I went to the library with him today, and I don't know how to get things."

The next day was Saturday, and we made a date to meet. I taught her how to use a card catalogue, the computer search, and showed her the numeric plan that catalogued the books. Finally, I introduced her to the information person at the desk.

"God sent you," Anna said with reverence and total belief. "Thank you, my teacher."

Starchy with purpose, she put her hand on William's shoulder and charged to the bookshelves. At about suppertime, I received another call.

"Ms. Bucher?" she began. "William and I went to three more libraries, and nobody knows anything about a silversmith named Paul Rivera."

I laughed so loud! It's one of those wonderful forever gifts that teachers get, linking them with a face, a willing heart, a kind spirit. She laughed, too, when I explained.

Of course she mastered the library system quickly, and William's completed diorama was a tiny cardboard hutch filled with pitchers, plates, silverware and candlesticks, fashioned from aluminum foil. And Paul Rivera was a period-dressed, hand-carved wooden figure, working at a table. William had carried on the traditions of his roots as the carver. Among the first settlers of New Mexico were deeply religious, master artisans who carved *Santos*, or saints. William's carving was beautiful, and so was his report and speech. He knew his silversmithing, and he added a bit about the northern New Mexico carvers of his family. Anna saw to that.

The last I heard, she was finishing her high-school education, with plans of becoming a fifth-grade teacher. Knowing Anna, she'll do it, and the world will have one more wonderful educator—who grades math with a vengeance.

Isabel Bearman Bucher

Born a Teacher

The people who influence you are people who believe in you.

Henry Drummond

Kelly woke up wet again from her own urine. A different household may have sent the six-year-old to the bathroom for a morning scrub before school, but not this one.

"Get on your clothes. Time for school." Her mother stood in her bedroom doorway, impatiently tapping her foot. A limp, unlit cigarette hung from between her red lips.

Kelly dug through her closet floor and found clothes that didn't look too bad. She put them on and then tried to smooth out the wrinkles with her small hands. Wetting a washcloth, she wiped away most of the mud from the leg cuffs. She combed her hair with the cat's brush and ate saltines her mother handed her as she left for school.

On the far side of the playground, Kelly drew with a stick in the dirt, making beautiful pictures while the other children played together on the swings. They often complained of odor whenever Kelly walked past. In class,

Kelly never had her homework done. She had a difficult time with her primer reader. Hardness, like a rock, grew inside her.

Everything seemed to be against Kelly. But she had one person on her side, her first-grade teacher. Mrs. Dina loved all her children and told them each day how remarkable they were. She took turns putting happy little sticky-notes on her students' desks. She smiled into their faces as she taught. She listened. She used a soft voice when correcting a problem. Then, at lunchtime, she marched them down the hall, straight as soldiers. "Keep in a line, children."

Mrs. Dina began to tutor Kelly each morning before school. She put her arm around the little girl in the dirty clothes, hugged the small body that smelled of urine, and whispered, "You are improving!" With heads together, they looked at picture books. How Kelly loved the shapes and colors. Then it was time to read. Kelly winced at those tricky words that kept somersaulting across her pages. But even those words couldn't take away the joy she felt from being with her teacher. It was the first time in her life she felt happy. It was good to sit in this room with clean windows and pictures of flowers hanging on the walls. Mrs. Dina smelled good. Bit by bit, the hardness inside began to soften.

Then one day, the unthinkable happened. Her mother came to take her out of this school, forever. "We're moving," was all she said.

Kelly ran to her teacher and held on to her hand. Mrs. Dina knelt down and with tears in her eyes said, "Don't ever forget how smart you are. Whenever you feel lonely, think of me for I will be thinking of you right then."

The following years were not kind to the young girl. Always on the move, she grew up in a handful of different schools throughout her elementary-school years. By middle school, her mother had abandoned her, and she was placed in foster care. Somewhere she found the fortitude to continue on with her education to become an art teacher.

Assigned to a familiar place for student teaching, she stood surrounded by paints and eager children on that first day of school. By lunchtime straight lines of children marched down the hall as soldiers. Then she heard a familiar, kind voice, "Keep in line, children."

There was Mrs. Dina, with a bit more gray in her hair than Kelly remembered, but other than that she looked basically the same. Then acting on instinct, Kelly walked up to the woman. "Hello, Mrs. Dina. Do you remember me?"

She studied the young woman's face for a minute then her usual smile broke across her face. "Why, Kelly! How wonderful to see you again!"

"I am so glad I finally have the chance to thank you."

"Thank me? Whatever for? I only had you for a few months."

"But it was more than enough, for those were the few months that rescued the rest of my life."

Robin Lee Shope

Begin at the Beginning

Anyone who stops learning is old, whether at twenty or eighty. Anyone who keeps learning stays young. The greatest thing in life is to keep your mind young.

Henry Ford

I had always wanted to go back to school. And one day, thirty years later, I did. I don't know what gave me the guts to do it, other than a burning desire to finish something I had started years ago. When the day came to register, I was terrified and got cold feet.

"I decided that I'm not going back to school," I told my family. "I don't really want this after all. I'm going to forget about it."

My daughter, who was a freshman in college at the time, sensed my apprehension. "Mom," she pleaded, "you've wanted to do this all your life. I'll go with you to register; I'll even stand in line for you." And that she did.

I had dropped out of college in my senior year, and now it was like starting all over again. I didn't know where to start. As chance would have it, in one of the first textbooks

I opened as "an older returning student," I came across a quote by Lewis Carroll (from his books, *Alice in Wonderland* and *Through the Looking Glass*): "Begin at the beginning," the King said gravely, "and go on till you come to the end; then stop." My sentiments exactly, Mr. Carroll. Thank you.

But it had been a long time since I had "cracked a book." I studied sometimes eight hours a day, forgetting to eat lunch or feed the goldfish. My husband and I would have to make dates (only on weekends) in order to see one another, and at times I felt guilty for choosing to spend an hour in the library and then having to make dinner from a box.

When my graduation day finally arrived, I was ecstatic. Not only was I fulfilling a lifelong dream, but my daughter was also graduating—on the same day. We had a mother-daughter celebration with family and friends, proudly displaying our newly acquired bachelor of arts degrees. I have never been so proud of my daughter. And when my daughter stood next to me at picture-taking time, our black robes melding into one, I could tell that she was very proud of her mother.

Shortly after graduation, I attained teaching credentials. And because I loved to learn and found teaching to be one of the best avenues to learning, I decided to continue my studies and go for a master of arts degree in education and creative writing. It was an excellent choice. I loved teaching, and I loved writing. With a degree in interdisciplinary studies, I could combine the two.

Graduate school was exhausting and overwhelming at times. I cut my hair short and got the first permanent of my life so that I wouldn't have to bother with setting my hair. I learned to make a two-hour spaghetti sauce rather than my usual six-hour one and learned that I could live without my nightly rendezvous with Ted Danson from *Cheers.*

The next two years flew by, but it wasn't easy. At one

point, I came home from school, threw my books on the kitchen counter, and announced to my family, "I'm quitting! I've had it!" After crying for a couple of hours and talking it over, I realized I had come too far to quit now. I had run the race well, and I was tired. I decided I would take one day at a time, resting along the sidelines.

I was in my final quarter of graduate school with only one class left to take when I was diagnosed with cancer. Cancer? Was I going to die? Would I have to leave my children before I wanted to? Would I be able to finish school?

A couple of days later, shaken and apprehensive, I appeared at my professor's door, leaving a puddle of tears and broken dreams on his shoulders. "Don't worry about it," he said. "We can work something out."

"But I have to go to Los Angeles for seven weeks of radiation therapy and won't be able to come to class." He suggested that I do my work in Los Angeles and send it to him through the mail. We could keep in touch by telephone.

"And don't give up," he said adamantly. "I have never met a student with so much determination. You are the kind of student teachers come to school for. And you have to use that same determination to fight this thing."

I promised him I would finish my schoolwork, and I would fight for my life. The kitchen table in my apartment in Los Angeles became my desk for the next seven weeks. I went for my treatment across the street then returned to my apartment and kitchen table to study and write my papers. I mailed my completed assignments from a post office nearby.

Right before Christmas, I graduated with honors and a master of arts degree in education and English. My graduation day was special for a lot of reasons. I had finished my radiation treatments and had finished my schoolwork. My husband and my children, along with my mother, sister and brother, were in the audience of the auditorium when they called my name and handed me my diploma. My eyes met theirs, and I wanted to shout, "Hey! Look at me! I did it!" After I passed my tassel to the left side of my cap from the right, I waved to them like I was royalty. Queen Elizabeth had nothing on me!

As I write this piece, I am three years clean of cancer. I take each day and live it, keeping my promise to my professor and to myself to fight for my life. I have lived to see my daughter become a teacher and my son graduate from college with a degree in psychology. Talk about pride!

And still today, I continue my own journey down the avenue of learning. I learn something new every day from my students who sit in front of me with questioning faces. They are my greatest teachers. I have taught many children in these past three years and have prayed daily that I have touched their lives as they have touched mine.

And in my quiet times, I can take a pen in my hand and write my thoughts and feelings on a clean sheet of paper, something I've loved to do since I was a child. Life doesn't get much better than this.

Lola De Julio De Maci

Once a Teacher, Always . . .

Mom was a teacher most of her life. When she wasn't in the classroom, she was educating her children or grandchildren: correcting our grammar; starting us on collections of butterflies, flowers or rocks; or inspiring a discussion on her most recent "Book of the Month Club" topic. Mom made learning fun.

It was sad for my three brothers and me to see her ailing in her later years. At eight-five, she suffered a stroke that paralyzed the entire right side of her body, and she went steadily downhill after that.

Two days before she died, my brothers and I met at her nursing home and took her for a short ride in a wheelchair. While we waited for the staff to lift her limp body back into bed, Mom fell asleep. Not wanting to wake her, we moved to the far end of the room and spoke softly.

After several minutes our conversation was interrupted by a muffled sound coming from across the room. We stopped talking and looked at Mom. Her eyes were closed, but she was clearly trying to communicate with us. We went to her side.

"Whrrr," she said weakly.

"Where?" I asked. "Mom, is there something you want?"

"Whrrr," she repeated a bit stronger. My brothers and I looked at each other and shook our heads sadly.

Mom opened her eyes, sighed, and with all the energy she could muster said, "Not was. Say were!"

It suddenly occurred to us that Mom was correcting brother Jim's last sentence, "If it was up to me . . . "

Jim leaned down and kissed her cheek. "Thanks, Mom," he whispered.

We smiled at each other and once again shook our heads—this time in awe of a remarkable teacher.

Kay Conner Pliszka

3

LOVE IN THE CLASSROOM

I am a teacher. A teacher is someone who leads. There is no magic here. I do not walk on water. I do not part the sea. I just love children.

Marva Collins

ABACALL@MSN.COM

"Your heart is slightly bigger than the average human heart, but that's because you're a teacher."

Reprinted by permission of Aaron Bacall.

3570486979

READER/CUSTOMER CARE SURVEY

CB2

We care about your opinions. Please take a moment to fill out this Reader Survey card and mail it back to us. As a special **"thank you"** we'll send you exciting news about interesting books and a valuable **Gift Certificate**

Please PRINT using ALL CAPITALS

First Name ____ MI. __ Last Name ____

Address ____

City ____ ST __ Zip ____ - ____

Phone # (___) ___ - ____ Fax # (___) ___ - ____

Email ____

(1) Gender:
- ○ Female
- ○ Male

(2) Age:
- ○ 19-29
- ○ 30-39
- ○ 40-49
- ○ 50-59
- ○ 60+

(3) Your children's age(s):
Please fill in all that apply.
- ○ 6 or Under
- ○ 7-10
- ○ 11-14
- ○ 15-18
- ○ 19+

(8) Marital Status:
- ○ Married
- ○ Single
- ○ Divorced / Widowed

(9) Was this book:
- ○ Purchased For Yourself?
- ○ Received As a Gift?

(10) How many Chicken Soup books have you bought or read?
- ○ 1
- ○ 3
- ○ 2
- ○ 4+

(11) Did you enjoy the stories in this book?
- ○ Almost All
- ○ Some
- ○ No

(12) How did you find out about this book? *Please fill in ONE.*
- ○ Personal Recommendation
- ○ Store Display
- ○ TV/Radio Program
- ○ Bestseller List
- ○ Website
- ○ Advertisement/Article or Book
- ○ Catalog or Mailing
- ○ Other ____

(13) What FIVE subject areas do you enjoy reading about most? *Rank only* ***FIVE****.*
Choose 1 for your favorite, 2 for second favorite, etc.

	1	2	3	4	5
Self Development	○	○	○	○	○
History	○	○	○	○	○
Military	○	○	○	○	○
Family and Relationships	○	○	○	○	○
Health and Nutrition	○	○	○	○	○
Sports	○	○	○	○	○
Business/Professional	○	○	○	○	○
Entertainment	○	○	○	○	○
Teen Issues	○	○	○	○	○

TAPE IN MIDDLE; DO NOT STAPLE

NO POSTAGE NECESSARY IF MAILED IN THE UNITED STATES

BUSINESS REPLY MAIL

FIRST-CLASS MAIL PERMIT NO 45 DEERFIELD BEACH, FL

POSTAGE WILL BE PAID BY ADDRESSEE

CHICKEN SOUP FOR THE TEACHERS SOUL
HEALTH COMMUNICATIONS, INC.
3201 SW 15TH STREET
DEERFIELD BEACH FL 33442-9875

FOLD HERE

7016486978

(18) Where do you purchase most of your books?
Please fill in your top ***TWO*** *choices only.*
- O General Bookstore
- O Religious Bookstore
- O Warehouse / Price Club
- O Discount or Other Retail Store
- O Website
- O Book Club / Mail Order

(20) What type(s) of magazines do you SUBSCRIBE to?
Fill in up to ***FIVE*** *categories.*
- O Military / History
- O Religious / Devotional
- O Parenting
- O Business / Professional
- O World News / Current Events
- O General Entertainment
- O Sports
- O Other (please specify) ________

(25) Are you:
- O A Parent?
- O A Grandparent

Do you have your own Chicken Soup story that you would like to send us?
Please submit separately to: Chicken Soup for the Soul, P.O. Box 30880, Santa Barbara, CA 93130

CB2

Let's Go, Daddy

We cannot teach people anything; we can only help them discover it within themselves.

Galileo Galilei

"Has it only been six months since he started at my child care center?" It felt to me more like six years since the day Jay Brewer came through my door for the first time. Even though it was his birthday, Jay was still his typical self. It was only 10:00 A.M., and he had already bitten Sarah twice, completely knocked over the art easels with a deafening crash, kicked Cedric and screamed loud enough to be heard in another time zone. And now he was attempting to run out our back door while repeatedly yelling, "See you! Wouldn't want to be you! See you! Wouldn't want to be you!"

After hearing this over and over, I was beginning to think he had a point.

My day started with the alarm ringing at 4:45 A.M. The next ninety minutes, like every day, were like a whirlwind of dressing, preparing and helping my wife Carol. Goodbyes were finally said, I searched for my car keys, finally found them, got in my car, and left for work.

Even though I arrived fifteen minutes early, there were already three cars with parents and children waiting in the driveway for me. One of the early arrivals was Jay Brewer.

I asked myself, *Why does Jay always arrive so early? Why does Jay always stay late? Why does Jay Brewer never, never, never ever miss a day? Is it just my imagination, or is it true that Jay Brewer seems to always be at my child-care center?*

I got out of my car and walked into the center with the parents and children. Jay's father reminded me that today was Jay's birthday and handed me a cake and a present. He whispered that he couldn't come to the party I had planned for Jay this afternoon. He had a meeting tonight so a sitter would be picking Jay up this evening. He asked me if it was okay if he left his present with me to open at the party. Before I could respond, he said, "Thanks," and left.

Now, several hours later, I was standing by the back door listening to Jay say, "See you! Wouldn't want to be you! See you! Wouldn't want to be you!"

I remembered how Jay's birthday morning began. I eased Jay from the back door to calm him down. He looked up at me and asked, "Is my daddy coming to my party today?"

I said, "No, Jay, he can't. He is very busy." Jay turned and ran a few steps and suddenly stopped, sadness plainly written over his entire body and face. That moment was the first time I actually saw the depth of his pain. Yes, I knew that his mother had died during his birth. Yes, I knew how often his daddy was busy with work. I surely knew how much difficulty Jay Brewer caused me. But now I saw something different—a fragile child in need of approval, trust and love. I decided to call Jay's father at work. It took all the courage I could muster. This wasn't going to be easy for me.

I dialed the number and talked softly as I asked to speak

to Mr. Brewer. My heart beat hard. *Don't blow this,* I told myself. The twenty seconds it took for him to come on the line seemed like an hour. Then I heard my voice say, "Mr. Brewer, this is Marty Appelbaum. I'm not sure how you see my role and what my place is with you, but I hope it's okay if I tell you this. Your son needs you today." I went on, "I know you're busy with work and meetings, but Mr. Brewer, you are important in the life of your child, and it is not going to be a party if you are not here to celebrate with him."

There was silence. I didn't know what to say, so I said nothing. I heard labored breathing. In a trembling voice, he softly said, "Thank you." I could tell he was sobbing. He said, "I'll be there," and there was a click.

I put the phone down and decided not to tell Jay his dad would be coming to the party. What a great surprise I hoped it would be for him. And what a great surprise it was! As Mr. Brewer entered the room, Jay ran to his father's open arms and was swept into a giant hug. There were tears of happiness in their eyes and in mine, too.

What a good time we all had with each other. Jay told me this was his "best birthday ever." As the day ended, Jay went to say good-bye to the other children one more time. Mr. Brewer came up to me and said, "Thank you for your phone call. Today meant a lot to Jay and to me." His voice trembled. "I have missed my wife so much. We had such plans. I never got a last chance to tell her I loved her. After hanging up the phone with you today, I realized that I've been running from life ever since her death. I am so thankful that you called and helped me to remember how much my son needs me."

Jay finished saying good-bye to the children and returned to his dad. He looked up at him with adoring eyes and said, "Let's go, Daddy," and so they did.

Marty Appelbaum

A Friday Night in May

You can pay people to teach, but you can't pay them to care.

Marva Collins

"Mr. Walker is coming to my jazz recital," announced Laura, my seven-year-old daughter, as I applied mascara to her blonde eyelashes.

Trying not to jab her eyeball, I asked, "What makes you think so?" Mr. Walker, her first-grade teacher, could do no wrong. He'd turned her into a reader, a thinker and an organized student. He was the one who encouraged my tomboy daughter to try dance. He'd told her she shouldn't settle for stereotypes. We settled on jazz—a dance experience that wasn't quite pink ballet slippers but more like rousing funk. She was leery, but decided to give it a try. Now, on the night of her big recital, it appeared she had her heart set on Mr. Walker attending. It's not that I doubted his dedication, it's just that I wouldn't attend a dance recital unless I'd given birth to one of the dancers. I'm not saying they are excruciating, I'm merely suggesting Mr. Walker probably had something more important to do on a Friday night.

I felt compelled to prepare my daughter for the real world. I couldn't let her go around thinking her happiness depended on the remote possibility he would attend.

"Did he say he'd come?" I inquired gently.

"No, but I asked him to," she said, flinching as I removed pink sponge curlers. I launched into a rambling lecture about how not everyone has the time or inclination to witness her stage debut.

"Mom," she sighed. "You don't understand. He wants to come. He's my teacher," she concluded, as if that was his sole reason for existence.

I figured she'd get over it. After all, you can't prepare your child for all of life's disappointments. And she did have grandparents in from Baltimore, cousins in from Nashville, and an aunt and an uncle attending. *It will have to be enough,* I thought, miserable because of the complete assurance she had shining from her blue eyes.

I got her safely backstage, lipstick applied, hair stiffly sprayed and cowgirl hat securely fastened. Cowgirls, istsy-bitsy-spiders and Arabian dancers crowded around, saying hello, touching each other's cemented curls. "I can't believe it's Laura," said her dance instructor, staring at the sight of Umbro shorts replaced with a fringed cowgirl skirt.

"Save a seat for Mr. Walker," she whispered, as I brushed some final blush onto her cheeks. I thought about telling her not to get her hopes up, to try to appreciate the accumulated frequent-flyer miles represented by members of her own family. But I didn't. *Maybe,* I thought, *she'll forget about it.*

The curtains were about to go up. Our extended family was gathered, when I happened to glance to the back of the theater. There, perusing a program, was Mr. Walker. I hurried to the back and half-dragged him down the aisle to the saved seat in the middle of our family. "You came,"

I whispered as the curtains rose. Smiling, he gave me the thumbs-up signal. When the little cowgirls came strutting on stage, he clapped and cheered, declaring them talented and wonderful.

"How did Mr. Walker like the dance?" was her first question as I retrieved her from the backstage crowd.

"How did you know he'd come?" I asked, still amazed.

"I just knew," she replied, a smile lighting her face like a candle in a dark room.

I know Laura will have a lot of dedicated teachers in her lifetime. She will have creative English teachers, brilliant college professors and inspired dance instructors. But I'm not sure she'll ever have another like Mr. Walker.

A teacher who obviously had something important to do on a Friday night in May.

Carolyn M. Mason

Love First, Teach Second

"You're going to have Mary in your room?" a fellow teacher asked. Her voice conveyed apprehension, as she added, "I feel sorry for you."

"She's on medication, you know," another teacher warned. "You will be, too, before the year's over!"

I'd heard similar comments during my eighteen years of teaching, but usually these first-grade children turned out to be normal in every respect.

So I began the year with calm assurance that I could handle whatever came.

Was I in for a surprise!

A few days before school started, Mary and her mother dropped by to "get acquainted." Golden blonde hair fixed to perfection cascaded down the little girl's back. Large, beautiful blue eyes gazed into mine. Between the outbursts from Mary, which frequently interrupted the conversation between her mother and me, I learned that Mary needed medication for both hyperactivity and asthma. She would need to take one pill after lunch.

Her mother agreed that the office would keep the medicine, and I would send her for it every day after lunch.

Mary's mother graciously volunteered as room mother. I was delighted.

Then came the first day of school.

Mary made her bouncy entrance and dropped purses, tablets, marking pens, hair barrettes and gimmicks of all kinds. Every time I turned around, it seemed that some child was crawling under a table to retrieve Mary's loot.

Whispering seemed impossible to Mary. She frequently blurted out her thoughts. "The answer is ahhh . . . one. No, two . . . No, threeeeeeeeeeee!"

I knew the scene by heart. She scrubbed vigorously with her eraser, usually tearing the paper, then started the whole procedure with a fresh sheet of paper, again and again.

One day, completely exasperated, I voiced my complaints to the office secretary.

"Mary's medication doesn't seem to help at all."

"What medication?" the secretary questioned. "She hasn't been in for it since school started."

"I send her for her pill every day after lunch," I protested, "and she comes back assuring me that she has taken it."

After that, I began sending a child I could depend on with her to see that she took her pill. Even with resumption of her daily medication, I still had to deal with Mary's repeated outbursts.

One day, after constant shushing, isolating and reprimanding, I stopped the class and said, "All right, Mary, come to the front. Take all the time you need to talk, wiggle or whatever, so you can settle down and we can get back to work."

Always before, this drastic method had worked. The student, embarrassed, would stand silently and be more than happy to sit down and resume working.

But not Mary. At first she jumped up and down,

growling like a caged bear. Then she pounded on the desks with her fists, screaming like Tarzan in the jungle. The children loved the show as Mary alternated between growling, screaming and laughing. This encouraged her to show off even more. After five minutes of these antics, I could stand no more. This little girl had outsmarted the teacher!

In the weeks that followed, I gave rewards, praise and reinforcement of positive behavior, when I could find any. Nothing seemed to work.

At the end of one particularly harassing day, I dismissed the children and slumped in the chair behind my desk, totally defeated. I had tried everything.

Everything, that is, except prayer!

With my head on my desk, I prayed, "Lord, help me with this child. Show me the key. Where have I missed it?"

In utter exhaustion, I dozed off. When I awakened a few minutes later, my frustration and weariness had disappeared. Two words kept coming to my mind: "Love her."

I was well aware that those who are the hardest to love are often the ones who need it the most. But I thought I had worked through this, and that I already loved her.

Yet, those two words, "love her," lingered in my mind. And they were there when I awakened the next morning.

"Lord," I prayed, "I already love her, so I'm going to take those two words to mean that I'm to love her . . . with hugs."

I hurried to school that morning, bursting with anticipation. God had answered, and I was eager to see God's plan unfold. When the bell rang, Mary bounded in with enough energy for the whole class. I gave her paper to write her spelling words on, and she jumped ten frog jumps to her seat.

Then she began to write and spell out loud, "D-o-w-n. Dddddd ooooo wwww nnnnnnnnnnn!"

"Mary, come to my desk, please," I said quietly.

With two hops, a skip, a side two-step and three giant

steps backward, Mary obeyed my command.

Silently, I pulled her toward me and held her close. In my thoughts, I was praying, "Lord, help this little child to calm down. Take away whatever is causing her hyperactivity." I continued this tactic. Sometimes these sessions lasted five minutes with no one saying a word. It was just Mary and I holding each other. The other children watched silently and seemed to understand. If Mary's behavior got out of control, we stopped and hugged, just Mary and I, while the class waited patiently and lovingly. There were times we did this four or five times a day.

One week later, Mary's reading teacher came running across the hall. "Whatever has happened to Mary? She isn't the same child!"

"It's called prayer and hug therapy," I explained. "I silently pray for her every day, and before I let her come to the reading class, I stop the children, hug her and say a silent prayer."

"Well, don't ever stop!" the teacher exclaimed.

In just a few short weeks, Mary's behavioral change was noticed by other staff members, too.

I knew in my heart that God was leading.

It is now spring. Last fall seems long ago. Now it's hard to think of Mary as ever having had problems. She acts perfectly normal in every way. When she raises her hand to answer a question, but instead says, "Teacher, I love you," I say a silent prayer of thanksgiving.

In a few minutes the bell will ring, and the children will come in—each with different needs. As I pass out their papers, I will pray silently for these little lives that have blessed mine so abundantly.

"Lord, bless this child today. Help me always to love first and teach second."

Joan Clayton

All Things Grow . . . with Love

Don't tell them how to do it, show them how to do it and don't say a word. If you tell them, they'll watch your lips move. If you show them, they'll want to do it themselves.

Maria Montessori

I once taught in a small private school located within the charming confines of a three-story stone mansion. Each morning at nine o'clock all the students gathered in the Great Room for a metaphysical warm-up in preparation for the day. Fifty-three children, ranging in age from three to seven years, sat on child-sized colorful chairs or in sun-flooded patterns on the thick carpet. Each bright face was illuminated by positive thoughts and feelings as he or she eagerly anticipated the morning's songs, meditations and exploration into yet another metaphysical cranny of the mind.

One morning the headmistress made an announcement to all the children gathered. "Today we begin a great experiment of the mind, of *your* mind." She held up two small ivy plants, each potted in an identical container.

"Here we have two plants," she continued. "Do they look the same?"

All the children nodded solemnly. So did I, for, in this way, I was also a child.

"We will give the plants the same amount of light, the same amount of water, but not the same amount of attention," she said. "Together we are going to see what will happen when we put one plant out in the kitchen, on the counter, away from our attention, and the other plant right here in this room on the mantel."

She placed one plant on the white wooden ledge, then led the children *en masse* to the kitchen where she sat the other plant on the white counter. Afterward she led the parade of wide-eyed youngsters back to their places in the Great Room.

"Each day for the next month, we shall sing to our plant on the mantel," she said. "We will tell it with words how much we love it, how beautiful it is. We will use our good minds to think good thoughts about this plant."

One of the smallest children jumped to her feet. "But, Ma'am, what about the plant out there?" She pointed a stubby finger toward the kitchen.

The headmistress smiled at all her charges. "We will use the kitchen plant as the 'control' in our great experiment. How do you think that will work?"

"We won't speak to it?"

"Not even a whisper."

"We won't send it good thoughts?"

"That's right. And then we'll see what happens."

Four weeks later my novice eyes were as wide and disbelieving as the children's. The kitchen plant was leggy and sick-looking, and it hadn't grown at all. But the Great Room plant, which had been sung to and swaddled in positive thoughts and words, had increased threefold in size with dark succulent leaves that fairly vibrated with energy when addressed with song, word or thought.

In order to prove the experiment—and also to dry the tears of the tender-hearted among us who feared for the life of the other plant—the kitchen ivy was rescued from its solitary confinement and brought to the Great Room to join the other ivy on the mantel, but at the opposite end.

Within three weeks, the second plant had caught up with the first ivy. Within four weeks, they could not be recognized, one from the other.

I took this lesson to heart and made it my own:

All things grow . . . with love.

Joan Bramsch

Sarah

Sometimes the heart sees what is invisible to the eye.

H. Jackson Brown, Jr.

I will never forget Sarah. In my eight years as a Head Start teacher, she was my most exceptional student.

One morning, the administrator had called my assistant and me into her office. She told us that we'd be getting a new student—a three-year-old named Sarah. "The girl has been abused," she said. Her father had poured a scalding bucket of hot water down her head, badly burning her neck, back, legs and scalp. She had no hair. Her back and legs would have to be wiped down with oil every few hours so they would not get stiff.

Sarah visited my preschool room the next day for an introductory meeting while the other students were out. Her facial features were petite, and she smiled up at me with innocent brown eyes, startlingly naked because her eyebrows were missing. The back of her bald head was badly scarred down to the neck. She wore a simple white sundress that showed her burnt arms. I seized with anger at her father. Then I worried about how the other children would react. I struggled to maintain calm in front of Sarah, her foster mother and my teaching assistant. After Sarah and her mom left, I gave into tears.

"We must prepare the students," my assistant reminded me. "We can't just let her walk in and be made fun of."

"To draw attention to her appearance would single her out," I said. After much discussion, we agreed to have Sarah come in for a half-day on her first day in order to ascertain how the children would react towards her.

The morning Sarah arrived she quietly took a seat. I watched her every second. During playtime, the other children talked to her and shared their toys. They didn't seem to notice she was different.

"It's dress-up time," one of my students reminded me. Every day before lunch, they all got to raid the closets and play in a collection of grown-up clothes and fanciful kid's costumes.

"Okay, everyone, let's get started," I agreed.

Sarah followed the other children and put on an Easter bonnet and princess outfit. I tried to smile, but the disparity between the delicate fabric and her scarred skin made me ache for her.

Sarah left after lunch. Here classmates had nap time, and then I led a vocabulary-building lesson.

Finally, I asked the children, "So how do you all like our new friend Sarah?"

One child answered. "Her hands are small."

Another added, "She picked the long skirt for dress-up."

Not one mentioned her thick skin or her missing hair.

The children's observations helped me realize something very valuable. We teachers saw Sarah as a child who had suffered greatly, a child who needed exceptional handling and assistance. We wanted to hold her, prove to her that not all adults were bad. The children, many of whom had also suffered in some way, saw beyond her scarred appearance. They saw another child, a peer, a new friend.

The next school day, during dress-up, Sarah put on the princess clothes again. She stood in front of a full-length mirror and danced in front of her reflection. "I am so beautiful," she murmured to herself.

The confidence of her whirling poses and self-compliment struck me. Here was a child who I thought should be shriveling in self-pity. Instead she was twirling around, having fun. I felt humbled by her inner strength and honored to witness her joy in just being alive. I reached out and embraced her. "Yes, Sarah, you are beautiful."

Michele Wallace Campanelli

A Bear and a Rock

"Attention all staff. There will be an emergency faculty meeting in the library in three minutes." My principal, Susan, rarely made this type of announcement over the intercom. It sounded serious. She repeated the announcement and clicked off.

I quickly finished putting out the paints so my creative center would be ready for the children when the bell rang and immediately went to the library. Susan began, "One of the mothers of a child in fourth grade was found dead in their home last night." Our eyes were glued on Susan. My heart beat faster. "It was Mrs. Colton, Whitney's mother."

"Jane Colton?" I asked not really believing it could be my neighbor one block away. I had chatted with Whitney's mom often when her child was in my kindergarten class four years ago.

Susan explained briefly the details surrounding her death then added, "There will be extra counselors available to help the kids deal with this tragedy."

Thoughts flooded my mind. *That poor child. Just nine years old and now without a mother. What can I do, God? What can I do?*

"I want to go and see her. If it's all right with you, I'd like to go visit Whitney right now. My student teacher can take over."

Susan agreed I should go. After signing out, I went back to my classroom to get my purse. The one haunting question was, *What can I give Whitney to help her through this?*

I looked around my classroom. There on my rocking chair sat our stuffed, much adored, Freedom Bear. For the past eight years, he had been to every child's home for an overnight stay. Occasional washings and sewing of holes had kept him soft and cuddly. I would give Whitney the Freedom Bear she'd hugged earlier in her life.

As I drove, I remembered how sad and fearful I was when I had been diagnosed with breast cancer. The day before my surgery, I knelt down in my backyard, picked up a small, smooth, ordinary rock, and squeezed it in my hand. It was solid, immovable, just like God. I frequently carried the rock in my pocket to remind myself I was not alone.

Suddenly, I pulled my car to the side of the road to find just the right rock for Whitney. I tried several different stones before I found her "perfect" rock.

I pulled in the driveway and saw Whitney in the doorway. She ran to me and threw her arms around my waist. I stroked her hair and through tears said, "I'm so sorry, Whitney. I loved her, too."

She looked up at me. "I can't cry anymore, Mrs. Wilkins."

"That's okay, Sweetheart. When my mom died five years ago, I cried a lot at first and then I didn't cry for awhile. But sometimes I still cry when I don't even expect to."

We stood there in silence, embracing.

Whitney began to share. "She's been sick lately, and she was in bed a lot. She didn't eat much either."

"She was very sick, Honey." I waited a few minutes to

see if she wanted to offer anything else about her mom. She didn't.

"I brought something for you, Whitney. I hope you snuggle with it—especially when you go to bed."

"What is it?" She smiled.

Reaching into the back seat of my car, I pulled out the big, soft, stuffed bear.

"Freedom Bear!" she exclaimed. "For me?" Then her sensitive nature led to another question. "What about the other kids in your class? Don't they need Freedom Bear?"

"They've all had him this year, so you can keep him as long as you want. Return him when you're ready, or keep him forever."

She squeezed him tightly and nestled her face next to his. "Thanks, Mrs. Wilkins." We walked hand-in-hand to the porch and sat down.

Whitney asked, "How did your mom die?"

"She had a bad heart."

"Did you cry a lot? I screamed when they told me."

"I cried a lot in the beginning. I think what I missed first was the sound of her voice." I placed my arm around her.

"We have videos of when we went camping," Whitney continued.

"Great! You'll enjoy watching your mom."

"My dad cries a lot. He doesn't want to see anybody."

"When my husband's mother died, he wanted to be alone, too. I guess everyone acts differently when someone they love dies. He even got angry sometimes, for hardly any reason. You and your dad might act different at times, too. It takes awhile."

That day we picked pieces of grass and threw them into the sunshine while we talked. I even painted her fingernails like her mom had probably done before.

"There's one more thing I want to give you, Honey, before I go."

I placed the rock in her hand. She looked a little puzzled. "Feel how solid it is." She looked down at the rock and wrapped her fingers tightly around it and smiled.

I told her about the time I had cancer and how a rock reminded me of God's strength and his promise to never leave me. "This is a rock for you to carry, Whitney. Remember, you are never alone."

Then her heartache became visible as tears streamed down her cheeks.

I dried her eyes, then mine. We rocked gently back and forth hugging each other and the Freedom Bear.

As I drove away, I blew her a kiss as she sat on the porch, squeezing Freedom Bear with one arm and waving good-bye with the rock in her other hand.

Two days later, my family attended Jane's funeral, and Whitney visited our home every day after school for two weeks. Our teenage daughter, Melissa, played basketball with her in our driveway, and we baked cookies and watched television. On Valentine's Day, I gave her a diary and encouraged her to write about her growing-up years.

Weeks passed, and I didn't see her. I wondered if she was sleeping with Freedom Bear or if she still carried the rock in her pocket. Then one day, I had to go into Whitney's classroom to talk with her teacher. As I left the room I felt a gentle tapping on my shoulder. I turned to see Whitney standing there with a smile. She slowly pulled an object from her pants pocket and opened her fingers to show me.

"I carry this rock with me every day," she whispered.

We smiled at the secret we shared. "I love you, Whitney."

"I love you, too, Mrs. Wilkins."

She put the rock back into her pocket, turned around and walked slowly back to her seat.

Sharon Wilkins

I Will Always Love You

Like most elementary schools, it was typical to have a parade of students in and out of the health clinic throughout the day. We dispensed ice for bumps and bruises, Band-Aids for cuts, and liberal doses of sympathy and hugs. As principal, my office was right next door to the clinic, so I often dropped in to lend a hand and help out with the hugs. I knew that for some kids, mine might be the only one they got all day.

One morning I was putting a Band-Aid on a little girl's scraped knee. Her blonde hair was matted, and I noticed that she was shivering in her thin little sleeveless blouse. I found her a warm sweatshirt and helped her pull it on. "Thanks for taking care of me," she whispered as she climbed into my lap and snuggled up against me.

It wasn't long after that when I ran across an unfamiliar lump under my arm. Cancer, an aggressively spreading kind, had already invaded thirteen of my lymph nodes. I pondered whether or not to tell the students about my diagnosis. The word breast seemed so hard to say out loud to them, and the word cancer seemed so frightening. When it became evident that the children were going to find out one way or another, either the straight scoop from me or possibly a garbled version from someone else, I decided to tell them myself. It wasn't easy to get the words out, but the empathy and concern I saw in their faces as I explained it to them told me I had made the right decision. When I gave them a chance to ask questions, they mostly wanted to know how they could help. I told them that what I would like best would be their letters, pictures and prayers. I stood by the gym door as the children solemnly filed out. My little blonde friend darted out of line and threw herself into my arms. Then she stepped back to look up into my face. "Don't be afraid, Dr. Perry," she said earnestly, "I know you'll be back because now it's our turn to take care of you."

No one could have ever done a better job. The kids sent me off to my first chemotherapy session with a hilarious book of nausea remedies that they had written. A video of every class in the school singing get-well songs accompanied me to the next chemotherapy appointment. By the third visit, the nurses were waiting at the door to find out what I would bring next. It was a delicate music box that played "I Will Always Love You."

Even when I went into isolation at the hospital for a bone marrow transplant, the letters and pictures kept coming until they covered every wall of my room. Then the kids traced their hands onto colored paper, cut them out and glued them together to make a freestanding rainbow of helping hands. "I feel like I've stepped into Disneyland every time I walk into this room," my doctor laughed. That was even before the six-foot apple blossom tree arrived adorned with messages written on paper apples from the students and teachers. What healing comfort I found in being surrounded by these tokens of their caring.

At long last I was well enough to return to work. As I

headed up the road to the school, I was suddenly overcome by doubts. *What if the kids have forgotten all about me? I wondered, What if they don't want a skinny bald principal? What if . . .* I caught sight of the school marquee as I rounded the bend. "Welcome Back, Dr. Perry," it read. As I drew closer, everywhere I looked were pink ribbons—ribbons in the windows, tied on the doorknobs, even up in the trees. The children and staff wore pink ribbons, too.

My blonde buddy was first in line to greet me. "You're back, Dr. Perry, you're back!" she called. "See, I told you we'd take care of you!" As I hugged her tight, in the back of my mind I faintly heard my music box playing . . . "I will always love you."

Suzanne M. Perry, Ph.D.

A Couple of Teachers

Many of the friends and acquaintances at the funeral of Sam Waterfield probably thought that his death had been a blessing. Sam had died slowly of a disease that robbed his once-vigorous body of its capabilities long before it challenged his mind. And for a couple as committed and in love with each other for over fifty years, as Gila and Sam had been, his illness had seemed especially cruel.

But I had come to know both Gila and her indomitable husband Sam well over the past five years since he had first been diagnosed with ALS. Gila and Sam, like me, were teachers. And I knew that Gila didn't view the death of her husband as a blessing. But, neither was she angry and overcome with her grief. No, Gila viewed Sam's death, I think, as simply a natural, inevitable end to the myriad lessons of a gifted teacher.

They had met just after World War II and married soon thereafter. Both of them had come to America having survived the concentration camps, and they both still bore faint blue tattooed reminders on their arms. Whatever other scars they carried remained hidden. They had each lost entire families, and they never had any children of their own. I think the reason both of them naturally gravitated toward teaching was that it was the perfect way for them to give vent to their loving and nurturing natures. And maybe they also felt that teaching children was a way for them to leave their personal mark on the future. I heard Gila quote Henry Adams more than once: "A teacher affects eternity; he can never tell where his influence ends." Sam taught biology at the university. Gila taught English, as I did, at the high school.

When Sam first became ill and Gila started teaching part-time, many of us wondered why she continued to teach at all. She could have stayed home with Sam, the two of them enjoying the good time he had left. After all, their first reaction to the news of his disease was to become as educated about it as they could. They knew what to expect. One of our colleagues speculated that perhaps Gila felt the need to work so that she could have a respite from the strain of caring for an increasingly incapacitated husband.

But those of us who were close to Gila and Sam knew that wasn't the reason. Gila continued to teach because she wanted to. And Sam encouraged her because he derived such joy from seeing her fulfilled, pursuing something she excelled at and loved.

But during the progression of Sam's disease, I came to see another reason why Gila continued to teach: Despite—or maybe because of—Sam's gradual deterioration, both of them still had a lot of lessons to offer. And it wasn't just her students who needed those lessons.

Gila incorporated what was happening to Sam into her teaching. As he lost each of his senses, Gila called upon her students to enhance the use of theirs, to become more aware of the gifts they possessed.

I had always found it interesting that Gila taught English because English is not her first language. And her class was always the one most requested by high-school juniors who were preparing for college entrance exams. The reason for this was that she never assigned lists of vocabulary words to be memorized by students. Instead, she just used her extensive, rich vocabulary to communicate the many stories and ideas that were always in her head. She never simplified her speech, believing that children rise to high expectations. She was right. Her students learned from context and scored consistently higher than their peers on tests. More important, her students were always enraptured by her stories. I often heard them in the halls or the lunchroom engaged in heated discussions about some point Gila had made in class. She made them think. And she had a love for language and a respect for the power of words that was contagious. And most of her stories were about her life with Sam.

Gila wasn't embarrassed by sharing the couple's range of emotions when Sam was first diagnosed. They had been frightened, then angry. Then, as Sam became sicker, he began to lose the ability to remember certain simple words. The couple's problem became one of communication. They had always been exceptionally close. But now Sam had to learn to share his thoughts and love in other ways, in other words.

Gila assigned her students a creative writing essay. They had to express a profound emotion to a loved one without using easy, key words like "love," "joy" and "happiness." The result was a series of essays using language worthy of professional writers. One of Gila's students remarked to me that she didn't know she was capable of such writing!

That's what it is really all about, I thought to myself when I heard that—raising a child's self-esteem, making that child see his or her own capabilities. High school is a stressful place; the world's influences can be overwhelming to young people. The teenagers coped with drugs, gangs, peer pressure, divorce and other sad facts of life. But

Gila's classes provided a respite from those pressures in many ways. She held optional classes outside, beside a lake at daybreak and at dusk, to give her students the joy of the experience. She let them see the beauty in the world, if only they would make the effort to seek it out and take the time to appreciate it. Every one of her students showed up at those special times.

As Sam lost each of his faculties—first speech, then sight, then hearing—Gila used innovative ways to teach her students to value the gifts they themselves still possessed. She brought in huge bouquets of wildflowers and adorned her classroom with them. She played music for her students as background for books that she read aloud. (She always believed that children of all ages like to be read to.) The triumphant strains of Mussorgsky's "Pictures at an Exhibition" swelled importantly as Heathcliff and Cathy found each other in the mist in *Wuthering Heights.*

Gila and Sam were good examples of courage and dignity. They were proof that there is a kind of love possible in this world that doesn't end when one of the partners changes or dies.

There are days when Gila says that the sadness she feels from Sam's absence threatens to engulf her, overpower her, drown her. Still, she continues to teach. It comforts her . . . and us.

A few days after Sam died, before Gila had returned to school, I noticed a young man—one of Gila's students—sitting outside on the steps leading up to the building. He was dressed in jeans and a leather jacket—black, I think. I can't quite remember. What I do remember distinctly was that the day was warm, unseasonably so, and for just a moment this boy had turned his face up to catch the warmth of the sun's rays. In his lap, open, was a copy of *Wuthering Heights.*

Marsha Arons

Coo-Coo-Ca-Choo

They say you never forget your first love. I know I'll never forget mine.

She was tall (which was important to me, because I was tall). She was beautiful (intense eyes, great hair, killer smile). She was athletic (best darn dodgeball player I ever saw). And she was exotic (I wasn't exactly sure where Canada was, but it was a foreign country, eh?).

She was also my fourth-grade teacher, which made our relationship forbidden—and exciting.

And we did have a relationship, make no mistake about it. I could see it in her eyes when she picked me to lead the Pledge of Allegiance. I could feel it when our hands "accidentally" touched while simultaneously reaching for the same Elmer's Glue bottle. I could sense it in the way she always seemed to call on me when I knew the answer. Folks said Miss Green was passionate about teaching. But I knew better. She was passionate about me.

It didn't matter that I was nine and she was twenty or forty or ninety or whatever. (When you're nine, adult ages are relative. They're all just old—even the cute ones.) It was the era of *The Graduate,* and society was abuzz with older women, younger men and coo-coo-ca-choo. Whatever that was.

And so, halfway through the school year, I decided it was time to quit being childish. One of us needed to be brave and daring. I could see that Miss Green was in an awkward position. It would be up to me to make the first move. But it would have to be the right move; bold, but not obvious; direct, but not impertinent; fearless, but not reckless.

At last, I came upon the perfect way to declare my love. Each week we were issued light-blue lunch tickets, which Miss Green kept until lunchtime. It was her job to make sure they were properly filled out and maintained. One day she passed them out early, and I took advantage of the opportunity to draw an elaborate design on the back. The centerpiece of the design was a heart with the initials "J. W. + M. G." (for "Miss Green"—teachers didn't have first names, did they?) etched on it. I was never much of an artist, but this was good work—elegant without being ostentatious.

I was confident that it communicated our mutual feelings. I anxiously awaited her response. I didn't have to wait long. When the bell rang for afternoon recess, Miss Green asked me to remain in class. My friends looked at me sympathetically as they rushed for the door. They assumed I was in trouble and probably couldn't understand why I was smiling. Nor could they have understood the pounding of my heart, the trembling of my hands or the heaviness of my breathing.

When the last of my classmates had left, Miss Green walked toward my desk slowly. Her eyes were focused on mine. There was earnestness there and just a trace of what was it? Passion?

Suddenly, I was afraid. I wasn't ready for this. She stood in front of me, her hands on her hips. She leaned toward me and slowly, deliberately, placed something on my desk.

It was my lunch ticket.

"Joe," she said firmly, pointing to my design, "this is inappropriate. You know that."

She was right, of course. The relationship never would have worked. Between the age thing and the Canadian thing, it didn't have a chance.

I was grateful she found some silly, obscure rule about not drawing on lunch tickets to hide behind. It made it easier to put it behind us and move on.

Not too long ago, I bumped into her. She's a grandmother now but still lovely. And there's still that incredible, passionate fire in her eyes. She introduced me to her husband.

I could tell he didn't know about "us," poor fool. But I know.

And deep in her heart, she knows, too. Coo-coo-ca-choo.

Joseph Walker

"I think you should know I no longer have a crush on you."

Reprinted by permission of Dave Carpenter.

The Bad Word Box

One of the most important things a teacher can do is to send the pupil home in the afternoon liking himself just a little better than when he came in the morning.

Ernest Melby

Mike was a very angry little boy. Though only seven years old, his heart and mind bore the burden of adult problems caused by his parent's unhappy marriage and tense home life. He thought it was his fault, and nothing he could do could make his father less angry or his mother less sad and distant.

As his second-grade teacher, I saw the outcome of his conflicted feelings in daily disruptive behavior in my classroom. The worse thing Mike did was to write swear words and bad language on little sheets of paper and put them in the desks of the other students, particularly the girls. Since most second-graders have learned to sound out words and read at an elementary level, most of the recipients of Mike's notes could read them and were offended by them. They would come up to me horrified or in tears saying, "Look what I found in my desk."

Mike never signed the notes, but it soon became evident that all of them were from him. He vehemently denied writing or passing out these notes. As a teacher, I had several choices. I could put him in time-out. I could send him to the office. I could reprimand him each time a note was discovered. Or, I could take an approach that allowed Mike to express his feelings in the only way he knew how but without offending any of his classmates. He was already slowly alienating the few friends he had left in the classroom.

One day after yet another nasty note was brought to my attention, I asked Mike to come up to my desk. I sat him on my lap and held him tight. At first he struggled, and I just held him closer, speaking very softly to him about what a neat little boy I thought he was and how it seemed to me that he was really worried about something. Did he want to tell me what it was? His squirming turned into struggling and then fighting with all his might to free himself from my arms.

Having learned a little bit about holding techniques in my graduate studies, I decided this was a case where perhaps I should hold Mike through his anger. So I held on gently but tight. After several minutes, he did stop fighting and began sobbing, nuzzling himself into my arms like a new puppy who wants to be held and loved. He never did tell me what was bothering him, but he did admit to sending the notes.

The next day I gave Mike a box with a slit cut in the top. I told him it was Mike's Bad Word Box. I told him that he could write as many bad notes as he wanted throughout each day as long as he put them in his special box. No one else in the classroom could put anything in it. The box was for him only as long as he put all the bad words that he wrote down in that box and nowhere else. If I found that he had violated this rule and given someone else a note with bad words on it, the box was no longer his.

Mike filled the box daily with notes filled with angry messages and horrible language. Two weeks after we started Mike's Bad Word Box, he came up to me and asked me if he could sit on my lap. Once there, he asked me if there were any jobs he could do in the classroom. I gave him two or three jobs that were not on our school helper list and asked him to do them daily. After completing each job, I complimented him. I told him what a great job he'd done and how important it was to me that he was such a good helper.

Shortly thereafter, the number of notes in the bad word box diminished. Slowly, they became fewer and fewer until there were no more bad words put into the box at all.

I don't know if Mike's parents ever resolved their marital problems. However, I do know that by listening carefully to Mike's inner plea, giving him the opportunity to express the emotions that had nowhere else to go and reinforcing the things he was doing right, Mike found our classroom a safe haven. For him, it became a place where anger wasn't necessary, and he could return day after day, to love.

Julie Wassom

Need a Hand?

Teaching can be a challenging profession. Some days there just doesn't seem to be enough of you to go around. Each little face is so eager, so trusting and *so* worthy of your attention. How can you reach them all? There just aren't enough minutes in the day—especially when the little faces come from kindergarten.

Kindergartners walk into a school ready to say "Wow!" to the world. They are excited by everything—from the chalk dust on your elbow to the bug crawling across their desk. They are loving, energetic, excited, energetic, intrigued, energetic, motivated, energetic, eager to learn—and did I mention they are also energetic? Working with kindergartners is like trying to keep a room full of ping-pong balls all underwater at the same time. But there are also those moments that make it all worthwhile. And Lucy created one of those moments.

Little Lucy (at least that's what we'll call her) had never been to kindergarten before. She was thrilled by the activities, the children, the classroom and the noise. Lucy especially liked the noise. At her house things weren't very noisy. When her family talked, there wasn't a sound. Her parents were deaf, and every conversation was conducted in sign language. Now Lucy was experiencing the excitement of a second language—she was getting to talk!

As the school year progressed, Lucy thrived. Her parents came in for conferences, they wrote notes, and the school even helped them get a special telephone so they could call the school with concerns about Lucy. All of this communication was wonderful, and Lucy benefited from it all!

Halloween came with pumpkins and costumes. Thanksgiving turkeys sported multi-colored feathers. But then came Christmas, the best of all. Santa was coming *very* soon, and the kindergartners were creating a Santa of their own to make him feel welcome. Dozens of tiny hands were traced onto colorful paper. Hundreds of tiny fingers were cut with blunt-tipped scissors. Proudly, the children brought their handprints to the teacher, who taped them on the door. There were red ones for Santa's suit, white ones for his beard, and even black hands to shape his boots. It was beautiful!

Lucy was thrilled. She loved the tracing and the cutting. It had been so much fun, she went home that night and traced and cut and traced and cut. When she was finished, she chose the best hand of all to take to her teacher.

The next morning Lucy could hardly wait. As soon as she reached the classroom she reached into her book bag and dug out her gift. Proudly, she presented her very best hand to her teacher. Her teacher bent down and gave Lucy a hug, but she was puzzled by the gift. The day before, Lucy had done such a wonderful job. Her tracing, her cutting, had been well within the skill level of her age group. But today's effort—well, it just wasn't Lucy's best work.

"Do you like it?" Lucy asked eagerly.

The teacher smiled.

"Yes, Honey," she replied. "But Lucy, there are some fingers missing. Did something happen?"

There *were* some fingers missing—it was obvious as soon as you looked at the hand. The thumb, the index finger and the pinky finger had been cut with perfection. The other two fingers, however, had been cut off at the palm.

"Yes, Teacher," Lucy said happily. "I wanted to give you my best hand—the one that says 'I love you.'"

And that's exactly what it did say—in sign language—"I love you."

Suzanne Boyce

"Congratulations. It's unanimously agreed that you put the kinder back in kindergarten."

4

DEFINING MOMENTS

My heart is singing for joy this morning. A miracle has happened! The light of understanding has shown upon my little pupil's mind, and behold, all things are changed.

Anne Sullivan

That's Just Roscoe

Children are our most valuable natural resource.

Herbert Hoover

In the fall of 1966, I began teaching in Wise County, Virginia, as a part of President Lyndon B. Johnson's Aid to Appalachia program. Along with a reading teacher and the bus driver, I traveled in a school bus that had been converted into a classroom on wheels. We served seven little schools surrounding Coeburn, Virginia, bringing music and reading once a week to the lives of the "educationally deprived" youngsters of the poverty-stricken southwest Virginia mountains. I was young, incredibly naive, and full of the vigor that only those born to teach possess.

Our first stop was at Tom's Creek School, which sat on the top of a hill, directly across from the coal mine of the same name. I went into the building to teach music to the first- and second-graders, while the reading teacher brought her charges out to the bus for instruction.

My first lesson was rhythms, using all sorts of rhythm instruments, recorded music, songs such as "The March of the Toy Soldiers" and several of Sousa's marches. The children responded as only six- and seven-year-olds can—with unbridled enthusiasm. I was euphoric! My first day was going to be a success!

However, I noticed a little boy sitting in the back of the room, isolated from the rest of the children. He didn't touch the musical instrument I had given him. But his blue eyes sparkled and his grubby little fingers moved with the beat of the music. He was without doubt the dirtiest little child I had ever seen. His hair was matted and greasy; his clothes had never seen soap and water; his shoes, barely covering his feet, were ragged, too large and tied with rough twine. His neck was so caked with grime that I wondered if anyone had ever held him down and scrubbed it like my grandmother did mine. All in all, he was a sad sight, a filthy little urchin in a classroom full of clean and shining faces.

After class, I questioned the teacher about him. Her reply startled and troubled me. "Oh, that's just Roscoe. He doesn't know anything. His whole family is retarded. He just comes to school so he can have a hot meal every day. He doesn't even talk. Don't mind him, Honey."

I left Tom's Creek but couldn't get Roscoe off my mind. How did the teachers at the school know he was retarded? Had he ever been tested? Had he just been shoved into the corner because of his family? What could I do to help him? I was sure I had seen him respond to the music. Had anyone even tried to help him?

When we arrived back in Coeburn, I made some inquiries. The principal at the high school told me that the family was an infamous one in the area. There was incest, alcoholism, mental illness and various other problems in the clan. Most of the agencies that tried to help had long since given up, because the grandfather, the patriarch of the group, was one to shoot first and ask questions later when "strangers" came too close to the home place.

The following week, as the bus pulled into Tom's Creek, the teacher I had talked to during the last visit was waiting eagerly on the front steps, smiling broadly.

As I approached her, she said, "I couldn't wait to tell you. This morning when Roscoe got here, he grabbed my dress, gave it a tug and said, 'Today's the day the music teacher comes.' I didn't even know he could talk, much less tell one day from another. It seems you and your musical instruments turned on a switch or something."

With tears of joy in my eyes, and a prayer of thanksgiving in my heart, I walked into the classroom for only the second time. Roscoe was sitting in the front row, still filthy, still different from the other children, but with blue eyes sparkling as he waited for "the music teacher."

As the year progressed, I took clothes to Roscoe, convinced the teacher to help me clean him up (in a washtub in the cafeteria, but that's another story), and watched as he began to blossom. His hair was a silky, platinum blond that women around the world would envy; his skin was peaches and cream. When the clothes began to look ratty, I brought more. The teacher made him change before he went home, because she said the other kids at home would take them or they would "just disappear" if he didn't.

Roscoe learned to read, learned his alphabet and his numbers, and showed an artistic nature that was superior to most of the other children in the class. He became a part of their games at recess and was no longer looked upon as "different."

I taught in the program for two years and was proud to see Roscoe progress. When I left to return to school in Tennessee, I lost track of him. I have no idea what happened to him, but I believe music—and soap and water—changed a life and maybe even a clan.

Sue L. Vaughn

Great Answer

If you must raise your voice, do it to cheer someone on.

Anonymous

In our kindergarten class, we constantly encouraged children to recognize and accept strengths in themselves and others. We daily promoted the concept of "family." We truly cared, nurtured, embraced and loved each other. One of our strongest class rules was, "We will say only kind things to each other." The children became cheerleaders for one another in attempts as well as successes. When someone had difficulty with a task, another child often said, "Just do your best." Standing ovations were given throughout the day for acts of effort.

One day the children were seated on the floor eagerly relating experiences about springtime when Michael raised his hand. Michael often raised his hand, but Michael couldn't speak. Because of the safe, inviting environment we had established, his enthusiasm and eagerness to learn never seemed to diminish. I recognized him each time he raised his hand, and we all gave him time to respond at his own comfort level, hoping this would be the time he'd talk. Then, after a few minutes, I would respond as if he had answered. "Michael, that was a good try." We then proceeded with our lesson.

When Michael raised his hand again this day, the class and I eagerly waited, as usual. And to our great surprise, he spoke! The children and I were so surprised and joyous, the energy in the room was overwhelming. One of my class angels, Nicole, spoke first, "That was a great wrong answer!" The class immediately stood and gave him a standing ovation.

Bonnie Block

Mother and Child

Teach as though you were teaching your own children.

Anonymous

It was Christmas 1961. I was teaching in a small town in Ohio where my twenty-seven bright-eyed, bushy-tailed third-graders eagerly anticipated the great day of gifts and giving.

A tree covered with tinsel and gaudy paper chains graced one corner. In another rested a manger scene produced from cardboard and poster paints by chubby, and sometimes grubby, hands. Someone had brought a doll and placed it on the straw in the cardboard box that served as the manger. It didn't matter that you could pull a string and hear the blue-eyed, golden-haired dolly say, "My name is Susie."

"But Jesus was a boy baby!" one of the boys proclaimed. Nonetheless, Susie stayed.

Each day the children produced some new wonder: strings of popcorn; handmade trinkets; and German bells made from wallpaper samples, which we hung from the ceiling.

Through it all, one little girl remained aloof, watching from afar, seemingly miles away. I wondered what would happen to this quiet child, once so happy and now so suddenly withdrawn. I hoped the festivities would appeal to her. But nothing did.

We made cards and gifts for mothers and dads, for sisters and brothers, for grandparents, and for each other. At home, the students made the popular fried marbles and vied with one another to bring in the prettiest ones.

"You put them in a hot frying pan, teacher. And you let them get real hot, and then you watch what happens inside. But you don't fry them too long or they break." So, as my gift to them, I made each of my students a little pouch for carrying their fried marbles.

And I knew they had each made something for me: bookmarks carefully cut, colored, and sometimes pasted together; cards and special drawings; liquid embroidery doilies, hand-fringed, of course.

The day of gift-giving finally came. We oohed and aahed over our handiwork as the presents were exchanged. Through it all, the quiet little girl sat quietly watching. I had made a special pouch for her, red and green with white lace. I wanted very much to see her smile. She opened the package so slowly and carefully. I waited, but she turned away. I had not penetrated the wall of isolation she had built around herself.

After school the children left in little groups, chattering about the great day yet to come when long-hoped-for two-wheelers and bright sleds would appear beside their trees at home.

She lingered, watching them bundle up and go out the door. I sat down in a child-sized chair to catch my breath, hardly aware of what was happening, when she came to me with outstretched hands, bearing a small white box, unwrapped and slightly soiled, as though it had been held many times by unwashed, childish hands. She said nothing.

"For me?" I asked with a weak smile, suddenly feeling very insecure for my thirty-odd years.

She said not a word, but nodded her head. I took the box and gingerly opened it. There inside, glistening green, a fried marble hung from a golden chain.

Then I looked into that elderly eight-year-old face and saw the question in her dark brown eyes. In a flash I knew—she had made it for her mother, a mother she would never see again, a mother who would never hold her or brush her hair or share a funny story, a mother who would never again hear her childish joys or sorrows. A mother who had taken her own life just three weeks before.

I held out the chain. She took it in both her hands, reached forward, and secured the simple clasp at the back of my neck. She stepped back then as if to see that all was well. I looked down at the shiny piece of glass and the tarnished golden chain, then back at the giver. I meant it when I whispered, "Oh, Maria, it is so beautiful. She would have loved it."

Neither of us could stop the tears. She stumbled into my arms and we wept together. And for that brief moment I became her mother, for she had given me the greatest gift of all: herself.

Patricia A. Habada

Promises to Keep

Knowledge is learning something every day. Wisdom is letting go of something every day.

Zen Saying

I'm a teacher. But there are days, like today, when I wonder why. It's been a tough day. The results of an English quiz taken by my fifth-graders were dismal. Despite my best efforts, the world of pronouns remains a mystery to them. How I wish there is a way to make the study of our language as exciting as a computer game, so the glazed looks would not appear in their eyes at the mention of the word "grammar."

I wanted to spend my lunch period thinking of a way to enrich the next day's lesson, but a child became sick and needed me to gather her assignments while she waited for her mother. It took longer than I thought so there wasn't time for lunch. Then an argument broke out at recess. Angry boys needed to be calmed and hurt feelings soothed before we could return to the classroom. We were all emotionally spent and found it hard to return to history books and Revolutionary War battles.

Hunger had given me a nagging headache, lingering long after the last child filed out for car pool. Now, hours later as I drive home, rubbing aching temples, I remember my husband's words, delivered like a lecture, after other days like this. "Why don't you quit? You'd probably make more money doing something else, and you wouldn't have papers to grade every night."

This late afternoon, I'm considering the wisdom of his words. I have a stack of papers to grade, which I promised my fifth-graders I would return tomorrow. But tonight a friend, whom I haven't seen in a year, is visiting from Belgium, and I told her I would keep this evening free.

Frustration builds as traffic slows, and I realize it's rush hour. No matter how hard I try, I can't seem to get out of my classroom ahead of the traffic. The world of my profession, a world filled with children, requires so much time. After school today, we had a faculty meeting. Events had to be planned, problems solved, new ideas discussed. So many details to remember. Just when I thought my day was over, a student peeked her head into the classroom to remind me I had promised to help her with a difficult assignment. The building was empty when I returned her to her waiting mother and wearily walked to my car.

Sitting in traffic threaded behind a distant stoplight, it's hard not to replay the day and revisit the tension. I turn up the air conditioner, hoping the coolness will ease my frustration and aching head. The last notes of a familiar melody are interrupted by news from the real world. Stock prices are down. Crime is up. The sound of gunfire fills the car as a broadcaster reveals the horror of life in a distant country. A strained voice reports the body of a local youngster, missing for weeks, has been identified. Click. Too much real world has invaded my space.

This missing child has had a profound effect on my fifth-graders. Every morning since she was first reported missing, my children have discussed news reports about her and prayed for her safe return.

Their concern was not only for her and her family but also for themselves. After all, she was one of them. A child believing herself to be safe and secure in her own neighborhood. My students, only one scant year younger than the tragic victim, wondered, "If it happened to her, could it happen to me?" Their thoughts and fears mirrored my own as I tried to find the right words to calm anxieties hoisted upon them by a world seemingly gone mad. There were no easy answers to quiet their apprehensions. How could I help them make sense out of senseless things and restore security to the small world of our classroom?

My children, ever wise with the innocence of youth, had found the answer themselves. They got out their pencils, markers and Crayolas and made cards. Cards written with words of compassion and love for a mother and father they didn't know. Cards that spoke of faith and the promise of peace. Cards adorned with ruby red hearts, golden crosses, spring flowers and rosy-cheeked angels. No grammar book, no lesson, could ever teach the beauty of the thoughts drawn and expressed by these children. Their cards, intended to comfort others, comforted the children themselves by leading them past the anxiety, back into the world of security that should be theirs.

As I sit in my car inching through the fumes of evening rush hour, I reflect on the strength of my students as they sought to right their world in the one way that made sense to them. I find myself smiling in spite of the heat, the traffic and the pile of ungraded tests. The rules of grammar might not have been learned today, but something bigger and better happened in my classroom. I just didn't recognize it at the time.

And then I remember. I remember why I'm still teaching. It's the children. They're more important than a lifetime filled with quiet evenings and more valuable than a pocket filled with money. The world of noise, pronouns, recess and homework is my world. My classroom, a child-filled world of discovery, of kindness and of caring is the real world. And I'm so lucky to be in it.

The traffic clears and I move past the stoplight, into the shady streets of my neighborhood. I'm glad to be home. It's time to call my friend and tell her I can't meet her tonight. I have promises to keep. She'll understand. After all, she's a teacher.

Kris Hamm Ross

Goals and Dreams—A Winning Team

After relocating to the suburbs of Atlanta, Georgia, I was fortunate to be offered a fifth-grade teaching position. When I accepted the job, I was warned that I was being given a "tough" group with behavioral problems and real attitudes. Being excited just to have a teaching job after relocating, I wasn't even discouraged even after warnings from former teachers and parents alike.

The year started out like any other year. Expectations were set, and my single rule of respect was imposed. Within two weeks, I began to notice the attitudes I had been warned about. This was a diverse group of students who were intolerant to differences of others. Getting them to work with partners or in groups was torture for them and for me.

I would not accept their intolerance. I insisted the students team up and respect one another and value their differences. This became my mission for the year. I had the time and situation to work through these skills with them. It was the year of the Olympics in Atlanta so there were teams from many nations all around us preparing for the games. We began to study the different countries that were participating. We talked about the history and values of each culture. We discussed how every person's role on a team was important. We talked about the respect for each person's talents as the means for success. We learned how winning was not as important as participating with effort. The feeling was contagious, and soon all the students were caught up in the Olympic fever and in doing their best. Away went the disputes when working together, and away went the name-calling, the racial slurs and the insults over mistakes. Instead, they shared feelings of encouragement for each other.

They were doing so well that other teachers and the parents began to notice. I heard things such as, "I used to see these kids and cringe when they came toward me. Now they are one of my favorite groups." I also heard, "A year ago I would never have expected Tricia to get a citizenship award." Parents reported that their children were no longer arguing with siblings or over chores and homework. The rebellious, intolerant attitudes had all but disappeared.

By spring, I felt these students were ready for their final test from me. I had received a small grant from the local community to support my plan. I began a project called Goals and Dreams. The idea was that the class would set a goal, and all the students would participate to make it happen. Having focused so much on sports with the Olympics, the students chose to get involved with a sports activity. Each year the school sponsored a five-kilometer road race to raise money for cancer research. This year my students were going to train for this road race and complete the 3.1-mile course, though none of them had ever run more than a mile and certainly none had ever been in a community road race before.

We began our training program learning about the body and the systems we would need to develop for us to run this race. We studied famous runners from the past and current runners training for the Olympics. We trained each day on the field and charted our endurance, pulse rate, heart rate and speed. Each student chose a running partner so they could encourage each other when one wanted to stop and walk. We kept training logs of activities done at home. We designed team T-shirts to wear on race day and did community service to raise money for the entry fee for the race. We all believed in our goal of participating in and completing the race.

Each day, lessons revolved around our goal, and the students were very excited about working to achieve it—except for one student.

Luke was not excited about running three miles on roads in the local neighborhood. He was not excited about running even one lap around the field. Luke was not a runner. He was the largest boy in the class by at least six inches and thirty pounds. To run for more than two minutes at any speed was a struggle for Luke. Despite this, he never complained and did each of the workouts with the class, always finishing last, always red-faced and gasping as he shuffled to join the class. Luke never seemed upset, and he trudged on like a real trooper each day.

No one in the class said much about Luke's struggle. It became accepted that Luke would come in last. There was never any pity or insults. It was just the way things were, and it didn't bother anyone—or so we thought.

The night before the big road race, Luke's mother called me. Her son was in tears over the idea of coming in last place in the community road race. Luke understood that winning didn't matter, but coming in last place would be humiliating. Luke's mom wanted me to be aware of this and know that she would walk the course so that she would come in last place instead of Luke.

The day of the race we excitedly lined up for team pictures and stretched our muscles. Everyone was confident about finishing the course and achieving our goal. Even Luke was a proud member of the team and showed no worry.

The gun went off and hundreds of runners started making their way around the course at different speeds. In front were runners from the community who had been running in races for years. In the crowd behind them were my twenty-six well-trained students and myself, a runner for several years.

After I crossed the finish line, I stood along with many parents to greet each student with a victory hug. One and two at a time they crossed, each bringing us closer to accomplishing our goal. I lost count of the students who had come across the line and started asking those who had finished to be on the lookout for classmates approaching. Gradually, each student crossed the finish line with gritty pride to be part of the success of our class as well as the personal success of finishing a 3.1-mile race. After some time, the finish line area started getting more and more quiet. Still, there was no sign of Luke. I looked around, and no longer saw my students or their parents. I was so disappointed. This was supposed to be a class goal, which meant that everyone had to cross the finish line, and then we would celebrate success.

Maybe this was too much to ask of ten-year-olds. Maybe parents who had hundreds of things to do on a Saturday morning did not understand the importance of having their child stay to cheer on every last classmate. I just knew I would not let Luke down. I would stay at the finish line until he crossed.

My disappointment soon turned to concern. What if Luke physically could not do it? As these thoughts ran through my head, I heard a huge commotion around the final bend before the finish line. A siren let off a screech that pierced my ears and turned my blood cold. Oh no, it must be Luke. Something was wrong with Luke! I started sprinting from the finish line toward the corner.

Suddenly, I stopped in my tracks to see Luke with the entire class gathered around cheering him on with every bit of energy they had left. Together, the group of twenty-six fifth-graders crossed the finish line screaming and celebrating their victory with Luke in the middle as the hero.

Every member of our team received a medal for our victory, and every time I look at mine in its special case, I am reminded of these special students, who learned and lived what it means to be a team, and of Luke, my running hero.

Jodi O'Meara

5

MAKING A DIFFERENCE

It's not how you live, it's whose life you change in the wake of yours.

Source Unknown

"I've had a very boring day so far, Ms. Kelley—I'm really counting on you to liven it up."

You Elevated My Spirit

A teacher who can arouse a feeling for one single good action, for one single good poem, accomplishes more than he who fills our memory with rows on rows of natural objects, classified with name and form.

Johann Wolfgang von Goethe

We sat in our crisp, new school clothes, hands folded in front, fidgeting slightly. We looked at the declarations of true love engraved on our desktops, bequeathed to us by last year's class. As if practicing Braille, we traced the carved initials with our fingertips. Our eyes burned through the large clock on the wall, willing it to speed up. Finally, the nine o'clock bell resounded through the halls and classrooms announcing the beginning of a new school year.

The seconds ticked away as we waited for our new teacher to enter. We dared not speak, expecting to be caught by a hunched-over schoolmarm in a sweater fastened with a gold chain. She would peer at us through thick glasses with pointed frames while wagging her finger in admonishment. Heavy sighs filled the room, knuckles cracked, eyebrows questioned, shoulders shrugged.

Your grand entrance, Mr. Barlow, was worth the wait.

We watched you dash in, long wavy hair flowing behind you, leather tassels hanging off each suede sleeve. A white ten-gallon hat crowned this relic of an era gone by or maybe yet to come; this was, after all, 1960. Removing the cowboy hat in a sweeping motion, you bent at the waist then raised yourself upright. With a baritone laugh, you smiled, twirling your handlebar mustache.

"My name is Mr. Barlow," you enunciated resonantly, then proceeded to write it on the board. Slapping chalkboard dust off your hands, you perched on the corner of your desk.

"Now tell me who you are and your favorite thing in the world."

One by one, we mumbled our answers, not knowing quite what to make of our new teacher. You taught the whole day, never explaining your get-up. We found ourselves smiling through geography, science, math, English and penmanship.

When we walked in the next day, you were in the same outfit and greeted us each by name: "Hello, Suzy, who loves her Barbie dolls. And aren't you Tommy, who has three GI Joes?" As quickly as you learned our names, you learned our strengths and our weaknesses, and you always found the positive in us.

Even Catherine. I had known Catherine since first grade. She would walk into a room with her head down, then slink into her chair to become invisible. The teachers rarely called on her because she broke out in tears when she didn't know the answers. That was usually the case in math. We were studying our times-tables one morning when . . .

"Catherine!" All eyes turned to the panicked child, then back to you, Mr. Barlow. "Would you tell me what your favorite number is?"

After an uncomfortable pause, she whimpered as if being tested, "Nine?"

"Excellent! That's my favorite number, too. Ask me why," you said with a sly grin.

"Why?" we all obliged in unison.

"Because." With a piece of chalk you quickly wrote a shortcut to learning the multiplication table for the number nine. Catherine's face shone with her newfound knowledge and understanding.

"So Catherine, if nine is your favorite number, what number should you like twice as much?" You pointed to the board helpfully.

"Eighteen?" she answered haltingly.

"Me, too! I like eighteen twice as much as nine. Which number do you think I like three times as much?"

And so it went, our heads ping-ponging from you to her until the lesson was completed.

Match over, you deferred to the little girl sitting up proudly. "Take a bow, Catherine," you said dramatically.

She did, and we broke out in spontaneous applause. From then on, we rooted for her and all the Catherines in our class. Mr. Barlow, you elevated us, then we took your lead and elevated each other.

I remember clearly the day you taught a lesson to Dennis, the class clown and occasional bully. Dennis had mercilessly teased a classmate, unaware you were witnessing the unacceptable behavior. We held our breaths waiting for our teacher to put an end to the cruelty.

"Stand up, Dennis," you said sternly. Startled, Dennis quickly collected himself and laughingly got up. "Repeat after me," you continued. "I am ashamed of myself for making Mary feel bad."

Dennis repeated the sentence with a grin on his face, causing some of the class to giggle uncomfortably.

A few seconds later the bell rang, and we were astonished to watch the usually unfazed Dennis slump into his seat, put his head in his hands, and sob in loud gasping heaves. No one was more astonished than you. Remember rushing to his side while we herded to recess? You, the frontiersman, held the Huck Finn look-alike in your arms and talked soothingly in his ear. After fifteen minutes of free play, we had almost forgotten about the scene that had taken place in class. We came back in the room wiping our mouths after a hasty drink from the fountain and looked over at Dennis. He was composed and looking very much like his old rascally self. We got out our science books and waited for you to teach us the day's lesson. You did.

"As you know, I embarrassed Dennis earlier today. I want all of you to know that I am very sorry. No one has the right to shame another person. If I had a problem with the way Dennis was acting, I should have spoken to him in private. Anyway," you smiled to lighten the mood, "we've both learned something today, haven't we Dennis?" You winked at the boy who turned scarlet and covered his face, his eyes shining brightly through his fingers.

All of us seemed to excel at something in your eyes. Often you'd let Dennis tell us a joke before three o'clock rolled around. Catherine recited the times-tables flawlessly by semester's end. And I, well, I got to follow in your footsteps. By that, I don't mean I became a teacher.

Do you recall the day when you gathered us around you and finally revealed the reason for your eccentric appearance? You told us that you had been playing Wild Bill Hickock in the ongoing musical *Annie Get Your Gun* at the Palo Alto Community Theater. Muffled "wows" escaped our lips, and we waited, eyes wide and mouths agape, knowing there was more to this story. Then you told us we were going to put on a production for our school. Our excitement couldn't be contained any longer. "What play are we going to do?" . . . "Will we put it on at night so that our parents can come?" . . . "Are we going to wear costumes?"

You listened patiently then showed us the title of our play, *Cinderella.* You wasted no time getting all the prospective actors to do a reading. When it was my turn I read with all the confidence you had instilled in me during the past few months.

At the end of the week you cast the parts. I got the lead! Looking back, I truly doubt, Mr. Barlow, that you would ever get a job as a casting director in a legitimate production.

I was a vision. White poster board adorned my head, topped with a trailing pink chiffon scarf. Stringy chestnut hair escaped the gold bobby pins entrusted to secure the peaked paper hat. For extra insurance, an elastic restraint went under my chin and encircled my already enormous ears, accentuating them even more. A borrowed taffeta prom dress, three sizes too big, tented over the hoop skirt. In my mother's dress heels, my spindly legs waltzed with each wobbly step. Blue eye shadow, expertly applied by a nine-year-old, caked my lids, and ruby lipstick smothered lips frozen in a permanent smile.

For one night, I was a beautiful princess; for a lifetime, I will be a self-assured woman.

On the outside, I looked more like one of Cinderella's evil stepsisters than Prince Charming's bride-to-be. On the inside, I glowed. A glow that you, Mr. Barlow, ignited and time will never diminish. A glow that Dennis and Catherine and I will pass on forever.

Adela Anne Bradlee

We Never Know

A master can tell you what he expects of you. A teacher, though, awakens your own expectations.

Patricia Neal

As long as I could remember, I'd wanted to be a teacher. On my list of "Most Respected," my teachers followed closely behind God and parents. That explains why, after four years in the air force during the Korean conflict, four years of college, one wife and a daughter, I found myself completing my student-teaching requirement in a small town in Illinois near the university campus.

I was in front of the class during a science demonstration, when a distinguished-looking man barged into the room and boldly stated that he was the superintendent of schools in a western suburb of Chicago and he wanted to hire me. (High-school chemistry and physics teachers were in demand. Russia had just launched *Sputnik,* and most secondary schools were rushing to upgrade their science curricula. They were competing with the large industries, which offered better starting salaries as enticements.) I told him I intended to teach in the central Illinois area and already had a job offer for thirty-six hundred dollars a year and was not interested in going to the Chicago area. He said, "I'll give you four thousand dollars." *Wow,* I thought. *Maybe I should go up north and take a look.* At that time, four hundred dollars a year was a huge difference.

I went north for an interview with the principal, who through my eyes, appeared to be Mr. Educator. He showed me the plans for the new addition to the physical plant with four new laboratories, which would be completed for my second year. Thrilled with the prospects, I signed a contract and agreed to attend graduate school during summers until I earned a masters of science degree.

My first year was hell. I was only given one chemistry class for non-college bound students, then two freshman general science classes of fifty-plus students each, and a senior physical science class. Since we were extremely crowded with students arriving and leaving all day, I was assigned two special duties: meeting the school bus and herding students into an auditorium until the bell, and study hall duty. My first class began at 7:30 and my last was over at 4:00.

But none of this caused me the most grief because I knew it was temporary until the new addition was added. Nor was it the fact that I didn't have a desk, a filing cabinet, a room of my own. I didn't mind that I somehow had to get more than one hundred freshmen to prepare science fair projects (a school requirement), or had to chair the homecoming parade, or wheel my science equipment on a lab cart between four different labs. My grief was my senior physical science class.

In my interview, I evidently made such an impression on my principal with my educational jargon about my aims, goals and dedication to the profession that he made the following proposal: "We have a dozen senior boys who will not graduate because they lack a credit in science. All plan to enlist in the army at the end of the year and don't care whether they get their diploma or not. I feel they will regret this for the rest of their lives. Could you design a science class in which they could succeed enough that we could give them a science credit?" Perhaps because of my lack of experience, I was eager to take on the task.

Forty years later I can still see their expressions as they seated themselves that first day of class and recognized each other. In that instant they knew what we were up to. From the back of the room I heard in a whisper, "If we stick together he can't flunk all of us."

I immediately reasoned that they had been treated as failures, and since I didn't know any of them personally, I would treat them as I would my top-notch college-bound seniors.

I spent most of my preparation time setting up physics equipment for the next day, each lab desk equipped with levers, pulleys, weights, etc. for a lab exercise dealing with forces. When they arrived and saw the equipment, the room buzzed with excitement. I was right! Now we will see some learning take place. I went into the storeroom for a piece of demo equipment. When I returned to the room I was excited to see them already actively engaged, then I was immediately disappointed to see them standing on their lab benches dueling with their meter sticks. Strike one.

Instead of sleeping, I spent most nights trying to come up with strategies that might work with that class. Since they carried rolled-up hot rod magazines in their hip pockets and constantly tried to read them during class, I came up with the plan to bring auto parts to class and base our study of physical principles around something more practical to them. I learned a *lot*:

1. How to lug a transmission up three flights of stairs and down a long hall to the room.
2. That they immediately could recognize it as a '57 Chevy.

But as soon as I began a discussion of the function of the parts of the transmission, they blacked out on me. Strike two.

After collecting the first test papers—twelve completely blank sheets with only the students' names on them—I realized that threats or ranting wouldn't work either. They had already had three years of that. But wait! I'd still been trying what every other science teacher had probably tried and failed to get through to them. I went to Mr. Johnson, the principal, and asked for permission to forget the textbook, classroom and laboratory during the class period and be allowed to leave the building to go to construction sites and telephone companies to take photographs and process the pictures. (I had been an air force photographer.) I could use these trips to teach physics, communications and even chemistry units. If these worked, we could continue with other units that I had in mind. He was all for it with one condition: We must not disturb other classes as we left the building.

I proposed this tactic to the class, and they were all for it. I stressed the importance of leaving the building quietly or that would be the end of our daily trips. It was winter with snow on the ground, so I asked them to bring their coats to class next day and we would walk to AT&T, which was close to the school.

As we moved through the hallways, the boys looked in many of the classrooms and made faces and waved. When we reached the street they threw snowballs at each other all the way. We never left the campus again.

I was so stressed out by Christmas break that I told Mr. Johnson I wasn't coming back after the holidays as I had realized I was not a good teacher and had failed miserably. He told me that he didn't want to lose me. He asked me to think about it seriously for the next two weeks, and if I did finish out the semester, he promised that as long as he was principal I would have all the advanced college placement chemistry classes since I was certainly qualified to teach them. After two weeks of rest and sleep, I decided to finish out my contract as well as thirty wonderful years of teaching at Downers Grove High School.

So what is the point of this story, which is typical for many beginning teachers?

Two years later I was selling tickets at one of our night football games to earn an extra five dollars when I noticed a handsome sharp-looking soldier over to one side of the ticket line. Eventually there was a break in the line, and he stepped up to the lighted booth so I could see his face.

"Sir, do you remember me?"

"My goodness, I certainly do. You are Jim. I remember every boy's name from that class."

"Sir, did you ever know that you were our favorite teacher, and your class was our favorite class?"

"Are you kidding? I have always felt that I let you boys down. I didn't teach you much of anything. I almost quit teaching because I failed you. So how can you say that?"

"But, Sir, you were the only teacher in high school who cared enough to keep trying, and you never gave up on us."

I wept unashamedly.

Larry L. Leathers

The Reader

That I may care enough to love enough to share enough to let others become what they can be.

John O'Brien

I remember it like it was yesterday, my first year of teaching. It was a third-grade class. All the preparation, all the textbooks and all of the classes I took did not completely prepare me for my first day.

Nervous does not begin to describe the anxiety I felt the days before meeting my class. One teacher added to that anxiety by telling me about a student on my roster. I'll call him Enrique. She explained to me that Enrique had come to that school only two months prior.

He was smaller than the other students. He was shy, in fact so shy that he often hid under his desk. Enrique could only count to five, didn't know the alphabet, could barely write his name, and had poor motor and communication skills. He'd go to a special class half of the day. The other half, he'd be with me. Yikes!

I recall asking Enrique's former teacher how to include him in the day's activities. She told me, "You don't." She'd purchased puzzles and preschool toys at yard sales and kept them in a box. When Enrique was in her class he had free access to the box.

I did not want this boy in my class. That must sound horrible, but it's true. I was scared enough as it was. I silently prayed he would not show up. "Just one year," I asked for, "just one year to get my bearings. After the first year, I could handle a student like Enrique with special needs."

That first day of school came. I think I was more afraid of the kids than they were of me, but I didn't let it show. Strangely though, there was no Enrique. A week went by and still no Enrique. A month, no Enrique. He was officially removed from my class roster. By the second month, the students and I were getting our routines smoothly into place.

At the beginning of my third month, I was about twenty minutes into teaching that morning when someone from the office came to my door with a little boy I'd never seen before. Before he was introduced to me I knew it was Enrique. With all of the fortitude I could muster, I forced a smile and welcomed him to our classroom, his classroom.

My entire routine was upset with assessing Enrique, getting his supplies, setting up his desk and learning his schedule. When I asked him to read me a passage from a book, he told me, "I can't read."

I assured him, "Sure, you can. Maybe this is just too difficult."

Enrique repeated, "I can't read."

As the days turned into weeks, I realized Enrique's presence was not nearly as traumatic as I thought it would be. There was no special "Enrique box." He participated in nearly every activity. I just modified them or paired him up with a partner. He wasn't a lost cause. He wanted to learn.

I started a special reading tutorial for Enrique. He learned the alphabet and phonics. For Christmas I bought him a board book about Santa Claus. It was the only book he owned. Although he could not read the story, he memorized it and repeated it at home every night.

Then one day we heard he had moved to another area of town. Enrique would be leaving our school to attend another in the district. Instead of the exuberance I certainly would have felt the first week of his arrival, I surprised myself with a resounding, "No! No he can't leave!" I pleaded my case. He was making progress and learning to read. He participated in class and was comfortable with the other students, who took him under their wings. Leaving the safe environment would surely send him back "under the desk," and all of our hard work would be lost. He'd have to start from ground zero again.

My pleas were effective. Enrique stayed. Somehow my principal and the district worked out a way to bus him to and from our school daily. I couldn't believe what I'd done. I'd fought to keep a child that I'd prayed I'd never have to teach.

As the school year continued, Enrique and I bonded. I'd start him on a project, then go help others. When I wasn't looking, he'd sneak a paper to his desk and draw a flower or a stick figure then secretly put it on my desk. When I'd find it, I'd peek over at him. We'd make eye contact, Enrique would smile, then return to his work.

One day in May I found a smiley face on yellow construction paper on my desk. It was decorated with stars and hearts. I recognized Enrique's work. Our eyes met, but this time I signaled for him to come to me. I whispered, "Enrique, did you draw this for me?" He nodded. I asked him why. He looked up at me and answered as if I should have known, "You help me read." He smiled, then went back to the work at his seat.

It was the most powerful moment of my teaching career. It was the moment I realized I really was a teacher, and what I did counted. I'd touched someone, and it was important. It also felt wonderful. I knew then I'd made a difference in someone's life. If I could touch one Enrique a year until I retired, I would be pleased with my life's work. Enrique taught me to expect the most from every one of my students, because each one has exactly that to give, the most. It's easy to get caught up with the politics and the struggles in education. But it's important to remember that we're all striving for that same goal. We all want the Enriques to learn, to feel confident, to be successful.

As my first year wound down, I pulled Enrique aside and asked him if he remembered telling me that he couldn't read when we'd first met. He said he remembered.

"Well, what about now?" I asked. Enrique lit up the room with his smile, then said, "I am a reader." He was right. He was a reader and much more.

Leon Lewandowski

Sergei

One of the beauties of teaching is that there is no limit to one's growth as a teacher, just as there is no knowing beforehand how much your students can learn.

Herbert Kohl

I had worried myself sick over Sergei's mother coming to see me. I was a new teacher, and I gave honest accounts of the students' work. In Sergei's case, the grades were awfully low. He was an extremely bright sixth-grader whose knowledge "leaked out at the elbow," as we said. He discussed adult subjects with nearly adult comprehension, but he couldn't read his own handwriting. His math grades were abysmal, for the same reason. His work in no way reflected his abilities, and I knew it. So when his mother made arrangements for a conference, I felt panicky, as if I were being called to account for Sergei's poor work.

Additionally, I knew his parents were communists, and I'd just finished teaching a unit on democracy. So I was trying to martial my resources, in case I had to have a political-philosophical discussion about the curriculum that I really would rather avoid. In short, I had new-teacher jitters. Defending one's actions in the face of a parent's opposition is one of the most difficult tasks of even the experienced, and I had taught for only about six months.

So when Sergei's mom entered the room, my palms were sweating. I was completely unprepared for her kisses on both my cheeks. "I came to thank you," she said, baffling me beyond speech. Because of me, she said, Sergei had become a different person. He talked of how much he loved me, he had made friends for the first time, and for the first time in his twelve years, he had recently spent an afternoon at a friend's house. I was responsible for all this. Sergei's psychologist had spoken at length with Sergei's mom, and she wanted to tell me how grateful she was for the self-respect I had nurtured in her son. She kissed me again and left.

I sat, stunned, for about a half-hour, wondering what had just happened. How in the name of all that's holy had I made such a life-changing difference to that boy—without even knowing it? It scared me more profoundly than any experience in my teaching career, before or since. And I knew I absolutely had to figure it out, because so much benefit, unthinkingly bestowed, could just as easily have been so much harm. And I never wanted to be the agent of a harm so huge, especially if it could be delivered essentially accidentally.

What I finally came to remember was one day, several months before, when some students were giving reports in the front of the class. Jeanne spoke quietly, and to encourage her to project her voice when it was her turn, I had said, "Speak up. Sergei's the expert on this; he's the one you have to convince, and he can't hear you in the back of the room." That was it. I knew it as soon as I remembered the incident, because from that day, Sergei had sat up straighter, paid more attention, smiled more, became happy. And it was all because he happened to be the last kid in the last row. Had another child sat there, I'd have probably said the same thing with the substitution of another name. God really does work in mysterious ways, and I thank God that the boy who most needed praise was the one who took the last seat that day, and that Jeanne, usually the class clown, spoke softly that day, too.

It taught me one of the most valuable lessons I've gleaned over the years, and I'm thankful that it came early and positively. We are so fragile. Our children are more so, and a small kindness can indeed make a life-determining difference. I became kinder that day. I became much, much more careful of what I say in front of students. And I hope that, though Sergei moved shortly thereafter, he did well in life, because he gave me more than I gave him.

Molly Bernard

A Tribute to Many Uncrowned Kings and Queens

The art of teaching is the art of assisting discovery.

Mark Van Doren

In the spring of 1962, I was in the seventh grade at Johnnycake Junior High School in Baltimore—Section 7B to be precise. In earlier years, the distinctions between classes had been the "redbirds" and the "bluebirds" in a vain attempt to avoid labeling one class the smart one and the other class (mine) the "dummy" group. But we all knew who was who in the hierarchy of redbirds and bluebirds. So in seventh grade the pretense was dropped in favor of 7A and 7B.

All my neighborhood friends were in the coveted A class. Me? I majored in playground. I was an "honor" student—as in, "Yes, Your Honor. No, Your Honor. I won't do that anymore, Your Honor."

I was a classic left-handed, dyslexic, hyperactive boy who consistently received "unsatisfactory" conduct scores under the category vaguely defined as "self-control." The letters M and N were indistinguishable to me, and a D masqueraded as B, P or Q. Classes were much too long, the desks far too small and the outdoor activities way too short. Like a prisoner about to be granted a three-month furlough, I was counting down the days until June.

The teacher for both 7A and 7B was like a great redwood tree to me; a colossal giant, who at six feet, two inches tall seemed twice as awesome from my diminished vantage point. Mr. King was his well-named title. He was kind, knowledgeable and revered by both sections A and B, a rare feat for any teacher.

One day, quite unexpectedly, Mr. King approached my 7A friends and observed that, "There is someone in 7B who is just as smart as any of you. Trouble is, he just doesn't know it yet. I won't tell you his name, but I'll give you a hint—he's the kid who outruns all of you and knocks the ball over the right-field fence."

Word of Mr. King's declaration reached me that afternoon as we boarded the school bus. I remember a dazed, shocked feeling of disbelief. "Yeah, sure. You've got to be kidding," I nonchalantly replied to my friends; but on a deeper, more subtle level, I remember the warm glow that came from the tiny flicker of a candle that had been ignited within my soul.

Two weeks later, it was time for the dreaded book reports in front of the class. It was bad enough to turn in papers that only Mr. King read, but there was no place to hide when it came to oral book reports.

When my turn came, I solemnly stood before my classmates. I began slowly and awkwardly to speak about James Fenimore Cooper's epic book *The Pathfinder*. As I spoke, the images of canoes on the western frontier of eighteenth-century America collided with lush descriptions of the forest and Native Americans who glided noiselessly over lakes and streams. No Fourth of July fireworks have ever surpassed the explosion that took place inside my head that day—it was electrifying! Excitedly, I began trying to share them all with my classmates. But just as I began a sentence to tell about the canoes, another scene of the land collided with one of Native Americans. I was only midway through one sentence before I jumped to another. I was "hyper" in my joy, and my incomplete sentences made no sense at all.

The laughter of my classmates at my "craziness" quickly shattered my inner fireworks. Embarrassed and humiliated, I wanted to either beat up my tormentors or to run home and cry in my mother's arms. But I'd learned how to mask those feelings long ago. So I returned to my desk, trying to become invisible.

The laughter ceased at the sound of Mr. King's deep, compassionate voice, "You know, Danny," he reigned forth, "you have a unique gift; the ability to speak outwardly and to think inwardly at the same time. But sometimes your mind is filled with so much joy that your words just can't keep up. Your excitement is contagious—it's a wonderful gift that I hope you can put to good use someday."

There was a pause that seemed to linger forever as I stood stunned, and then it began—clapping and congratulatory cheers from my classmates. A miracle of transformation occurred within me on that great day.

Forty years later, I now have fancy-sounding words like "encouragement," or "turning a perceived minus into a plus" to describe what Mr. King did for me that day. Today, I take my turn to say "thank you" to all the Mr. and Ms. Kings—the teachers who helped me and countless others reframe our lives forever.

Daniel Eckstein, Ph.D.

The Sunday School Teacher

I am not a teacher but an awakener.

Robert Frost

Miss Swan couldn't take being a Sunday school teacher any longer. Not for another Sunday! This handful of disrespectful teenagers snapped their gum during prayer time and read magazines during Bible study. But most awful of all, at prayer request time they asked the Lord to increase their weekly allowances!

"I have had it with you. I quit!" she screamed at the students.

"Cool," Rick said nodding in approval. He was the rudest kid she'd ever met.

It took two months to find a new replacement for that Sunday school class. The pastor escorted Miss Betty Ray in to meet the pseudo-angelic-looking group. New in town, she hadn't heard of their reputation for chasing off teachers. By the look of her pink dress, one size too small, and her bad blonde bleach job, the students obviously felt they had an easy mark. Soon bets were being taken as to how long Miss Betty would last with them.

Betty introduced herself, stating she recently came from the South. She certainly looked like a southern belle who wore outdated clothes and whose beauty had peaked a decade earlier, only she didn't know it yet. Snickers rippled in the room as she rummaged through the huge shoulder bag she carried for a purse.

"Have any of you ever been *out* of state?" she asked in a friendly tone. A few hands went up.

"Anyone travel *beyond* five hundred miles?" One hand went up as the snickering diminished.

"Anyone visit *outside* the country?"

No hands went up now. The silent teens were puzzled. What did this have to do with anything? Was she using psychology on them, or was she just plain clueless?

Finally, Betty's bony hand struck on what she had been searching for in her handbag. Pulling up a long tube, she unrolled a map of the world.

"What else do you have in there? Lunch?" someone cracked.

Betty smiled lightly and answered, "Cookies for later."

"Cool," Rick quipped.

Then she pointed with a long fingernail to an odd-shaped continent.

"I was born here," she tapped with her finger. "And I lived here until I was about your age."

Everyone craned their neck to see where it was.

"Is that Texas?" someone sitting in the back asked.

"Not even close. It is India." Her eyes twinkled with joy.

"How did you get way over there to be born?"

Betty laughed. "My parents were missionaries there, and that is where my mother was when I came into the world."

"Cool!" Rick leaned back in his chair duly impressed.

Betty fumbled again in her purse, this time pulling out a handful of old wrinkled pictures along with a tin of chocolate chip cookies. They passed the pictures around, viewing each with great interest. Dark faces stared up from the photos, frozen in time. The kids studied them as they bit into the sweets.

"You don't have to be a missionary—everyone can do something in this world to help another," Miss Betty said.

The hour quickly slid by as she told them her stories about faraway places and what the people were like there and how they lived.

"Wow, this is as exciting as TV!" one young girl told her.

Sunday after Sunday, Betty came to class, tying her lessons to their everyday lives. She told the teens how they could make a difference right now. The students grew to love her, bleached blonde hair and all. The more they liked her, the lovelier she became.

Betty taught that Sunday school class for twenty years. Though she never married, or had children of her own, the town came to think of her as a surrogate parent since she taught two generations of children.

At last, her hair grew into a natural gray. Increasing wrinkles about her mouth and eyes added character to her cherub face. Her hands began to shake with age. Every now and then, she received a letter from a former student. There was a doctor, a research scientist, a homemaker, a businessman and many teachers among them.

One day she reached into her mailbox and pulled out a blue envelope with a familiar foreign stamp in the upper right-hand corner. In the left corner was the name of a boy in that very first Sunday school class, years ago. She recalled how he'd always liked her cookies and seemed so interested in her lessons. A picture slid out of the envelope and onto her lap. Squinting her eyes, she smiled at the man in the photo, still seeing the teenage boy in him. Standing in rubble, in the city of Delhi, India, he stood with other volunteers who had come to help earthquake victims.

The caption read, "Because of you, I am here now."

Robin Lee Shope

Every Student Can Learn

The great thing in this world is not so much where we are, but in what direction we are moving.

Oliver Wendell Holmes

For every student, there is one special teacher, one who reaches them in just the right way or at just the precise time they are ready to learn. If we are lucky, we find our special teacher, the one who lights a fire within us, who kindles burning desire to learn and a faith that we can, indeed, learn the subject. For me, it was my mentor, Sue.

I began working as a special education teacher in a small rural school in Northern California. My students were challenged by communication and learning disabilities. Sue, a veteran teacher, worked with students with similar challenges. She was no ordinary teacher. She had a vision unlike many teachers I had previously experienced.

While it's the common wisdom to say every student can learn, Sue had faith in those words. She organized her classroom around the idea that learning occurs best in a social context. She put challenged students side-by-side with typically developing students. Not only were her students successful across all curriculum settings, they weren't treated any differently from kids who weren't learning-challenged, and, most importantly, they fit in with their peers and were not made to feel different. She worked from each student's strengths rather than working from their deficits. Truly, I had never before seen such students so happy or so successful.

Children who learn in different ways engender far less sympathy than those who have disabilities that can be seen. People with these kinds of challenges are often judged as dumb or lazy, which is far from the truth. It is such a struggle to sound out the letters to the words and by the time you finish the sentence, you've forgotten what you've read. The letters can look different from paragraph to paragraph, and information can come in at such a rapid pace that it is challenging to hang onto it all.

Learning disabilities run in families, particularly among males. Sue had two brothers in her program. Both boys were progressing, and feeling hopeful after having struggled for years, when it was discovered that the baby of the family, the last boy, had a communication and learning disability, too. Sue passed this little guy on to me because of my background in communication skills, and we worked as a team to support him.

It was during this same time period that Sue had stayed late one evening to ready her classroom for open house. She was startled by a knock at her door. There, in her doorway, awkwardly and nervously, stood the father of the family. "Ms. Lyon, I'm sorry to trouble you at this hour," he stumbled, hesitating and searching for words. "Usually my wife comes to see you about the boys for conferences while I'm working. I want you to know how much we appreciate the work you are doing with them. They can read because of you, and that is something we are all grateful for."

Sue invited him in and offered him coffee and a chair. His face showed his internal struggle. Clearly, he was trying to say something that was very difficult for him to communicate.

He took a few sips of coffee while the silence and anticipation of what he was trying to say hung heavily in the air. To reassure him, Sue said, "Your boys are bright and hard-working, and I really enjoy getting the chance to work with them. I think that they trust me enough to tease me about my choice in professional football teams," which brought a smile to the father and broke the tension a little bit.

The father spoke quietly, "I was a hard-working kid in school, and I still work hard today. When I first started in school, I was so happy to be there that I didn't want to miss a day, for any reason. When I started moving up in the grades, school got harder and harder for me. I knew I wasn't dumb because I could remember anything that was said to me, I was athletic and I could do most arithmetic in my head, but I really struggled with reading.

"I would wake up each morning and tell myself, *Today I'm going to try harder to make the letters stand still.* By the end of the day the result was the same, and I couldn't read. As I got into high school, my teachers showed their sympathy for me by just passing me on. They knew I'd mastered the information, and I was not a behavior problem.

"I coped by pretending to need to go to the bathroom during tests, or asking for help from my friends. I even pretended to be asleep sometimes. I started to believe the taunts of 'retarded' from classmates I had heard early on in school. Once I started believing those words, my whole life changed. I was a nonreader in a reading world, and many doors closed to me, or I thought they were closed to me. I learned to hide my disability well; in fact, I'm a master at it. My own wife didn't know for a long time.

"I think reading must be like a secret code, and I just can't make sense out of it. It just looks like a jumble to me. But I've been watching my boys, and they're getting it, with your help.

"I just got a new job at my company, and I really like it; it means a better life for my family. I need to take a test in order to move up the ladder, and I came here to ask for your help. Could you teach me to read? My employer is even willing to give me some time off to work on my reading so that I can better myself."

Sue was stunned. She sat silently, thinking, for a long moment. Then she smiled as she obviously came to a decision. "Yes, of course, you come in twice a week, and I'll work with you. I can't promise you'll succeed, but I can promise to give you all my support."

Every week for two years, the father came to school to work with Sue. It was a struggle for him at first, but with the sense of hope and success he'd witnessed in his sons, plus the trust and encouragement he received from Sue, slow and steady progress ensued. She even wrote to his employer thanking him for investing in his employee and supporting his literacy. She also reassured the boss that he was a very hard worker who was making significant progress.

The day of the test came. Sue was at work, teaching her young students all day but was certainly distracted with the tension of waiting for the news. Would he pass? He was making significant progress, but was it enough? As the day ended, Sue quietly cleared her desk, erased the boards and put away all the materials. She grabbed her coat and was about to turn off the lights and leave when the door opened and in came the father, followed by his whole family.

She looked at him, and the tension broke. He couldn't keep his delighted smile hidden. "I guess you can tell," he said, beaming, "I passed it! I did real well, they told me.

And I've got you to thank for it!" He hugged her and, patiently waiting in line, the rest of his family took their turns hugging her, too.

"No sir, while I do appreciate your thanks, I just want to point out to you and to the kids that you were the one with the courage to ask for support, and you were the one with the commitment to come in here every week for two years and spend all that time studying. You're the real hero, it seems to me."

Sue noticed the two boys looking up at their dad with a newfound sense of respect. It reminded her of why she chose to be a teacher: a special place and a time with a lot of caring that she alone could fill. Yes, for every student there is one teacher, one special teacher who can light the fire of learning.

Meladee McCarty

Awakening

Education is not preparation for life; education is life itself.

John Dewey

A new moon has just slipped behind West Hill, and I wonder what I am doing out at this early hour. It is not an unusual hour, I suppose for most people, but for me it is.

Headed for the Bath, New York, veteran's hospital, to conduct a creative writing workshop for patients who are in an intensive rehabilitation program, I am not only half-asleep, but feeling inadequate. I ask myself what I have accomplished in the year I have spent volunteering.

As I near the old red brick buildings, I come upon David, a fortyish Vietnam veteran and amputee, peddling a bike furiously with his one leg. It is slow going for him, and as I pass, he waves and smiles.

"I have a story!" he shouts, peddling faster. The jeans folded over the stump of his left leg flap in the wind.

Pulling into the parking area I watch him quickly lock up the bike and undo the crutches fastened onto the back of the old three-speed.

I step out of the warm car and shiver in the early mist, waiting as he struggles to reach me.

"I was afraid you weren't coming today," he greets me, gasping.

"Well, here I am," I say, looking into his dark eyes. Eyes that are usually averted or clouded in pain from the ulcers on the stump that keep him here. Today those eyes are bright, swept clear by the wind and the excitement he seems to be feeling.

He reaches into an inside pocket and pulls out a tightly folded paper. He has been coming to the group for months but has never shared any of his writing. He always says he can't write but is a good listener.

I unfold the paper and glance at the title. My eyes fill, and I turn toward the door quickly.

There are only a few lines on a wrinkled notebook page, but they make me see that it has been worthwhile making the early morning trip.

The title of his story is *You Have Helped Unlock the Silence in My Heart.*

Beatrice O'Brien

Easter in Jackson

Even if it's a little thing, do something for those who have need of help, something for which you get no pay but the privilege of doing it.

Albert Schweitzer

The pounding rain began in the middle of the night. The people of Jackson, Ohio, awoke to the sound then went back to sleep. The next day the rain continued, and the water began to rise. Statistics said Jackson floods once every one hundred years, but no one believed this would be the flood of the century.

People were evacuated from their homes to higher ground, leaving everything behind. Buildings in the low-lying areas were immersed in water. People watched as dogs, cats, cows and other animals were swept away. Cars and trucks were carried miles away from their homes. The people felt helpless as they watched Mother Nature show her power.

My roommate, Susan, was home in Jackson that weekend of March third, 1997. When she returned to our house in "The Ghetto" of the University of Dayton, she told us of the floods and how her powder blue Beretta had been destroyed. Her grandmother was rescued while standing on her bed holding her oxygen tank, immersed to her chest in water.

I was a senior at the university, in the second phase of my student-teaching experiences. I worried about lesson plans, finding a job, where to go after graduation and leaving my friends. My worries suddenly seemed to pale in comparison to the problems of Jackson.

Susan returned to her sixth-grade student-teaching experience the following Monday. She told the story to her students and showed them pictures from the newspaper. Her inspired and compassionate students took action. They stopped raising money for their trip to Camp Kern and began raising money for the flood victims. They sold lollipops, wrote letters to the community asking for donations and collected their own money. Even first-graders donated money. Mountains of clothes, furniture and food piled up. Susan's class made Easter baskets from shoeboxes and filled them with candy and toys as well as toothpaste, soap, toothbrushes and shampoo.

She and I loaded her mom's black Chevy Beretta to the ceiling with the Easter baskets. On the trip there, I wondered what I would see; I couldn't imagine losing almost everything. Dusk was beginning to set in, and I felt nervous when we arrived. My stomach dropped when I saw some houses reduced to the railroad ties that had been their foundation. The smell of river water permeated the air. No carpet, furniture, plumbing or appliances remained. Knowing that only days ago this had been someone's home pained my heart. How many children had grown up here? What kind of memories lingered? Would the house ever be rebuilt? The monster flood had dulled its roar and retreated, but its impact would be long-lasting.

We drove from house to house, knocking on doors, ready to begin our mission. I was filled with trepidation. Would families who had been devastated by floodwater want an Easter basket? The gesture was beginning to seem useless.

"Hello, I'm Susan Moore, and this is my friend, Allison. My sixth-graders at Pennyroyal Elementary made Easter baskets for you when they heard about the flooding because they wanted to help."

Their faces lit up as they opened their gifts. As we entered one home, a husband and wife were crouched over their floor with hammer and nails. When he opened the box, he began to cry. "I can't believe those kids did this. Let me give you some money for their school." As I glanced at what was left of his home, I could not believe his generous spirit. He eventually conceded to write a thank-you note instead.

One woman ran out to find us after opening her box, tears rolling down her face. "I collected bunny rabbits, and I lost them all in the flood. There was a small pink rabbit in my box. I can start my collection again. Thank you." The burly man standing next to her also had tears in his eyes.

My heart was warmed as I played the small role of messenger in this tribute to the good in the human spirit. So often we hear of the shortcomings of our youth, but these youngsters answered a cry for help and gave proof that generosity and love prevail.

Allison C. Miller

Changing the World—One Clip at a Time

Never doubt that a small group of committed people can change the world; indeed it is the only thing that ever has.

Margaret Mead

In 1998, principal Linda Hooper wanted to start a project that would teach the students at Whitwell Middle School (Whitwell, Tennessee) about tolerating and respecting different cultures. Mrs. Hooper sent her eighth-grade history teacher and football coach, David Smith, to a teacher-training course in nearby Chattanooga. He came back and proposed that an after-school course on the Holocaust be offered at the school. This in a school with hardly any ethnic and no Jewish students.

Mr. Smith and eighth-grade English teacher Sandra Roberts held the first session of the project in October of that year. The teachers began by reading aloud from Anne Frank's *Diary of a Young Girl* and Elie Wiesel's *Night.* They read aloud because most of the students could not afford to buy books.

What gripped the eighth-graders most as the course progressed was the sheer number of Jews put to death by the Third Reich. Six million. They could hardly fathom such an immense figure.

One day, Roberts and Smith were explaining to the class that some compassionate people in 1940s Europe stood up for the Jews. After the Nazis invaded Norway, many courageous Norwegians expressed solidarity with their Jewish fellow citizens by pinning ordinary paper clips to their lapels, as Jews were forced to wear a Star of David on theirs.

Then someone had the idea to collect six million paper clips to represent the six million Jewish Holocaust victims. The idea caught on, and the students began bringing in paper clips from home, from aunts and uncles, and friends. They set up a Web page. A few weeks later, the first letter arrived—then others. Many contained paper clips. By the end of the school year, the group had assembled 100,000 clips. But it occurred to the teachers that collecting six million paper clips at that rate would take a lifetime.

The group's activities have long spilled over from the classroom. It's now called the Holocaust Project. Down the halls, students have created a concentration camp simulation with paper cutouts of themselves pasted on the wall. Chicken wire stretches across the wall to represent electrified fences. Wire mesh is hung with shoes to represent the millions of shoes the victims left behind when they were marched to death chambers. And every year now they reenact the "walk" to show their love and respect for those victims they never had a chance to meet. The "walk" also gives students at least an inkling of what people must have felt when Nazi guards marched them off to camps.

Meanwhile, the paper clip counting continues. Students gather for their Wednesday meeting, each wearing a paper clip on the lapel of their group's polo shirt emblazoned: "Changing the World, One Clip at a Time." All sorts of clips arrive: silver- and bronze-colored clips, colorful plastic-coated clips, small clips, large clips, round clips, triangular clips, and even clips fashioned from wood. The students file all the letters they receive in ring binders. With the collected paper clips, the students wanted to honor the victims with a memorial.

It was decided that the memorial would be more meaningful if the clips could be housed in an authentic German railroad car. With help from German citizens, the school obtained an authentic German railroad car from the 1940s, one that was actually used to transport victims to the camps. The car, transported from Berlin, Germany, to the tiny town of Whitwell, now sets in front of the middle school loaded with eleven million of these symbolic paper clips from all over the world. The principal, teachers and students took their vision and turned it into a reality. Having collected over twenty-nine million paper clips and over twenty thousand letters, the students and teachers at Whitwell Middle School have achieved a response that no one could have predicted.

For generations of Whitwell eighth-graders, a paper clip will never again be just a paper clip. Instead, it will carry a message of perseverance, empathy, tolerance and understanding. One student put it like this: "Now, when I see someone, I think before I speak, I think before I act and I think before I judge."

Can one person, or one small group, truly do anything to help bring humanity together in understanding and peace? Just ask the students at Whitwell and all of those around the world who are helping them collect paper clips!

Steve Goodier

6

THE CLASSICS

To teach is to learn again.

Oliver Wendell Holmes

All the Good Things

A child's life is like a piece of paper on which every passerby leaves a mark.

Ancient Chinese Proverb

He was in the third-grade class I taught at Saint Mary's School in Morris, Minnesota. All thirty-four of my students were dear to me, but Mark Eklund was one in a million. Very neat in appearance, he had that happy-to-be-alive attitude that made even his occasional mischievousness delightful.

Mark also talked incessantly. I tried to remind him again and again that talking without permission was not acceptable. What impressed me so much, though, was the sincere response every time I had to correct him for misbehaving. "Thank you for correcting me, Sister!" I didn't know what to make of it at first, but before long I became accustomed to hearing it many times a day.

One morning my patience was growing thin when Mark talked once too often, and then I made a novice-teacher's mistake. I looked at Mark and said, "If you say one more word, I am going to tape your mouth shut!"

It wasn't ten seconds later when Chuck blurted out, "Mark is talking again." I hadn't asked any of the students to help me watch Mark, but since I had stated the punishment in front of the class, I had to act on it.

I remember the scene as if it had occurred this morning. I walked to my desk, very deliberately opened the drawer and took out a roll of masking tape. Without saying a word, I proceeded to Mark's desk, tore off two pieces of tape and made a big X with them over his mouth. I then returned to the front of the room.

As I glanced at Mark to see how he was doing, he winked at me. That did it! I started laughing. The entire class cheered as I walked back to Mark's desk, removed the tape, and shrugged my shoulders. His first words were, "Thank you for correcting me, Sister."

At the end of the year I was asked to teach junior-high math. The years flew by and before I knew it, Mark was in my classroom again. He was more handsome than ever and just as polite. Since he had to listen carefully to my instruction in the "new math," he did not talk as much in ninth grade as he had in third.

One Friday, things just didn't feel right. We had worked hard on a new concept all week, and I sensed that the students were growing frustrated with themselves—and edgy with one another. I had to stop this crankiness before it got out of hand. So I asked them to list the names of the other students in the room on two sheets of paper, leaving a space between each name. Then I told them to think of the nicest thing they could say about each of their classmates and write it down.

It took the remainder of the class period to finish the assignment, but as the students left the room, each one handed me the papers. Charlie smiled. Mark said, "Thank you for teaching me, Sister. Have a good weekend."

That Saturday, I wrote down the name of each student

on a separate sheet of paper, and I listed what everyone else had said about that individual. On Monday I gave each student his or her list. Some of them ran two pages. Before long, the entire class was smiling. "Really?" I heard whispered. "I never knew that meant anything to anyone!" "I didn't know others liked me so much!"

No one ever mentioned those papers in class again. I never knew if they discussed them after class or with their parents, but it didn't matter. The exercise had accomplished its purpose. The students were happy with themselves and one another again.

That group of students moved on. Several years later, after I returned from a vacation, my parents met me at the airport. As we were driving home, Mother asked the usual questions about the trip, the weather, and my experiences in general. There was a slight lull in the conversation. Mother gave Dad a sideways glance and simply said, "Dad?" My father cleared his throat as he usually did before saying something important. "The Eklunds called last night," he began.

"Really?" I said. "I haven't heard from them for several years. I wonder how Mark is."

Dad responded quietly. "Mark was killed in Vietnam," he said. "The funeral is tomorrow, and his parents would like it if you could attend." To this day I can still point to the exact spot on I-494 where Dad told me about Mark.

I had never seen a serviceman in a military coffin before. Mark looked so handsome, so mature. All I could think at that moment was, *Mark, I would give all the masking tape in the world if only you could talk to me.*

The church was packed with Mark's friends. Chuck's sister sang "The Battle Hymn of the Republic." Why did it have to rain on the day of the funeral? It was difficult enough at the graveside. The pastor said the usual prayers and the bugler played taps. One by one, those who loved

Mark took a last walk by the coffin and sprinkled it with holy water.

I was the last one to bless the coffin. As I stood there, one of the soldiers who had acted as a pallbearer came up to me. "Were you Mark's math teacher?" he asked. I nodded as I continued to stare at the coffin. "Mark talked about you a lot," he said.

After the funeral, most of Mark's former classmates headed to Chuck's farmhouse for lunch. Mark's mother and father were there, obviously waiting for me. "We want to show you something," his father said, taking a wallet out of his pocket. "They found this on Mark when he was killed. We thought you might recognize it."

Opening the billfold, he carefully removed two worn pieces of notebook paper that had obviously been taped, folded and refolded many times. I knew without looking that the papers were the ones on which I had listed all the good things each of Mark's classmates had said about him. "Thank you so much for doing that," Mark's mother said. "As you can see, Mark treasured it."

Mark's classmates started to gather around us. Charlie smiled rather sheepishly and said, "I still have my list. It's in the top drawer of my desk at home." Chuck's wife said, "Chuck asked me to put his in our wedding album." "I have mine, too," Marilyn said. "It's in my diary." Then Vicki, another classmate, reached into her pocketbook, took out her wallet and showed her worn and frazzled list to the group. "I carry this with me at all times," Vicki said without batting an eyelash. "I think we all saved our lists."

That's when I finally sat down and cried. I cried for Mark and for all his friends who would never see him again.

Helen P. Mrosla
Chicken Soup for the Soul

Miss Hardy

There comes that mysterious meeting in life when someone acknowledges who we are and what we can be, igniting the circuits of our highest potential.

Rusty Berkus

I began life as a learning-disabled child. I had a distortion of vision that we label "dyslexia." Dyslexic children often learn words quickly, but they don't know they don't see them the way other people do. I perceived my world as a wonderful place filled with these shapes called words and developed a rather extensive sight vocabulary of words, which made my parents quite optimistic about my ability to learn. I discovered to my horror in the first grade that letters were more important than words. Dyslexic children make them upside-down and backwards, don't even arrange them in the same order as everybody else, and so my first-grade teacher called me learning disabled.

She wrote down her observations and passed them on to my second-grade teacher over the summer so she could develop an appropriate bias against me before I arrived.

Another problem I faced is that dyslexic children often see the answer to a math problem, but they don't see the busy work in between like everyone else does. I arrived in the second grade able to see math answers, but having no idea what the busy work was to arrive at them and discovered the busy work was more important than the answer. Now I was totally intimidated by the learning process, so I developed a stutter. Being unable to speak up assertively, being unable to perform normal math functions, and arranging letters inappropriately, I was a complete disaster and developed the strategy of moving to the back of each class, staying out of sight and, when apprehended and called upon, muttering or mumbling, "I d-d-don't kn-kn-know." That kind of sealed my fate.

My third-grade teacher knew before I arrived that I couldn't speak, write, read or do mathematics, so she had no real optimism toward dealing with me. I discovered malingering as a basic tool to get through school. This allowed me to spend more time with the school nurse than the teacher or find vague reasons to stay home or be sent home. That was my strategy in the third and fourth grades.

Just as I was about to die intellectually, I entered the fifth grade and God placed me under the tutelage of the awesome Miss Hardy, known in the western United States as one of the most formidable elementary teachers ever to walk the Rocky Mountains. And this awesome six-foot-tall woman put her arms around me and said, "He's not learning disabled, he's eccentric."

Now, you view the potential of an eccentric child far more optimistically than a plain old disabled one. But she didn't leave it there. She said, "I've talked with your mother, and she says when she reads something to you, you remember it almost photographically. You just don't do it well when you're asked to assemble all the words and pieces. And reading out loud appears to be a problem, so when I'm going to call on you to read in my class, I'll let you know in advance so you can go home and memorize it the night before, then we'll fake it in front of the other kids. Also, Mom says when you look something over, you can talk about it with great understanding, but when she asks you to read it word for word and even write something about it, you appear to get hung up in the letters and stuff and lose the meaning. So when the other kids are asked to read and write those worksheets I give them, you can go home and, under less pressure on your own time, do them and bring them back to me the next day."

She also said, "I notice you appear to be hesitant and fearful to express your thoughts and I believe that any idea a person has is worth considering. I've looked into this and I'm not sure it will work, but it helped a man named Demosthenes—can you say Demosthenes?" "D-d-d-d . . ." She said, "Well, you will be able to. He had an unruly tongue, so he put stones in his mouth and practiced until he got control of it. So I've got a couple of marbles, too big for you to swallow, that I've washed off. From now on when I call on you, I'd like you to put them in your mouth and stand up and speak up until I can hear and understand you." And, of course, supported by her manifest belief in and understanding of me, I took the risk, soon tamed my tongue and was able to begin to speak thoughts.

Then, the year I went on to the sixth grade, for the first time so did Miss Hardy; so I had the opportunity of spending two full years under her tutelage.

I kept track of Miss Hardy over the years and learned a few years ago that she was terminally ill with cancer. Knowing how lonely she would be with her only special student over one thousand miles away, I naively bought a plane ticket and traveled all that distance to stand in line (at least figuratively) behind several hundred other of her special students—people who had also kept track of her and had made a pilgrimage to renew their association and share their affection for her in the latter period of her life. The group was a very interesting mix of people—three U.S. senators, twelve state legislators, a number of chief executive officers of corporations and businesses. The interesting thing, in comparing notes, is that three-fourths of us went into the fifth grade quite intimidated by the educational process, believing we were incapable, insignificant and at the mercy of fate or luck. We emerged from our contact with Miss Hardy believing we were capable, significant, influential people who had the capacity to make a difference in life if we would try.

H. Stephen Glenn, Ph.D.
A 2nd Helping of Chicken Soup for the Soul

To Beth's First-Grade Teacher

The secret of education is respecting the pupil.

Ralph Waldo Emerson

I didn't know the man in front of me that morning. But I did notice that we both walked a little straighter, a little more proudly, as our daughters held our hands. We were proud but apprehensive on that important day. Our girls were beginning first grade. We were about to give them up, for a while at least, to the institution we call school. As we entered the building, he looked at me. Our eyes met just for a minute, but that was enough. Our love for our daughters, our hopes for their future, our concern for their well-being welled up in our eyes.

You, their teacher, met us at the door. You introduced yourself and showed the girls to their seats. We gave them each a good-bye kiss, and then we walked out the door. We didn't talk to each other on the way back to the parking lot and on to our respective jobs. We were too involved thinking about you.

There were so many things we wanted to tell you, Teacher. Too many things were left unsaid. So I'm writing to you. I'd like to tell you the things we didn't have time for that first morning.

I hope you noticed Beth's dress. She looked beautiful in it. Now I know you might think that's a father's prejudice, but she thinks she looks beautiful in it, and that's what's really important. Did you know we spent a full week searching the shopping malls for just the right dress for that special occasion? She wouldn't show you, but I'm sure she'd like you to know that she picked that dress because of the way it unfurled as she danced in front of the mirrors in the clothing store. The minute she tried it on, she knew she'd found her special dress. I wonder if you noticed. Just a word from you would make that dress all the more wondrous.

Her shoes tell you a lot about Beth and a lot about her family. At least they're worth a minute of your time. Yes, they're blue shoes with one strap. Solid, well-made shoes, not too stylish, you know the kind. What you don't know is how we argued about getting the kind of shoes she said all the girls would be wearing. We said no to plastic shoes in purple or pink or orange.

Beth was worried that the other kids would laugh at her baby shoes. In the end she tried the solid blue ones on and, with a smile, told us she always did like strap shoes. That's the first-born, eager to please. She's like the shoes—solid and reliable. How she'd love it if you mentioned those straps.

I hope you quickly notice that Beth is shy. She'll talk her head off when she gets to know you, but you'll have to make the first move. Don't mistake her quietness for lack of intelligence. Beth can read any children's book you put in front of her. She learned reading the way it should be taught. She learned it naturally, snuggled up in her bed with her mother and me reading her stories at naptime, at bedtime and at cuddling times throughout the day. To

Beth, books are synonymous with good times and loving family. Please don't change her love of reading by making the learning of it a burdensome chore. It has taken us all her life to instill in her the joy of books and learning.

Did you know that Beth and her friends played school all summer in preparation for their first day? I should tell you about her class. Everybody in her class wrote something every day. She encouraged the other kids who said they couldn't think of anything to write about. She helped them with their spelling. She came to me upset one day. She said you might be disappointed in her because she didn't know how to spell "subtraction." She can do that now. If you would only ask her. Her play school this summer was filled with positive reinforcement and the quiet voice of a reassuring teacher. I hope that her fantasy world will be translated into reality in your classroom.

I know you're busy with all the things that a teacher does at the beginning of the school year, so I'll make this letter short. But I did want you to know about the night before that first day. We got her lunch packed in the Care Bear lunch box. We got the backpack ready with the school supplies. We laid out her special dress and shoes, read a story, and then I shut off the lights. I gave her a kiss and started to walk out of the room. She called me back in and asked me if I knew that God wrote letters to people and put them in their minds.

I told her I never had heard that, but I asked if she had received a letter. She had. She said the letter told her that her first day of school was going to be one of the best days of her life. I wiped away a tear as I thought: *Please let it be so.*

Later that night I discovered a note Beth left me. It read, "I'm so lucky to have you for a dad." Well, Beth's first-grade teacher, I think you're so lucky to have her as a student. We're all counting on you. Every one of us who left our children and our dreams with you that day. As you take our youngsters by the hand, stand a little taller and walk a little prouder. Being a teacher carries with it an awesome responsibility.

Richard F. Abrahamson, Ph.D.
A 3rd Serving of Chicken Soup for the Soul

The Magic Pebbles

It is the habitual thought that frames itself into our life. It affects us even more than our intimate social relations do. Our confidential friends have not so much to do in shaping our lives as the thoughts, which we harbor.

J. W. Teal

"Why do we have to learn all of this dumb stuff?"

Of all the complaints and questions I have heard from my students during my years in the classroom, this was the one most frequently uttered—I would answer it by recounting the following legend.

One night a group of nomads were preparing to retire for the evening when suddenly they were surrounded by a great light and they knew they were in the presence of a celestial being. With great anticipation, they awaited a heavenly message of great importance they knew must be especially for them.

Finally, the voice spoke, "Gather as many pebbles as you can. Put them in your saddlebags. Travel a day's journey, and tomorrow night will find you glad and it will find you sad."

After having departed, the nomads shared their disappointment and anger with each other. They had expected the revelation of a great universal truth that would enable them to create wealth, health and purpose for the world. But instead they were given a menial task, which made no sense to them at all. However, the memory of the brilliance of their visitor caused each one to pick up a few pebbles and deposit them in his saddlebag while voicing his displeasure. They traveled a day's journey, and that night while making camp, they reached in their saddlebags and discovered every pebble they had gathered had become a diamond. They were glad they had diamonds. They were sad they had not gathered more pebbles.

It was an experience I had with a student, who I shall call Alan, early in my teaching career that illustrated the truth of that legend to me.

When Alan was in the eighth grade, he majored in "trouble" with a minor in "suspensions." He had studied how to be a bully and was getting his masters in "thievery."

Every day I had my students memorize a quotation from a great thinker. As I called roll, I would begin a quotation. To be counted present, the student would be expected to finish the thought.

Alice Adams—"There is no failure except . . ."

". . . in no longer trying. I'm present, Mr. Schlatter."

So by the end of the year, my young charges would have memorized fifty great thoughts.

"Think you can, think you can't—either way you're right!"

"If you can see the obstacles, you've taken your eyes off the goal."

"A cynic is someone who knows the price of everything and the value of nothing."

And, of course, Napoleon Hill's, "If you can conceive it, and believe it, you can achieve it."

No one complained about this daily routine more than Alan—right up to the day he was expelled and I lost touch with him for five years. Then one day, he called. He was in a special program at one of the neighboring colleges and had just gotten off parole.

He told me that after being sent to juvenile hall and finally being shipped off to the California Youth Authority for his antics, he had become so disgusted with himself that he had taken a razor blade and cut his wrists.

He said, "You know what, Mr. Schlatter, as I lay there with my life running out of my body, I suddenly remembered that dumb quote you made me write twenty times one day. 'There is no failure except in no longer trying.' Then it suddenly made sense to me. As long as I was alive, I wasn't a failure, but if I allowed myself to die, I would most certainly die a failure. So with my remaining strength, I called for help and started a new life."

At the time he had heard the quotation, it was a pebble. When he needed guidance in a moment of crisis, it had become a diamond. And so it is to you I say, gather all the pebbles you can, and you can count on a future filled with diamonds.

John Wayne Schlatter
A 2nd Helping of Chicken Soup for the Soul

Mr. Washington

One day in eleventh grade, I went into a classroom to wait for a friend of mine. When I went into the room, the teacher, Mr. Washington, suddenly appeared and asked me to go to the board to write something, to work something out. I told him that I couldn't do it. And he said, "Why not?"

I said, "Because I'm not one of your students."

He said, "It doesn't matter. Go to the board anyhow."

I said, "I can't do that."

He said, "Why not?"

And I paused because I was somewhat embarrassed. I said, "Because I'm Educable Mentally Retarded."

He came from behind his desk, and he looked at me and he said, "Don't ever say that again. Someone's opinion of you does not have to become your reality."

It was a very liberating moment for me. On one hand, I was humiliated because the other students laughed at me. They knew that I was in Special Education. But on the other hand, I was liberated because he began to bring to my attention that I did not have to live within the context of what another person's view of me was.

And so Mr. Washington became my mentor. Prior to

this experience, I had failed twice in school. I was identified as Educable Mentally Retarded in the fifth grade, was put back from the fifth grade into the fourth grade, and failed again when I was in the eighth grade. So this person made a dramatic difference in my life.

I always say that he operates in the consciousness of Goethe, who said, "Look at a man the way that he is, he only becomes worse. But look at him as if he were what he could be, and then he becomes what he should be." Like Calvin Lloyd, Mr. Washington believed that "Nobody rises to low expectations." This man always gave students the feeling that he had high expectations for them, and we strove, all of the students strove, to live up to those expectations.

One day, when I was still a junior, I heard him giving a speech to some graduating seniors. He said to them, "You have greatness within you. You have something special. If just one of you can get a glimpse of a larger vision of yourself, of who you really are, of what it is you bring to the planet, of your specialness, then in a historical context, the world will never be the same again. You can make your parents proud. You can make your school proud. You can make your community proud. You can touch millions of people's lives." He was talking to the seniors, but it seemed like that speech was for me.

I remember when they gave him a standing ovation. Afterwards, I caught up to him in the parking lot, and I said, "Mr. Washington, do you remember me? I was in the auditorium when you were talking to the seniors."

He said, "What were you doing there? You are a junior."

I said, "I know. But that speech you were giving, I heard your voice coming through the auditorium doors. That speech was for me, Sir. You said they had greatness within them. I was in that auditorium. Is there greatness within me, Sir?"

He said, "Yes, Mr. Brown."

"But what about the fact that I failed English and math and history, and I'm going to have to go to summer school. What about that, Sir? I'm slower than most kids. I'm not as smart as my brother or my sister, who's going to the University of Miami."

"It doesn't matter. It just means that you have to work harder. Your grades don't determine who you are or what you can produce in your life."

"I want to buy my mother a home."

"It's possible, Mr. Brown. You can do that." And he turned to walk away again.

"Mr. Washington?"

"What do you want now?"

"Uh, I'm the one, Sir. You remember me, remember my name. One day you're gonna hear it. I'm gonna make you proud. I'm the one, Sir."

School was a real struggle for me. I was passed from one grade to another because I was not a bad kid. I was a nice kid; I was a fun kid. I made people laugh. I was polite. I was respectful. So teachers would pass me on, which was not helpful to me. But Mr. Washington made demands on me. He made me accountable. But he enabled me to believe that I could handle it, that I could do it.

He became my instructor my senior year, even though I was Special Education. Normally, Special Ed students don't take Speech and Drama, but they made special provisions for me to be with him. The principal realized the kind of bonding that had taken place and the impact that he'd made on me because I had begun to do well academically. For the first time in my life I made the honor roll. I wanted to travel on a trip with the drama department and you had to be on the honor roll in order to make the trip out of town. That was a miracle for me!

Mr. Washington restructured my own picture of who I

am. He gave me a larger vision of myself, beyond my mental conditioning and my circumstances.

Years later, I produced five specials that appeared on public television. I had some friends call him when my program, "You Deserve," was on the educational television channel in Miami. I was sitting by the phone waiting when he called me in Detroit. He said, "May I speak to Mr. Brown, please?"

"Who's calling?"

"You know who's calling."

"Oh, Mr. Washington, it's you."

"You were the one, weren't you?"

"Yes, Sir, I was."

Les Brown
A 3rd Serving of Chicken Soup for the Soul

The Royal Knights of Harlem

We cannot always build the future for our youth, but we can build our youth for the future.

Franklin D. Roosevelt

Within walking distance of my Manhattan apartment but also light-years away, there is a part of New York called Spanish Harlem. In many ways, it is a Third World country: infant and maternal mortality rates are about the same as in say, Bangladesh, and average male life expectancy is even shorter. These facts it shares with the rest of Harlem, yet here, many people are also separated from the more affluent parts of the city by language. When all this is combined with invisibility in the media, the condescension of many teachers and police who work in this Third World country but wouldn't dream of living there, and textbooks that have little to do with their lives, the lesson for kids is clear: they are "less than" people who live only a few blocks away.

At a junior high that rises from a barren patch of concrete playgrounds and metal fences on East 101st Street, Bill Hall teaches the usual English courses, plus English as a second language to students who arrive directly from Puerto Rico, Central and South America, even Pakistan and Hong Kong. Those kids are faced with a new culture, strange rules, a tough neighborhood, and parents who may be feeling just as lost as they are. Bill Hall is faced with them.

While looking for an interest to bind one such group together and help them to learn English at the same time, Bill noticed someone in the neighborhood carrying a chessboard. As a chess player himself, he knew this game crossed many cultural boundaries, so he got permission from a very skeptical principal to start a chess club after school.

Few of the girls came. Never having seen women playing chess, they assumed this game wasn't for them, and without even a female teacher as a role model, those few who did come gradually dropped out. Some of the boys stayed away, too—chess wasn't the kind of game that made you popular in this neighborhood—but about a dozen remained to learn the basics. Their friends made fun of them for staying after school, and some parents felt that chess was a waste of time since it wouldn't help get a job, but still, they kept coming. Bill was giving these boys something rare in their lives: the wholehearted attention of someone who believed in them.

Gradually, their skills at both chess and English improved. As they got more expert at the game, Bill took them to chess matches in schools outside Spanish Harlem. Because he paid for their subway fares and pizza dinners, no small thing on his teacher's salary, the boys knew he cared. They began to trust this middle-aged white man a little more.

To help them become more independent, Bill asked each boy to captain one event, and to handle all travel and preparation for it. Gradually, even when Bill wasn't around, the boys began to assume responsibility for each other: to coach those who were lagging behind, to share personal problems, and to explain to each other's parents why chess wasn't such a waste of time after all. Gradually, too, this new sense of competence carried over into their classrooms, and their grades began to improve.

As they became better students and chess players, Bill Hall's dreams for them grew. With a little money supplied by the Manhattan Chess Club, he took them to the State Finals in Syracuse. What had been twelve disparate, isolated, often passive, shutdown kids had now become a team with their own chosen name: The Royal Knights. After finishing third in their own state, they were eligible for the Junior High School Finals in California.

By now, however, even Bill's own colleagues were giving him reasons why he shouldn't be spending so much time and effort. In real life, these ghetto kids would never "get past New Jersey," as one teacher put it. Why raise funds to fly them across the country and make them more dissatisfied with their lives? Nonetheless, Bill raised money for tickets to California. In that national competition, they finished seventeenth out of 109 teams.

By now, chess had become a subject of school interest—if only because it led to trips. On one of their days at a New York chess club, the team members met a young girl from the Soviet Union who was the Women's World Champion. Even Bill was floored by the idea that two of his kids came up with: If this girl could come all the way from Russia, why couldn't The Royal Knights go there? After all, it was the chess capital of the world, and the Scholastic Chess Friendship Games were coming up.

Though no U.S. players their age had ever entered these games, officials in Bill's school district rallied round the idea. So did a couple of the corporations he approached for travel money. Of course, no one thought his team could win, but that wasn't the goal. The trip itself would widen the boys' horizons, Bill argued. When Pepsi-Cola came up with a $20,000 check, Bill began to realize that this crazy dream was going to come true.

They boarded the plane for the first leg of their trip to Russia as official representatives of the country from which they had felt so estranged only a few months before. But as veterans of Spanish Harlem, they also made very clear that they were representing their own neighborhood. On the back of their satin athletic jackets was emblazoned not "U.S.A.," but "The Royal Knights."

Once they were in Moscow, however, their confidence began to falter badly. The experience and deliberate style of their Soviet opponents were something they had never previously encountered. Finally, one of the Knights broke the spell by playing a Soviet Grand master in his thirties to a draw in a simulation match. The Russians weren't invincible after all; just people like them. After that, the Knights won about half their matches, and even discovered a homegrown advantage in the special event of speed chess. Unlike the Soviet players, who had been taught that slowness and deliberation were virtues, the Knights had a street-smart style that made them both fast and accurate.

By the time Bill and his team got to Leningrad to take on the toughest part of their competition, the boys were feeling good again. Though they had been selected at random for their need to learn English, not for any talent at chess, and though they had been playing for only a few months, they won one match and achieved a draw in another.

When the Knights got back to New York, they were convinced they could do anything.

It was a conviction they would need. A few months later when I went to their junior high school clubroom, Bill Hall, a big, gentle man who rarely gets angry, was furious about a recent confrontation between one of the Puerto Rican team members and a white teacher. As Bill urged the boy to explain to me, he had done so well on a test that the teacher, thinking he had cheated, made him take it over. When the boy did well a second time, the teacher seemed less pleased than annoyed to have been proven wrong. "If this had been a school in a different neighborhood," said Bill, "none of this would have happened."

It was the kind of classroom bias that these boys had been internalizing—but now had the self-esteem to resist. "Maybe the teacher was just jealous," the boy said cheerfully. "I mean, we put this school on the map."

And so they had. Their dingy junior high auditorium had just been chosen by a Soviet dance troupe as the site of a New York performance. Every principal in the school district was asking for a chess program, and local television and newspapers had interviewed The Royal Knights. Now that their junior high graduation was just weeks away, bids from various high schools with programs for "gifted" kids were flooding in, even one from a high school in California. Though all the boys were worried about their upcoming separation, it was the other team members who had persuaded the boy who got that invitation to accept it.

"We told him to go for it," as one said. "We promised to write him every week," said another. "Actually," said a third, "we all plan to stay in touch for life."

With career plans that included law, accounting, teaching, computer sciences—futures they wouldn't have thought possible before—there was no telling what continuing surprises they might share at reunions of this team that had become its own support group and family.

What were they doing, I asked, *before* Bill Hall and chess playing came into their lives? There was a very long silence.

"Hanging out in the street and feeling like shit," said one boy, who now wants to become a lawyer.

"Taking lunch money from younger kids, and a few drugs now and then," admitted another.

"Just lying on my bed, reading comics, and getting yelled at by my father for being lazy," said a third.

Was there anything in their schoolbooks that made a difference?

"Not until Mr. Hall thought we were smart," explained one, to the nods of the others, "and then we were."

Gloria Steinem
Chicken Soup for the Soul

How Could I Miss? I'm a Teacher

A master can tell you what he expects of you. A teacher, though, awakens your own expectations.

Patricia Neal

In the early 1960s in New York City, I worked with a group of eighth- and ninth-grade students who were only reading at the second- to third-grade level. I found it difficult not to experience despair, working with them, trying to tutor kids who had basically given up on school. Their attendance was spotty at best. I believe many of them came to school simply because this is where most of their friends were that day, rather than because they thought they might learn something.

Attitudinally, they were a disaster. Anger, cynicism, sarcasm and the expectation of being failed, ridiculed or put down was the tenor and content of their talk. I tried to tutor them in small groups and one-on-one, and I must confess the results were not encouraging with most. Oh, there were a few who seemed to respond more positively on an occasional basis, but it was impossible to tell when that marginally positive attitude might disappear, replaced by sullenness or unaccountable flashes of anger.

One of my other problems was the fact that, at the time, almost no age-appropriate remedial reading materials were available for junior high school students at such a low level. They wanted to read about relationships, dating, sports and cars, not materials like "Run, Spot, run! See the ball. It is bouncing." The kids regarded the materials I had as too babyish and beneath them. Unfortunately, more interesting materials were way too difficult in reading level for them to handle without much frustration. Several of them complained continuously about the reading material. Jose, a tall, lanky boy with a pronounced accent, captured the essence when he said, "Hey, man, this stuff is boring. And it's dumb, too! Why do we got to read this junk, man?"

A glimmer of an idea crept into my mind. I sought help from my department chairman on how to write a proposal for funding a little tutoring project. We didn't get a huge sum of money, but it was enough for a pilot program for the last eight months of the school year. It was simple and it worked.

I "hired" my students as reading tutors. I told them that the nearby elementary school had students in the first, second and third grades who needed help in reading. I had some money that I could pay to anyone who'd help me work with these children. My students asked whether this would take place during or after school. "Oh, *during school.* In fact, it will be instead of our class period together. We'll just walk over there each day and work with the kids there.

"You've got to know that if you don't show up, you don't get paid. And you also have to understand that it would be very disappointing to a young child if you were his or her tutor and you didn't show up or if you didn't work caringly with that child. You'll have a big responsibility!"

All but one of my eleven students jumped at the chance to be a part of this program. The lone holdout changed his mind within one week when he heard from the other students how much they were enjoying working with the young kids.

The elementary kids were grateful for the help but even more so for some attention from these older kids from their own neighborhood. Clearly you could see a version of hero worship in their eyes. Each of my students was assigned two or three younger children to work with. And they worked, reading to them and having them read aloud as well.

My goal was to find a way to legitimize eighth- and ninth-graders reading such young material. I thought that, if I could get them to read that material and read regularly, they would surely improve. As it turned out, I was right. At the end of that year, testing showed almost all of them had improved one, two or even three grade levels in reading!

But the most spectacular changes were in my students' attitudes and behavior. I hadn't expected that they would start to dress better, with more care and more neatness. Nor had I expected that the number of fights would decrease while their attendance dramatically increased.

One morning, as I was entering school from the parking area, I saw Jose walking toward the door. He looked ill. "What's the matter, Jose?" I asked. "You look like you might have a fever." This was a student whose attendance had been the second worst in the group.

"Oh, I guess I'm feeling kind of sick, Mr. McCarty," he replied.

"So why are you here today? Why didn't you stay home?" I asked.

His answer floored me. "Oh, man, I couldn't miss today. I'm a *teacher!* My students would miss me, wouldn't they?" He grinned and went in the building.

Hanoch McCarty, Ed.D.
A 4th Course of Chicken Soup for the Soul

THE BORED OF EDUCATION

Reprinted by permission of Benita Epstein.

A Gift from Brandon

A teacher affects eternity; he can never tell where his influence stops.

Henry Adams

While my son was in college we would talk a couple of times a week. We always had great conversations, but on this particular day it was very special! He was twenty-one years old, about to turn twenty-two, and a senior at Linfield College in Oregon. His name is Brandon. He's studying to be an elementary education teacher, and he had just finished his first day in the classroom as a student teacher.

His phone conversation started out, "Mom, I had my first teaching experience today," and the rest of the conversation went something like this.

"I was pretty apprehensive, not knowing what to expect, but Mr. Schindler, the older teacher in the classroom and the person assigned to help me get started in the world of teaching, assigned me to several young male students to help them with their math.

"Not realizing, Mr. Schindler had told the students

before I entered the classroom that I was a football player for the college. When I entered the room, the students began asking me for my autograph. It made me laugh, but obviously, it made me feel great, too; and the way the students acted, you would have thought I was one of the 49ers or something. I enjoyed the moment and signed some autographs, and then we got down to work.

"I started working with this particular young fellow who was around eight years old. He was having some difficulty getting a grasp on a math problem, and he sadly looked up at me and said, 'I'm so stupid, aren't I?' I told him he wasn't stupid at all and that math hadn't been my favorite subject either. He was really struggling, but he smiled at my comment and we carried on.

"Several hours had zoomed by, and I heard Mr. Schindler say, 'Well, it's time to have some lunch.' He called out, 'Brandon, let's get ready to go.' When he called out Brandon, I immediately came to attention, turning around to see Mr. Schindler coming towards me with a wheelchair. He brought it up to the little guy I was working with. I had no idea that this young student had special needs; no one had mentioned it. We proceeded to move Brandon from his desk to his wheelchair. I was hiding it, but my heart was feeling very heavy at that moment. Mr. Schindler looked up at me and said, 'Brandon, why don't you and Brandon have some lunch.' Mr. Schindler reached down and gave little Brandon two peanuts, a little treat he gave out when they worked hard, and those treats were really special to the kids because they had received Mr. Schindler's approval.

"Rolling down the hallway, Brandon looks over his shoulder and said, 'Wow, I have your name!' Mom, he seemed to be so proud that we shared the same name. By the time we reached the cafeteria, he had a million questions, but one that stayed with me was, 'How's it feel to run and catch a football?' Little Brandon told me he had never been able to walk, so all he knew was that wheelchair.

"The slammer came when we reached the cafeteria door and little Brandon called out, 'Wait, Mr. Flood,' and believe me I was still adjusting to being called *Mr. Flood* . . . that's my dad's name, not mine. Stopping the wheelchair while little Brandon wiggled around so he could look me in the eyes, reaching up and opening his small hand, he handed me his two peanuts and said, 'I want you to have these for helping me so much today.' It stopped me in my tracks, and I must have glued my eyes to those two peanuts, feeling the lump in my throat, I could hardly look at little Brandon at that moment.

"Here was a little boy, who had never felt his feet touch the ground, never had the use of his legs, never experienced so many things in his young life as I had, yet his heart was filled with so much kindness to hand me his two special peanuts! Mom, he had no idea the impact he had on me my first day of teaching. All I could say was 'Thanks, Brandon!'"

Listening to my son tell his story, as I was going through a box of Kleenex, I realized that *my* Brandon had grown up! I had no doubts whatsoever, after that conversation, what a wonderful, caring *teacher* my son would become!

Myrna Flood
Chicken Soup for the Parent's Soul

I Am a Teacher

I am a teacher.

I was born the first moment that a question leaped from the mouth of a child.

I have been many people in many places.

I am Socrates exciting the youth of Athens to discover new ideas through the use of questions.

I am Anne Sullivan tapping out the secrets of the universe into the outstretched hand of Helen Keller.

I am Aesop and Hans Christian Andersen revealing truth through countless stories.

I am Marva Collins fighting for every child's right to an education.

I am Mary McCloud Bethune building a great college for my people, using orange crates for desks.

And I am Bel Kaufman struggling to go *Up the Down Staircase.*

The names of those who have practiced my profession rings like a hall of fame for humanity... Booker T. Washington, Buddha, John Dewey, Leo Buscaglia, Moses and Jesus.

I am also those whose names and faces have long been forgotten but whose lessons and character will always be remembered in the accomplishments of their students.

I have wept for joy at the weddings of former students, laughed with glee at the birth of their children, and stood with head bowed in grief and confusion by graves dug too soon for bodies far too young.

Throughout the course of a day, I have been called upon to be an actor, friend, nurse and doctor, coach, finder of lost articles, money-lender, taxi driver, psychologist, substitute parent, salesman, politician, and a keeper of the faith.

Despite the maps, charts, formulas, verbs, stories and books, I have really had nothing to teach, for my students really have only themselves to learn, and I know it takes the whole world to tell you who you are.

I am a paradox. I speak loudest when I listen the most. My greatest gifts are in what I am willing to appreciatively receive from my students.

Material wealth is not one of my goals, but I am a full-time treasure seeker in my quest for new opportunities for my students to use their talents and in my constant search for those talents that sometimes lie buried in self-defeat.

I am the most fortunate of all who labor.

A doctor is allowed to usher life into the world in one magic moment. I am allowed to see that life is reborn each day with new questions, ideas and friendships.

An architect knows that if he builds with care, his structure may stand for centuries. A teacher knows that if he builds with love and truth, what he builds will last forever.

I am a warrior, daily doing battle against peer pressure, negativity, fear, conformity, prejudice, ignorance and apathy. But I have great allies: intelligence, curiosity, parental support, individuals, creativity, faith, love and laughter all rush to my banner with indomitable support.

And who do I have to thank for this wonderful life I am so fortunate to experience, but you the public, the parents. For you have done me the great honor to entrust me with your greatest contribution to eternity, your children.

And so I have a past that is rich in memories. I have a present that is challenging, adventurous and fun because I am allowed to spend my days with the future.

I am a teacher . . . and I thank God for it every day.

John Wayne Schlatter
Chicken Soup for the Soul

7

OVERCOMING OBSTACLES

The object of education is to prepare the young to educate themselves throughout their lives.

Robert Maynard Hutchins

"I love my students, I love them not."

Reprinted by permission of Donna Barstow.

Standing by Mr. Donato

An education is not a thing one gets, but a life-long process.

Gloria Steinem

If an important measure of success is how much people respect and think of you, if it's the lengths they will go to stand firmly in your corner and never budge an inch from your side, then Richard Donato is one of the most successful men in the San Fernando Valley today.

No one at Calahan Street Elementary School would let this thirty-eight-year-old custodian go without a fight. When they learned he would lose his job as plant manager unless he passed a high school equivalency test, everyone from the principal's office to the cafeteria workers got involved. Mr. Donato had to score an eighty-one on the test, but on his first try, the best he could muster was a weak forty-one. This high school dropout from New York, who had made such an impact on this school with his hard work, humor and sage advice to kids, was about to be cut loose. The road uphill was steep, and time was short.

Calahan Street Elementary rolled up its sleeves and got

to work. Teachers came in early and stayed late, tutoring Mr. Donato on their own time. Kids stopped him in the hallways and told him to hang in there. "Study hard Mr. Donato, just like you always tell us to do."

Mr. Donato gave up his lunch and recess breaks to study with teachers Mandy Price, Linda Babb and others. Then he went to night school classes designed to help him pass the test.

The results began to show.

The forty-one score moved up to a fifty on his next try. The fifty became a sixty-four on the test after that. And the sixty-four became a seventy-six.

Five points. So close. But the clock had just about run out. Word spread throughout school that if Mr. Donato didn't pass the test this Saturday, he was gone from Calahan—transferred to another school and a custodial job that didn't require a high school diploma.

Calahan Street went into a full-court press.

Kids got out their crayons and wrote letters to anyone with any clout in the school district, telling them how much Mr. Donato meant to them, how they loved him, and please, let him stay.

Teachers and office workers wrote letters of their own, detailing how Mr. Donato was the first to arrive in the morning and the last to leave at night; how there wasn't a speck of graffiti on this campus, and every classroom was swept clean every morning.

The school custodian may have no high school diploma, they wrote, *but that doesn't mean he isn't one of the sharpest, wisest employees on this campus.*

We aren't asking that Rich be excused from the test, only that he be allowed to stay at Calahan until he passes, Mandy Price wrote. *We all know he can do it.*

But, as educators, they also knew the flip side of their efforts. They knew the anxiety that comes to anyone, from

CEOs to custodians, when success is so close. Would Mr. Donato's score continue to rise, or would the pressure be so great that his grade would drop, depriving him of those precious five points he desperately needed to keep his job?

On Friday, the day before the test, the telephone in Principal Rick Wetzell's office rang. There had been a miscommunication, he was told. Because Mr. Donato had been with the school district for ten years, he was "grandfathered" in. Only new hires needed to have a high school diploma.

Mr. Donato's job was safe.

By midday Friday, the entire school knew Rich would be staying. He didn't need to pass the test anymore.

"Yes, I do," Richard Donato said respectfully. "I have to pass it for my wife and three young children. I have to pass it for myself."

It's like he always told the troubled kids who teachers brought to him for a little talking to. Kids headed down the same wrong road he had taken growing up in New York City. "You gotta stay in school and you gotta try," Donato would say. "The other way is the loser's way."

Now, the sage custodian had a chance to show all the kids at Calahan with action, not words.

Mandy Price answered her phone at home Saturday at noon.

"Is this Mrs. Price, the woman who helped me *pass this test?"*

Too choked up to respond, Mandy could only smile and cheer inside for everyone at Calahan Street Elementary School. Richard Donato scored an eighty-one.

Dennis McCarthy

One of My Early Teaching Jobs

The object of teaching a child is to enable him to get along without his teacher.

Elbert Hubbard

One of my early teaching jobs involved teaching at an alternative school. This school had "the worst of the worst," the students that even public alternative schools had expelled. The students who straggled in the door every day were living lives of quiet desperation, labeled as failures and never expected to amount to anything. Our school had an on-premise day care, so we had a lot of teen mothers who were trying to break free of their cycle of poverty. Every student who came to us realized we were the last chance they had to make something of their lives.

As a fairly new teacher, I was terrified of them. They were mostly African-Americans from the inner-city, and I was a white teacher who grew up in the affluent suburbs. I had visions of what they were like gleaned from countless hours of television and movies. I was sure these kids were violent, amoral people, and somehow I envisioned myself as their savior, the person who would turn their lives from violence and poverty to peace and prosperity. I couldn't have been more wrong.

My first day there, the students knew they had me in a corner and took advantage of every misstep I made. The first scene in *Dangerous Minds* could have been my classroom, and I had no ex-Marine moves to get their attention. I was scared and nervous, and I wondered why I ever thought I could teach these incorrigibles. As I was about to leave, certain that I would turn in my resignation that afternoon, one of my students came over and said, "Oh, you'll be okay. They's just testin' you." With a smile, he sauntered out.

I have never been a person to turn down a challenge, so I came back the next day and the next and the day after that. After a while, the challenges came less often, and I knew I had "made it" when I heard one of our students tell another, "You got Miz Nelson? Yeah, she cool."

I came to the school determined to teach the students how to read. Instead, the students taught me how to live. I learned what it is like to be truly poor, to be told that you are nothing and to have suspicion and fear follow you every day of your life. I learned about the joy you can find in the little things in life and why teenagers want to have babies. I learned what makes a young man join a gang and even take a life. When the student who had reassured me that first day was cut down in a drive-by shooting, I learned a lot about grief. I learned even more about the human spirit and how truly resilient it could be.

My homeroom students were the most special to me. I saw them every morning when we prepared for the rest of their day. We talked about what was going on at home, at school, and everything and anything they wanted or needed to discuss. In the afternoon, before they left, we had study hall and again talked about what was going on in their lives.

Each homeroom teacher was responsible for his or her homeroom kids. We were their advocates, their friends and, for some, very much their "parents" since many of these kids didn't have an available parent figure. If they didn't come to school, we found out why. We visited their homes to meet their families, and we were available at every turn at school to give whatever assistance was needed.

Then, midway through the year the announcement came. The organization that had sponsored us had sold the land, and at the end of the year, our school would be closed.

We teachers were devastated. We loved our kids like our own, and we hated to let them go. The students were even more destroyed. This school was their last chance. Many of them literally had nowhere to go. The public schools had expelled them, and no one else would take them either. Once again, they would fail.

The students responded to the news with one of two attitudes. Many just dropped out, feeling rejected again. Those who stayed decided to work until their last breath and get as much as they could from school. When protest after protest failed, they finally resigned themselves to the fact that they would be moving on. They chose new schools or stepped up their work so they could graduate with the final class.

As the school year came to a close, I wondered what I could give to these kids who had given me so much, who had taught me about myself, and about my prejudices, and about what is really important in life. I didn't have much money, and I knew that material gifts wouldn't impress many of them anyway. So I wrote each student a letter telling them about the wonderful qualities I saw in them, my hopes and dreams for their futures, and the ways they had changed my life. I told each of them that I loved them.

The day before the last day, I handed out the letters and waited calmly, expecting these "tough" kids to reject my words and toss them into the trash. Instead, I was met with absolute silence.

"Do you really mean this?" one asked.

"Of course. Every word."

"Wow."

One big hulking boy, who had never succeeded in school until he came to us, sat silently in a corner of the room. I thought he was just waiting for the moment I wasn't looking so he could throw my letter out. Instead, he came over, hugged me and sobbed. I heard him say, "No one ever told me that I was this good before."

My heart broke. Imagine living your life for eighteen years and never having anyone tell you how valuable and special you are, to not be recognized for being important in the world. I couldn't fathom the despair with which this child had lived his life.

That day, I determined that my role as a reading teacher was not merely to teach students to read, but much more importantly, to teach them of their value in life. To this day, every holiday, I write every one of my students a letter telling them about the gift they are to me and their classmates. It never fails that a few kids cry, and most of them are amazed that someone cared enough to tell them they are valuable people. The letters are tucked quietly into notebooks and some even stapled into binders, lest the letter be lost and the reminder of their value be gone forever.

I often think of those kids and wonder if they know how many lives they have truly touched by having first touched mine.

Angela K. Nelson

Near the end of 1st period, substitute teacher Brenda Angsley was confronted with the undeniable fact that this was a tough school.

The Big Kid

I was only twenty and weighed about 102 pounds when I started teaching. One of the students in my first speech class was twenty-one years old and weighed about 290 pounds. The principal brought him to my class, told him to take a seat and said: "We have to get rid of this kid, this year . . . so pass him no matter what!"

This was my first experience as a high school teacher. I was one day on the job. Because "pass this kid, no matter what" was against my principles, I said to the principal, "No, I will pass him because he deserves to pass. He will pass, I guarantee it."

This "kid" was the youngest of seven brothers. They were all as big as he was, and they would not let him quit school until he graduated. He had taken every class in the school and was teetering on a D average.

After everyone settled in their seats, I introduced myself, set my standards and assigned them to share something good they had done for someone else.

The Big Kid, as he was not so affectionately called, didn't start to work when I said, "You can start preparing what you want to say." He just sat there.

As I approached him, one of the students stopped me

and said, "He never does anything. Don't bother him."

I thanked the student for his advice but ignored his well-meaning words and sat down beside the Big Kid. I looked him in his eyes as if I were definitely his size and said, "Let's begin."

"I ain't goin' ta give no speech," he said with a grin to let me know that this was a very firm and absolute final resolution.

"There is no way out," I responded as I looked at him with the same resolve, as if I were bigger, taller and stronger then he was. I also smiled, paused and then continued as if he agreed with me that he was indeed going to give that speech. (To me this was not a power of wills, but a power of right.) "Let me see, something good that you have done for someone . . ." We started talking and soon he told me about making a tree house for his nephew. His brothers were all carpenters and made everything around the house that anyone wanted except a tree house for their nephew. So he decided one day to do it on his own. The way he told the story was beautiful, filled with love and goodness for his nephew and with a rare insight into the needs of another. He described his nephew in every detail, and added with a smile that broke across his entire face, "That little kid would smile inside out when I'd lift him into his tree house. He'd look down at me as if I had made him King of the Mountain." The Big Kid added shaking his head in disbelief, "You know, everyone thought I was crazy making that tree house for him on account of because he was so crippled."

Our eyes meet. Mine filled with tears. I thanked him with a smile "inside out" for sharing his beautiful story with me and said, "I have a reward for you: you get to be . . . first!" Before he could say a word, I stopped the class and announced, "We have our first speech ready." He looked terror-struck, as if he was facing the biggest hurdle of his life. I quickly ushered the Big Kid to the front of the room. "Tell it exactly the way you told me," I whispered to him. "Have the courage to be 'King of the Mountain' like your little nephew has taught you." Encouragingly, I added, "I believe you can do this!"

After some delay, he opened his mouth to speak. His hands were on top of his head, his old torn, shabby T-shirt revealed a bulging fat stomach hanging over his pants. He twisted and turned; he was definitely uncomfortable and struggling.

I nodded my head. "Begin," I mouthed. "No way out" . . . only a way into the hearts of everyone in that class.

When he finished his speech, there was not a dry eye in the class of those sophisticated seniors and their teacher—me. There was silence. He just stood there with a helpless or hopeless expression on his face, then the class exploded in applause as they jumped to their feet with a standing ovation. He savored, or I should say we all savored, the moment.

I gave him an A. Then he cried, "Nobody ain't never gave me no A before."

"You gave us the gift of telling us your story," I sniffed. "You earned the A." From that point on you had to wrestle the Big Kid for "first speaker position" with every assignment. I have never seen anyone improve so much in my life. The students became his friends, and he became theirs. They still called him the Big Kid, but the meaning had a big heart in it, now. There was such unity and support in that class that everyone was eager to speak.

But that's not all . . .

The next semester, there he was in my journalism class, front and center. We were to produce the school newspaper. Help! I had never had a journalism class in my life. I had never put together a newspaper and never worked on a yearbook, even when I was in high school. The students who were in second-year journalism asked me where the dummy sheets were. I said, "Show them to me when you find them." I didn't have the faintest idea what a dummy sheet was. I studied the book and learned a lot.

But I didn't learn half as much as the Big Kid did. It was in this class that I discovered he couldn't read or write. I was horrified by the "pass-'em-out-of-here-and-forget-'em" policy in place in our schools at that time.

How could he do his assignments without being able to read or write?

No way out.

Okay! I accepted the challenge. To fulfill his assignments, the Big Kid collected his stories by interviewing the students. We confided in one of the second-year journalism students that he could not write, and that person wrote his story each week from his dictation. Soon other students found out about his inability to read and write, and they eagerly offered to help him, as well.

At that time, there were no teachers assigned to teach reading or writing to nonreaders in high school, so the students helped him learn to read and write.

By the end of the year he could read and write. He wrote:

Something Good You Have Done for Me

Thank you. The good you have done for me, I hope I can repay to others.

The Big Kid has learned to read and to write and gets to graduate!

He received an A and the Most Improved Student Award.

Joyce Belle Edelbrock

Only a Shadow in His Past

The student armed with information will always win the battle.

Meladee McCarty

Each August many new students come to us with warning labels. The long list of students and their medical ailments is handed out the first day. Teachers highlight the names in their class and file the list away.

One Monday, five days before semester's end, my seniors began their final exam speeches in my speech class. I sat in the last seat of the center row to evaluate them. Rick sat sideways in the desk in front of me and placed one arm on my desk. He was a mainstreamed special education student, painfully shy, who agonized through every minute of the required speech class.

Rick didn't look at the speakers but stared at my paper as I wrote the evaluations. I was mildly irritated by his scrutiny but didn't say anything. If this attentiveness meant he was coming out of his shell, I didn't want him to retract.

Then a movement on my desk caught my eye. Rick's

hand was stiff and a single finger twitched. A fleeting recollection—Rick's name on the warning list—epilepsy. A millisecond of fear flitted through my body. Rick's head fell back. His legs twitched. No time for fear.

I stood up. "Rick is having a seizure. Help me get him to the floor. Move the desks away from him."

Trevor and Mark lifted Rick to the floor. Everyone pushed desks out of the way. Trevor took off his new jacket, of which he was so proud, crumpled it and placed it under Rick's head. I turned his head to the side. My eyes sought out Amanda, the hyper-responsible overachiever. "Go get Mrs. Leonard, *now!*" She was out the door without a backward glance.

Rick was into a full grand-mal seizure, his entire body rigid and twitching, frothy saliva pouring from his mouth. I knelt next to him and looked up at the frightened faces. "Thank you all for helping. Now go stand quietly in the hallway." The class filed out.

Dolly Leonard, the special education teacher contact, arrived and went to Rick. She looked up at me. "You did the right things here." She paged the office. "Call an ambulance. We have a student in room 212 who's having an epileptic seizure."

Dolly stayed with Rick, and I went to my students. They were quiet, concern etched in their young faces. "An ambulance is on its way. Rick will be fine. Please go sit in the library for the rest of the hour."

Trevor refused to leave. He and I went back into the classroom and waited. The ambulance arrived. The medics strapped Rick to a stretcher and carried him out. Dolly left to call Rick's mother.

Trevor picked up his saliva-drenched jacket and balled it up.

"Sorry about your jacket," I said.

"That's what washing machines are for." He stared at

the floor where Rick had been. "I'm going to the restroom." He came back with handfuls of paper towels and soaked up the saliva. We put all the desks back in order. The bell rang.

"Thanks, Trevor."

He nodded and went to his second-hour class.

Rick was absent on Tuesday. I gave the first speech of the day, praising my class for keeping calm and thanking them for helping. Knowing that a shared significant emotional event bonds a class, I said, "You will undoubtedly learn something about yourselves and each other from this experience."

When he returned on Wednesday, Rick asked if he could change the topic for his speech. My brain ran through all the teacherly reasons why he shouldn't. My vocal chords didn't listen. "If you're sure you can have it prepared in two days, go for it."

Rick delivered the last speech on Friday—an informative presentation on epilepsy. When he finished he placed his notecards on the lectern and looked up at the class. He spoke of when he was diagnosed, of the various medications he had tried, how he found one that worked, how he hated taking it. "In fact, I had stopped taking it. That's why I had the seizure. Guess I'll have to take it the rest of my life." He looked around at the class. "I figured you should know since you were here. I really want to thank all of you for helping me." He looked down for a few seconds before saying, "Do you want to ask me anything?" Questions came, tentatively at first, and then poured forth.

Seated in the center row, last desk, I watched Rick speak with confidence and authority. That painfully shy boy only a shadow in his past.

Melinda Stiles

Let a Miracle Happen

When the pupil is ready, the teacher will come.

Chinese Proverb

"There's a new student waiting in your room," my principal announced, hurrying past me on the stairs. "Name's Mary. I need to talk to you about her. Stop in the office later."

I nodded and glanced down at the packs of pink, red and white paper, and the jars of paste and boxes of scissors I held in my arms. "Fine," I said. "I've just come from the supply room. We're making valentine envelopes this morning. It'll be a good way for her to get acquainted."

This was my third year of teaching fourth-graders, but I was already aware how much they loved Valentine's Day (now just a week away), and making these bright containers to tape to the fronts of their desks was a favorite activity. Mary would surely be caught up in the excitement and be chatting cheerfully with new friends before the project was finished. Humming to myself, I continued up the stairs.

I didn't see her at first. She was sitting in the back of the room with her hands folded in her lap. Her head was down and long, light-brown hair fell forward, caressing the softly shadowed cheeks.

"Welcome, Mary," I said. "I'm so glad you'll be in our room. And this morning you can make an envelope to hold your valentines for our party on Valentine's Day."

No response. Had she heard me?

"Mary," I said again, slowly and distinctly

She raised her head and looked into my eyes. The smile on my face froze. A chill went through me and I stood motionless. The eyes in that sweet, little-girl face were strangely empty—as if the owner of a house had drawn the blinds and gone away. Once before I had seen such eyes: They had belonged to an inmate of a mental institution, one I'd visited as a college student. "She's found life unendurable," the resident psychiatrist had explained, "so she's retreated from the world." She had, he went on, killed her husband in a fit of insane jealousy.

But this child—she could have been my own small, lovable niece except for those blank, desolate eyes. *Dear God,* I thought, *what horror has entered the life of this innocent little girl?*

I longed to take her in my arms and hug the hurt away. Instead, I pulled books from the shelf behind her and placed them in her lap. "Here are texts you'll be using, Mary. Would you like to look at them?" Mechanically, she opened each book, closed it and resumed her former position.

The bell rang then, and the children burst in on a wave of cold, snowy air. When they saw the valentine materials on my desk, they bubbled with excitement.

There was little time to worry about Mary that first hour. I took attendance, settled Mary into her new desk and introduced her. The children seemed subdued and confused when she failed to acknowledge the introduction or even raise her head.

Quickly, in order to divert them, I distributed materials for the envelopes and suggested ways to construct and decorate them. I placed materials on Mary's desk, too, and asked Kristie, her nearest neighbor, to offer help.

With the children happily engrossed, I escaped to the office. "Sit down," my principal said, "and I'll fill you in." The child, she said, had been very close to her mother, living alone with her in a Detroit suburb. One night, several weeks ago, someone had broken into their home and shot and killed the mother in Mary's presence. Mary escaped, screaming, to a neighbor's. Then the child went into shock. She hadn't cried or mentioned her mother since.

The principal sighed and then went on. "Authorities sent her here to live with her only relative—a married sister. The sister enrolled Mary this morning. I'm afraid we'll get little help from her. She's divorced, with three small children to support. Mary is just one more responsibility."

"But what can I do?" I stammered. "I've never known a child like this before." I felt so inadequate.

"Give her love," she suggested, "lots and lots of love. She's lost so much. There's prayer, too—and faith, faith that will make her a normal little girl again if you just don't lose hope."

I returned to my room to discover that the children were already shunning this "different" child. Not that Mary noticed. Even kindly little Kristie looked affronted. "She won't even try," she told me.

I sent a note to the principal to remove Mary from the room for a short time. I needed to enlist the children's help before recess, before they could taunt her about being "different."

"Mary's been hurt badly," I explained gently, "and she's so quiet because she's afraid she'll be hurt again. You see, her mother just died, and there's no one else who loves her. You must be very patient and understanding. It may be a long time before she's ready to laugh and join in your games, but you can do a lot to help her."

Bless all children. How loving they can be once they understand. On Valentine's Day, Mary's envelope overflowed. She looked at each card without comment and replaced it in her container. She didn't take them home, but at least she looked at them.

She arrived at school insufficiently dressed for the bitterly cold weather. Her raw, chapped hands—without mittens—cracked and bled. Although she seemed oblivious to sore hands and the cold, I sewed buttons on her thin coat, and the children brought caps, scarves, sweaters and mittens. Kristie, like a little mother, helped Mary bundle up before she went outdoors, and she insisted on walking to and from school with her.

In spite of our efforts, we seemed to be getting no closer to Mary as the cold, dreary March days dragged by. Even my faith was wearing thin. My heart ached so desperately, wanting this child to come alive, to be aware of the beauty the wonder, the fun—and, yes—even the pain of living.

Dear God, I prayed, *please let one small miracle happen. She needs it so desperately.*

Then on a late March day, one of the boys excitedly reported a robin in the schoolyard. We flocked to the window to see it. "Spring's here!" the children cried. "Let's make a flower border for the room!"

Why not? I thought. *Anything to lift our spirits.* This time the papers we selected were beautiful pastel colors—with brown strips to weave into baskets. I showed the children how to weave the baskets and how to fashion all the flowers we welcome in early spring. Remembering the valentine incident, I expected nothing from Mary; nevertheless, I placed the beautifully colored papers on her desk and encouraged her to try. Then I left the children to do their own creating, and I spent the next half-hour sorting scraps of paper at the back of the room.

Suddenly, Kristie came hurrying to me, her face aglow. "Come see Mary's basket," she exclaimed. "It's so pretty! You'll never believe it!"

I caught my breath at its beauty. The gently curled petals of hyacinths, the daffodils' fluted cups, skillfully fashioned crocuses and violets—work one would expect from a child much older.

"Mary," I said. "This is beautiful. How did you ever manage?"

She looked at me with the shining eyes of any normal little girl. "My mother loved flowers," she said simply. "She had all of these growing in our garden."

Thank you, God, I said silently. *You've given us the miracle.* I knelt and put my arms around the child. Then the tears came, slowly at first, but soon she was sobbing her heart out against my shoulder. The other children had tears in their eyes, too, but theirs—like mine—were tears of joy.

We fastened her basket in the very center of the border at the front of the room. It remained there until school ended in June. On the last day, Mary held it carefully as she carried it out the door. Then she came running back, pulled a crocus from her basket and handed it to me. "This is for you," she said, and she gave me a hug and a kiss.

Mary moved away that summer. I lost track of her, but I'll never forget her. And I know God is caring for her.

I've kept the crocus in my desk ever since—just to remind me of Mary and of the enduring power of love and faith.

Aletha Jane Lindstrom

Special Needs

Every student can learn, just not on the same day, or the same way.

George Evans

School had been in session about two weeks when my principal came to tell me I would be getting a new student. A new inclusion policy adopted by the district meant Kim, a special needs student, was to be placed in a regular classroom for the first time.

Records provided us with some information. Kim had been abandoned by her alcoholic and drug-dependent mother shortly after birth. She had been shuffled from institutions to foster homes for several years before finally being adopted by a distant relative. Kim had been in a special school for retarded children, where she was often restrained to keep her from running away or hurting other children. Her IQ was estimated to be about forty.

"Kim can't be expected to do very much. Just do your best under the circumstances. The special education teacher will help all she can," the principal said.

I spoke to my class the next day, preparing them for the

new student. I explained that she was a special needs student and would need all our help in order to adjust to her new surroundings. I enlisted the help of two sweet girls, Deirdre and Rene. They volunteered to sit by Kim and help her in any way they could. They would be Kim's special friends.

The next day, when Kim was guided into my fifth-grade classroom, my heart sank. She walked with a shuffling gait resembling that of a prehistoric man. Her lank blonde hair was pulled up in a "Pebbles" style. Spittle drooled from her mouth. Her startlingly blue eyes seemed vacant. She clutched a dirty baby doll in her hand.

Whatever will I do with this child in my classroom? I thought to myself. Recovering quickly, I welcomed her and asked Deirdre and Rene to come forward. I introduced them to Kim, and they helped her to her desk.

Children never cease to amaze me. The students acted as if having Kim in our class was as natural as could be. I don't recall anyone ever being unkind, teasing or hurting her in any way. Instead, they accepted Kim as one of them and treated her with love. We carried on with our lessons every day as usual, coping with her occasional outbursts as best we could.

As time passed, we noticed changes in Kim. She walked more upright. She rarely drooled anymore. She began to experiment with a pencil and crayons and became interested in books and magazines. At lunch, Kim no longer ate with her fingers, but used a fork or spoon. She still got food all over her face, but Rene and Deirdre taught her to wipe her mouth with a napkin. The vacant look left her face, and she smiled and even laughed once in a while. Kim learned to trace over letters to write her name. She began to speak in short sentences rather than pointing and saying one word. Each day seemed to bring improvement.

The changes not only occurred in Kim but in everyone in our class. Students were more willing to help one another, more kind and patient. We became almost like a family, not a class.

One day, as I sat on my high stool at the front of the room calling out words for the spelling test, Kim got out of her seat and walked to me.

"Yes, Kim. What is it?"

"Kim say words," she replied.

"Certainly, Kim. You may help me. Come and sit on the stool."

Then, as I called out each spelling word, Kim repeated the word in her own special way. The class smiled and continued with the test. Kim's face was aglow! From then on, Kim and I gave the spelling test together each Friday.

Kim left school at the end of the year and headed for middle school. Though I've never seen her again, I think of her often and carry her picture in my wallet. It reminds me of the great blessing she brought to my students and me—the knowledge that everyone, regardless of race, religion, socioeconomic or intellectual level, is a "special needs" person, and that the greatest of all those "special needs" is love.

Frankie Germany

Moment in the Sun

Billie Jo Johnson was a rather nondescript, somewhat homely sophomore in my drama class the one year I taught in her high school. While several of the other girls in that class had been active in speech festivals and play contests and were quite good, Billie Jo had never involved herself, and I was surprised to find her in my class.

I decided that for the one-act play contest that year, we would produce *Medea,* the Greek tragedy wherein Medea stabs to death her two little boys to gain revenge against Jason, her husband, who had abandoned her but loved the children very much.

It would have been an ambitious effort even for a well-trained college troupe, but I felt we could pull it off with the likes of Virginia, or Carol, or Sharon playing the part of Medea.

On a Monday, I passed out the scripts and told the students we would hold tryouts on Friday. Friday came, and the old "troopers" like Virginia did a very credible job; I was relieved, sure we could at least win an honorable mention at the subdistrict play contest.

Then it was Billie Jo's turn. She had memorized the part of the script she wanted to use for the tryouts. She stood in front of the class, waited for silence, and began.

She became transformed. She was no longer Billie Jo, age fifteen; she was Medea, a middle-aged, vengeful woman, eyes flashing evil, willing to go to any length to avenge her abandonment, even to the point of killing her children, and when she pantomimed the stabbing, the kids and I all screamed. We were stunned. Billie Jo, now having become Medea, looked out over the class with her malevolent smile and held us transfixed for probably half a minute. Then she let us go. Wow!

Billie Jo would play the part, voted for by even the other girls who, up to this point, had wanted it. Rehearsals began.

We found a Jason, the two nurses and recruited two little six-year-old boys, the children of Kenny Frair, the newspaper editor, to play the part of the victims.

The little boys were a delight to direct, as children are natural actors, and while they did not have speaking parts, they died quite convincingly at Medea's hands.

We took the play to the subdistrict contest at Lockwood, where we won first place handily, and then on to the district contest at Springfield, where we won again. Now we were entitled to compete in the state contest at the University of Missouri at Columbia.

That was quite an accomplishment for a little school like Miller High. Here we could be competing against the big "powers." The agenda would be St. Louis, Kansas City, St. Joseph, Springfield and (snicker) Miller.

The plays were presented in Jesse Hall auditorium to a full house, mostly academic types. All the plays were excellent, and Springfield finished to great applause. Then it was Miller's turn.

The curtain went up, Billie Jo began, and within a minute or so, the little auditorium had become the Old Vic, Carnegie Hall and The Royal Opera House. And when

Billie Jo, seeming to glow from the evil aura of Medea, stabbed the children, people in the audience rose to their feet in terror. When the curtain came down, there was dead silence in the audience, and then, when the spell broke, thunderous applause.

The judges awarded Miller first prize, and as they handed me the trophy, one of the judges asked me if it was difficult to direct the little boys.

I asked, "What little boys? The weather was so bad their parents didn't want them to come."

"But I saw them," she said.

"No, you didn't. Billie Jo just had you so much under her spell you only thought you saw them. She pantomimed that part, just like she did in tryouts."

A few weeks later, Billie Jo received an offer of a full four-year scholarship to the MU drama department. But her parents wouldn't hear of it. They said Billie Jo needed to stay on the farm like a decent girl should. She'd marry a local boy and would inherit the property and be a farmer like them. They meant well.

I don't know whatever happened to Billie Jo. She'd be in her late fifties, now, and I suspect she's on that farm cooking dinner for the hay haulers, it being fall.

But at least she had her one moment in the sun.

Joe Edwards

"No one has played hookey since we put that sign above the door."

The Substitute's Surprise

We ask for strength and the Great Spirit gives us difficulties, which makes us strong.

Native American Prayer

Our ringing phone broke the early morning silence. I raised my head from the pillow. Bright orange numbers glared from the clock radio—6:00 A.M.

Must be a school. But I just applied yesterday.

"Tell them no," mumbled my husband. He rolled over and pulled the blanket over his ears.

"I can't. It's my first assignment." I grabbed the phone with one hand and picked up a pencil with the other. Scooting a notepad within reach, I tried to sound awake. "Hello."

"This is the secretary from Braden Middle School," a pleasant woman's voice explained. "We need a substitute for an eighth-grade health class. Are you available today?"

Not my favorite grade or my favorite subject, but in a new city and new school system . . . "Sure," I responded.

"I know it's late but can you be here by 7:30?"

An hour and a half to shower, dress, drive half an hour,

find the new school and look over lesson plans. My head shook no. My voice answered, "Yes."

When I walked into the school office just before 7:30, the secretary shoved a note with a phone number at me. "The teacher requests that you call immediately." She led me to a phone and left me alone.

I dropped my shoulder bag of substitute time-fillers and dialed the number. "This is your sub for the day. The secretary said you wanted to talk to me."

A hoarse male voice asked, "How often have you taught eighth grade?"

The image of teaching my son's eighth-grade PE class and umpiring his baseball game flashed in my head, followed by a picture of me playing basketball with an eighth-grade girls' class. "Enough," I responded.

"Well . . . Well . . ." the voice sputtered.

I waited. *What's the problem? Why can't he say it?*

At last he blurted, "Today is human development."

I slumped into the nearest chair. "You mean sex education?"

"Yes." He quickly proceeded with instructions. "Divide the class into groups and have them discuss the questions you'll find on my desk. Good-bye." Then he added sympathetically, "Have a nice day."

I hurried into the classroom—a chemistry lab. A male teacher peeked around the door between our rooms. "I teach math next door. Holler if you need anything."

I nodded my head, checked my watch, frantically scribbled my name on the chalkboard, then searched for the questions. On a scrap of paper I found the first question, obviously written by a student. "You are the girl, and you are pregnant. You are the boy, and you are responsible. What do you do?"

Oh, my gosh! What do you do? What do I do?

The first bell rang.

I gathered the questions, class roster and seating chart and placed them on a lab table. Quickly, I squared my shoulders and stretched to my full five-feet, seven-inches just as the first students drifted in and found their seats. The second bell rang.

My stomach flip-flopped with each new name I called from the roll.

Hidden behind the table, my knees shook as I stared at thirty pairs of eyes above "oh-boy-we-have-a-sub" smiles.

I tried to remember discussions of sex with my own boys. None came to mind—I had at least four more classes after this one.

Taking a deep breath, I divided the class into groups and spelled out the directions. In the discussion that followed, they giggled, laughed, whispered and teased about off-color subjects. I had no control—a situation new to me.

When the bell rang and the students bolted for the door, I heaved a quick sigh of relief. Five minutes to revise the lesson. I checked the class schedule.

"A planning period. Hallelujah!" I cried to the empty room. I outlined a new plan and after fifty minutes felt relatively prepared.

The bell rang. Another set of students sauntered into the room. I stood behind the table again, my knees still clattering.

After the second bell, I introduced myself and called the roll without smiling. "Today we'll be having an adult conversation. I'll accept no slang, only proper terminology." The strength and calmness of the words spilling from my mouth stunned me.

Whispers dominoed around the room, "Sex . . . Sex . . . Sex." My heart pounded in my throat. *At least I have their attention. Now I'll shock them.*

"Why sex?" I asked.

Silence. Mouths flew open, eyes looked at the floor or

toward the ceiling, and smiles turned to smirks.

"What d'ya mean?" sneered a good-looking blond boy.

"Just what I said." I repeated slowly, "Why sex?"

He smiled, "Fun!"

"That's one reason," I countered quickly. "Why else?"

The smiles faded; no one laughed. I could almost see the wheels turning inside their heads. My tense shoulders relaxed—a little. I was in control.

A young lady softly volunteered, "Reproduction?"

"Good answer," I acknowledged. "Have any of you ever seen an African sculpture?" A few students snickered but mostly their faces reflected questioning looks. I was sure they wondered what African sculptures had to do with sex. I continued, "What's different about them?"

Silence again. Finally, a voice answered, "They make some parts of the body big."

"What parts are exaggerated?" I glanced around the room.

A girl's hand slowly raised. "The head is out of proportion."

"African cultures enlarge those parts of the body which are important. Why is the head important?"

"That's where your brain is?" suggested a boy.

I nodded. "The brain is the seat of knowledge. What else is enlarged?"

Another shy voice offered. "The breasts."

"Yes, because breasts provide food for their babies." Moving from behind the table, I continued, "If I'd lived in Africa about one hundred years ago, or even in some places today, my three boys would have died. My body didn't produce enough milk to feed my children."

Two girls stole glances at each other, then looked me over as if they didn't believe me. But they remained close-lipped.

"Reproduction is very important in African cultures as

well as in our own," I explained. "If our boys don't marry and have sons, my husband's name will die out." Behind my back, I crossed my fingers—*not exactly the whole truth.* "Do you want your name to die, or do you want it to live on after you're gone?"

By sharing my own experiences openly, a feeling of camaraderie formed between the class and me. The students' discomfort and embarrassment seemed to subside.

Finally, I divided the class into groups with a discussion leader and group reporter. I handed out one question at a time. They shared their feelings maturely and openly, then proposed solutions for difficult problems.

For the rest of the classes, I stood in front of the lab table rather than hide behind it.

At the end of the day, I left the teacher a note then closed and locked the classroom door. A familiar male voice said, "Bye, Mrs. O. Have a nice day." The handsome, blond young male smiled and waved. No sneer this time.

A few mornings later, the ringing phone woke me again. The clock's numbers glimmered 5:30 A.M.

My husband rolled over pulling all the covers with him. "Tell them no."

I grabbed the phone and a pencil.

"Mrs. Osmundson, this is the Braden Middle School where you taught on Monday. You don't teach eighth-grade math, do you? The teacher asked specifically for you."

After sex education, I can teach anything!

"I'll grab my calculator and be there by 7:00."

Linda L. Osmundson

Miracle in the Gym

What's done to children, they will do to society.

Karl Menninger

Doesn't it seem a bit cruel to send a child in a wheelchair to physical education class? That's what I used to think until I found myself eavesdropping on a class one day. Steve Schulten has been the physical education teacher at Little Harbour School in Portsmouth, New Hampshire, for many years. Popular with the parents as well as the children, Steve is known for his energy, his compassion and his love of teaching. When my youngest child, Jonathan, started kindergarten, he could hardly wait until "gym day," and together we would cross the days off his calendar, one by one. My daughter Elizabeth attends the same school. And she, too, has a fondness for Steve and for the gym class. On our way home from school one day, she mentioned something that struck me as odd.

"I got to push Tyler's wheelchair in gym today," she said nonchalantly.

"Tyler goes to gym class?" I asked, completely astonished. This boy's senses were severely impaired. Unable to speak, how was he supposed to gain anything from this gym class? I was certain that this constituted some kind of abuse, but trusting Steve and the principal of our school, I kept my big mouth shut.

A few days later, I arrived a little early when picking up my kids. Wandering through the foyer, I realized my daughter's class was in the gym. Yes, this was in fact "gym day," and I was in the perfect spot to peek through the door and see what they were doing.

What I witnessed was a miracle in the making. As the class participated in their relay race, my daughter approached the boy in the wheelchair. When his turn came, she pushed him with all her might to the other side of the gym. Although the boy never seemed to notice, something even greater than that was happening. Reaching the other side of the gym, my daughter and some of her friends surrounded Tyler's wheelchair immediately.

"Way to go, Tyler!" they exclaimed.

"Was that fun, Tyler?" another one asked.

They hugged him and patted his shoulders in congratulations. I don't know if Tyler felt their touch. I don't know if he enjoyed the wind on his face when his wheelchair was pushed quickly across the gym. And I don't know if he experienced fun or laughter inside his quietude.

What I do know is this: The other children in that gym class were making miracles happen. They were showing evidence of complete tolerance in a world of discrimination. They treated this mentally and physically challenged boy the way they would like to have been treated. In return, they were learning compassion. And they were learning a form of communication that is so natural and innocent coming from young children. They were learning to communicate with their love. For although Tyler was unable to speak with words, something about him told these kids that he knew love and could understand its language.

Steve watched all of this as though it was an ordinary day. I hid behind the door so no one would see this misty-eyed mother as she eavesdropped on her daughter's gym class.

I don't know if he is aware of the lessons he has taught these children. In addition to instructing them in the rules of the games, and in the importance of good health, physical fitness and good sportsmanship, he has allowed an aura of joy to be created inside that gymnasium. He has made sighted and hearing children feel right at home with a child who cannot see and cannot hear. And he has fostered their sense of compassion.

In the future, when this man looks to his retirement days, I pray that one child or one parent will laud his accomplishments enthusiastically. For throughout his many years of teaching physical education, he has been responsible for far more than stronger muscles and agility. He has taught his students to maintain healthy hearts, both physically and emotionally. A gym isn't the first place one would imagine for the teaching of compassion. Yet at Little Harbour School, both this teacher and his students get an A-plus.

Kimberly Ripley

Benjamin

Even before school started, I knew all about my incoming first-graders. Their kindergarten teachers spoke of the students in glowing terms, except for one. Benjamin, they said, wasn't like other children; he didn't like stories, he couldn't sit still and he didn't have respect for other people's property. He was like a wild animal, eating out of the garbage and running amok. They sympathetically wished me luck.

On the first day of school, I talked with the children about the routines and procedures of first grade. Benjamin, as advertised, had a hard time sitting at group time, staying in his seat or following directions.

After story time, I asked if anyone felt like sharing his or her fears or hopes for the new school year. I got the ball rolling by telling them that I couldn't sleep the night before because I had butterflies in my stomach. The children shared their thoughts, and we decided to draw pictures of what we wanted to happen during first grade. I figured the pictures would make a good class book and remind us of our goals for the year.

Most children drew themselves playing with friends,

eating in the cafeteria or reading a book. I cautiously approached Benjamin, who had been alternately drawing with and nibbling on his crayons. We'd only been in school about two hours, and his area already looked like a disaster.

"Benjamin, you've used beautiful colors," I said, helping him pick up his scattered crayons. "Tell me about your drawing." It looked like a jumble of scribbles, lines and dots.

"It's you'n me," he said, his eyes on his work. "See? I'm over here with my net, and there's butterflies livin' in your stomach."

I laughed, taken by surprise.

"So there are," I said, striving for a serious expression. "I like your picture, but I was hoping you'd draw what you want to happen this year."

"I did," was all he'd say.

"He never does what he's supposed to," Laurie informed me. Soon other children began telling me how awful Benjamin had been the previous year. It was clear to me that Benjamin carried major baggage from kindergarten, and he'd need all of our help to clear it away.

"Everything's different in first grade," I said, giving Benjamin a conspiratorial wink.

I showed Benjamin's picture to his kindergarten teacher when she asked if I survived my first day. She smiled and said, "Well, it's better than a picture he drew last year. I felt so bad—he drew our school on fire and told me that's how I felt about him. I truly wish you better luck with that child than I had."

Her words pierced my heart. It became my mission to help Benjamin relate to other children, feel safe and secure in school, and learn to read and write.

When I called to discuss Ben's difficulties, his stepmom assured me he was stubborn, not stupid. She made him sit for two hours at home so he'd know how to sit at school. I stopped calling when she suggested, "Just hit him, he'll settle down." I knew she was receiving parenting classes in her home, and I prayed that Benjamin would benefit from them one day.

In time, most kids began to accept Benjamin, but no one beside me called him "friend." He learned some social skills, but no matter what accommodations, incentives or one-on-one support I offered, Benjamin wasn't able to concentrate on learning. I sent him to second grade, sure he'd end up friendless and in special education classes. I felt like I failed him.

During his second-grade year, Benjamin visited me every day before school. He'd come in munching on a muffin from the school cafeteria, crumbs flying everywhere and say, "Good morning, Mrs. Courtney. Have a good day." I'd give him a hug and send him on his way with whatever inspirational words of wisdom I had handy.

At the whole-school assembly on the first day of his third-grade year, Benjamin told me he was going to be a good boy. I told him he'd always been a good boy.

"No," he said, as if I was a little slow. "I'm goin' to listen 'cause I wanna learn." I told him I thought that was a good plan. And incredibly, Benjamin did learn to read that year. He carried around a notebook and wrote constantly—wonderful, imaginative stories.

Benjamin's in fourth grade now and doesn't visit me anymore. I asked him why and he said simply, "I'm in fourth grade." I was saddened by his cavalier attitude but had to admit that he was entitled to make his own decisions.

When asked to write letters of encouragement to fourth-graders taking the in-depth standardized tests required by our state, I chose Benjamin. I told him I was proud of how hard he was working in school and that he'd do well on the test if he used the strategies he'd been taught. I concluded by saying I didn't know what had caused him to take school seriously, but I was really glad he had.

The next day, Benjamin came into my room, munching on a cinnamon roll, crumbs trailing behind him, and handed me a large envelope. I said, "Good morning Benjamin. Read your test carefully today, okay? I know you'll do your best." He just smiled and gave me a thumbs-up.

Later that morning, while my students were at art, I looked at the envelope. Benjamin had written a note on the outside. It said:

Dear Mrs. Courtney,

The answer is in here. Please be careful with it. I'll pick it up at the end of the day.

Love, Benjamin

The envelope held a picture of his first-grade class, a letter from his Sunday school teacher asking where he'd been and hoping he'd return soon, three copies of newspaper articles he'd appeared in during first grade, a certificate from his brother's teacher commending him for helping her clean her room and earning himself a yearbook, a beautifully drawn picture of Benjamin and his stepmom, several notes from me, and a certificate for reading to my class. Everything was in pristine condition. I stood staring at the contents of the envelope trying to decide how the mementos added up to success in school as his note indicated.

Then it struck me, the items came from people in his life who cared about him. I had a good cry that day, and I don't think I'll worry about students in the same way again. No, I hadn't taught Benjamin to read as I had hoped. But, somehow, I had helped prepare him for learning. The envelope told me Benjamin knew that.

Dori Courtney

"Ms. Willis, remember me? Matt? From last year? I've gotten big over the summer."

The Virtue of Excellence

Every person is gifted in some area. We just have to find out what.

Evelyn Blose Holman

Maggie was assigned to the inner-city classroom in the middle of the year. All the principal had told her was that the former teacher had left suddenly, and this was a class of "special" students. She walked in on bedlam, spitballs flying through the air, feet on desks, the noise deafening. She strode to the front of the classroom and opened the attendance book. Next to each name on the list were numbers from 140 to 160. *Oh,* she thought to herself. *No wonder they are so high-spirited. These children have exceptional IQs.* She smiled and brought them to order.

At first, the students failed to turn in work, and assignments that *were* handed in were done hastily and sloppily. She spoke to them about their innate excellence, their giftedness, that she expected nothing short of the best work from them. She continually reminded them of their responsibility to use all the extra intelligence God had given them.

Things began to change. The children sat up tall, and they worked diligently. Their work was creative, precise and original. One day, the principal was walking by and happened to look into the classroom. He observed students in rapt attention, composing essays.

Later, he called Maggie into his office. "What have you done to these kids?" he asked. "Their work has surpassed all the regular grades."

"Well, what do you expect? They're gifted, aren't they?"

"Gifted? They're the special-needs students—behavioral disordered and retarded."

"Then why are their IQs so high on the attendance sheet?"

"Those aren't their IQs. Those are their locker numbers!"

"Whatever," said Maggie.

Linda Kavelin-Popov
Submitted by Susanne M. Alexander

8

BEYOND THE CLASSROOM

I am not a teacher, only a fellow traveler of whom you asked the way. I pointed ahead—ahead of myself as well as of you.

George Bernard Shaw

In Case of Darkness

What the pupils want to learn is as important as what the teachers want to teach.

Lois E. LeBar

One of the good things about being in the fourth grade was I got to go to Miss Roebuck's house. Some teachers stuck gold stars or little butterflies on your work whenever you did something especially well. Some wrote notes on your paper so you could show your parents. Miss Roebuck believed in achievement that lasted longer than one paper or one social studies project. If you kept up in her class you got invited to her house three times a year. Once just before Thanksgiving. Once just before Christmas and once the Sunday before Good Friday. You had to be working all the time.

She lived in a two-story white-frame farmhouse with dark green shutters at the east end of town. It had a porch that looked out over a wide valley and the Ohio River beyond. Only two acres of the old farm remained in her family. The rest had been sold to a developer from Cincinnati who built a bunch of townhouses on it for city people who wanted to live in the country.

Both Miss Roebuck and I thought it odd that you would move out of the city into exactly the kind of place you were trying to get out of. "Ironic . . . look it up," she called it. When she added "look it up" to something she said she always made it sound like part of the mysterious word in question. You spent a lot of time looking things up if you wanted to stay in Miss Roebuck's good graces.

When you went to her house you could swing in her hammock, fish in her pond, scare other kids in the meadow grass or in the woods, but most of all you got to eat pie. Miss Roebuck liked to bake pie, and she could do that better than anyone I've ever known.

The secret of cooking, she said, was to be prepared before you set out to do it. Ingredients, equipment, recipe . . . everything lined up. Preparation was a very big and important thing to Miss Roebuck.

"Doors will open in your life, and if you are not prepared, you won't be able to walk through them." Or "You never know what's going to happen to you or for you. You'd better be prepared." She applied maxims like this to almost everything we did, from multiplication tables to knowing that tin was important to the economy of Venezuela.

I could not imagine myself ever needing to know that, but Miss Roebuck insisted that I didn't know if I would or not. So it was better to know it than to not know it.

On the windowsill above her old white sink with the soapstone countertop was a red flashlight. It sat upside down. That is with its bulb end on the sill. And it had a piece of white adhesive tape wrapped around it. I was not able to reach it or to read what was written on the tape. But that flashlight sure did rouse my curiosity.

It was in the winter just before Christmas that five of us were invited to spend Saturday at Miss Roebuck's when the really bad thing happened. There was a good ten inches of snow on the ground and the storm that produced it had wind so fierce it sounded like screaming. We were worried our day would be called off. But two days afterward, the sun was bright, the roads were cleared and six lucky kids were dropped by our parents at ten in the morning on Miss Roebuck's porch.

She gave us hot chocolate, dark and creamy. After that we got bundled up, our chins forced high by scarves, our hands sheathed in mittens and gloves, and we set out on a trek through the woodlot. We had to stay with our assigned buddy but were allowed to explore the woods and the hillside below at will. Miss Roebuck stayed pretty much in the middle of our group as we went slogging though the woods, kicking up snow, yelling to each other when we found fox tracks or uncovered a squirrel's cache of hickory nuts.

"Squirrels prepare well for winter," Miss Roebuck said to me and my buddy Arnold as we passed. *Harping on one of her themes,* I thought. Her determination to drill stuff into our heads sort of pleased me in a funny way.

"And they don't mix up their larders either. Hickory nuts are all you'll find in this place. They'll have put their acorns someplace else." She was still talking when Arnold and I headed over the crest of the hill, and I was never seen again.

That's what I thought anyway. Just as we started down the other side of the rise I fell through a hole in the snow and ended some six feet or so below the surface in the most complete darkness I have ever known. I heard Arnold start yelling. But that was not much comfort. I had no doubt I would never be found, would perish here, my bones discovered centuries later by aliens from some distant planet.

I was dizzy and really frightened. The hole smelled like wet fur. I could be in a black bear den for all I knew. I sat with my knees tucked up, breathing hard. The blackness terrified me.

In a few moments I heard voices. The kids yelling and Miss Roebuck's voice, calm and easy. "Doc are you all right?" That was my nickname.

"I dunno," I said weakly. "I can't see anything."

"You've fallen through the roof of what was an old root cellar. There's nothing to be afraid of. We'll have you out in a few minutes. Now sit still." I was too scared to do anything else, and my teeth started to rattle.

And then from almost directly above me came a beam of light. A thin, frail shaft of light that fell just past me and dispelled my fear in an instant.

I could see rough stone walls, a floor of hewn slate and, just beyond the light, the outline of the oak root-cellar door. I tried to push against it, but it didn't budge. I pushed harder and harder. Nothing happened.

Then I heard Miss Roebuck say, "Doc, move away from the door, please." As I did that, the door slowly opened, and I could see daylight and Miss Roebuck standing outside, holding her red flashlight, waiting for me.

"Some doors open in." She said this so softly and with such gentleness that it didn't make me feel like the idiot I knew I was.

There was a lot of laughing then. My friends were relieved, I guess, so they made fun of me. We continued to walk for a little while more and then we headed back to Miss Roebuck's fine big kitchen. She'd made a deep dish apple pie. We had that and warm apple cider. The most amazing thing was that the kids didn't just wolf it down. They ate the pie as if they wanted to make it last forever.

I helped clean up after we were all finished. And as I put some glasses on the counter I saw the flashlight was right back in its familiar place. I asked if I could see it and Miss Roebuck handed it to me without a word.

I wanted to know what was written on the instrument of my deliverance. I turned the flashlight in my hand so I could read the writing. There in perfectly crafted script—Miss Roebuck learned her own lessons well, I thought—was written, "In case of darkness, do something."

And in all the years since, whenever I set out on a task that required me to be prepared for some unknown turn of events, the image of that inscription has come into my mind like a beacon of light. I remember to prepare myself well. And I remember the splendid times I had at Miss Roebuck's house when we were out of the classroom, enjoying some spirited adventure, having a good time and being taught, somehow, everything we needed to know.

W. W. Meade

Perils of a Preschool Husband

When someone is taught the joy of learning it becomes a lifelong process that never stops, a process that creates a logical individual. That is the challenge and joy of teaching.

Marva Collins

My beloved and I were zipping along, about ten miles above the speed limit, two hundred miles north of San Francisco. Behind us was Andrew, our college sophomore; ahead of us was six hundred miles of the dullest driving west of Kansas, and then, home.

It was just before nine in the morning, and my not-yet-caffeinated eyes were fighting the tourist-torpor brought on by four days of Andrew's excited shouts, "Hey, look at this! Ever see anything like that before?" Our twenty-year-old was proudly guiding us through the verdant splendor of the astonishing redwoods of Northern California's Humboldt County.

To my right, my wife Jan, was enjoying one of those, "You start the driving, I'll catch a snooze until you get tired," naps. Suddenly, I heard an anxious, imperative voice, punctuated by a piercing elbow to the ribs, "Oh, look. Stop!" Three thoughts overloaded my brain in the same millisecond that I floored the brakes and slid toward the road's shoulder. "What did I hit?" "Are you all right?" "What did we forget?" It was nothing of the sort. She pointed to the sawmill across the road and the piles of redwood sawdust—sawdust that would go great in the pouring table of her home away from home, room 2 at the Growing Place Preschool.

Five minutes later we had made an illegal U-turn through the weeds of the road divider; made a deal to buy some sawdust from a guy who never quite understood what we were all about; stripped the pillow cases off the two pillows in the car to carry the damp chips home; and slathered through the beginnings of yet another rain shower to scoop soggy sawdust into the never-to-be-used-again pillow cases.

My wife, beatifically smiling, said, "The kids will love it." That single thought made the slipping, sliding and purging of slimy sawdust out of her shoes worthwhile for her. Her smile made it worthwhile for me. You accept the inexplicable when you're married to a preschool teacher.

It isn't the sort of thing that you expect when you propose to a beautiful girl who had majored in dance education and went on to be a Radio City Music Hall Rockette. When our son Andrew turned three, we enrolled him at the Growing Place Preschool. Jan started working at the school as an assistant teacher. Andrew enjoyed preschool, and my wife found a new career.

The die was cast on the afternoon when she came home and said, "I think I'd like to keep teaching preschool after Andrew moves on. It'll keep me young." That was nineteen years ago. She still loves it, and without question, it has kept her young!

As a writer, I have written and produced more than one

hundred children's records, written for two honored children's television series and created or cocreated three network children's series. One would expect that I know a lot about kids. And I do. However, I've learned more about young children by sharing my life with a teacher who cares about the kids in her class just as if they were her own. She worries about their welfare both in and out of school. So, for all practical (and many impractical) purposes, her three- and four-year-old tikes become our extended family.

As our son moved on through schools and life, Jan's classes gave us other kids to laugh with and care for. Jan's school is not a day-care center, but rather a school where the entire staff is truly involved in the program and with the children, collectively and individually. It's a requirement.

I know this because for nineteen years now, I've heard about what Sarah said, Peter did, Jennifer painted, and what Jason A. and Jason W. accomplished. I've heard about Melinda's improvements and Jake's shenanigans in the play yard. I've heard seemingly endless phone calls between Jan and other teachers as they tried to solve a child's problem, to reach over the horizon to find some new way to help.

Nineteen years of this, and for some reason, I love it more than ever. I know that I must be part of an army of men who never go into a store without keeping an eye open for stuff that might be useful to their preschool-teacher wives.

"Wow! Dinosaur-shaped sponges . . . I'll get six packages." "Smelly markers at three bucks a pack; I wonder if three will be enough?" Every trip, to any kind of store, has the additional enticement of knowing that I might stumble onto something that we've never thought of before and that the kids would love. Guys who aren't married to preschool teachers never know the delight of holding up a package of wooden clothespins in all colors of the rainbow and saying hopefully, "Whaddayuh think? Only a buck and a half for twenty-eight of them." Then the joy of success that comes with the magic reply, "Great! I love 'em. Can you get six more?"

A man who isn't married to a preschool teacher can't comprehend the magic moments as she tosses out ideas of how best to use his latest shopping discovery. "I wonder what we could do with those pins in the pouring table?" "With play-dough?" "Maybe if we glued two together?" It's a whole new area in which a husband can be creative and, as a bonus, keep his mind young and active.

Jan's preschool accepts children with special needs, and there have been a scattering of autistic students. And attention deficit disorder? Where was it, or what was it called when I was in school? She brings home the problems of these special students, their hopes and their accomplishments, and we've shared all these things together. Nowadays, dinner table conversation at our place might focus on the autism or ADD article we saw in Sunday's paper.

Jan's concerns about her students have become part of our lives. As a result, our life together has been richer and more fulfilled. Jan's career as a preschool teacher has given us an expansive vista of shared joys, accomplishments and memories. Especially rewarding is the prospect that in spite of my getting ever older, each September I can look forward to a new group of names, faces and personalities to hear about, laugh at, and love—Jan's classes, our extended family.

I would never have experienced that joy if my beloved hadn't thrown away the tap shoes and picked up the flannel board. As a job, it doesn't pay as much. As a life, the riches are unparalleled.

Roy Freeman

Excellence Is Love in Action

Inside every great teacher is an even greater one waiting to come out.

Source Unknown

On the wall next to the door of the principal's office hung a paddling stick with a bad reputation. This intimidating wooden board was displayed in the open for all students to see, a reminder that law and order was enforced in this building. We definitely did not want to get sent to the principal's office because there court was held, and if you were found guilty of the crime for which you were accused, the paddle was used to carry out your sentence.

I couldn't imagine being reprimanded in this way. Mrs. Hood, my former teacher at Newark #7, rarely had to do so much as raise her voice. We children had never wanted her to be upset with us, so we simply did what she expected.

The stick had more than a bad reputation; Brian and Tommy and Henry and Clyde told us firsthand about the wooden stick. It was not just a *symbol* of justice. This paddle had seen active duty.

Mr. Pierson was the principal and the judge at this

school. He was a very tall, very muscular and very handsome man with gleaming white straight teeth, dark brown eyes, shiny jet-black disheveled hair and a shapely mouth. Unfortunately, good looks were wasted on this man. Mr. Pierson dressed in the same dark suit, alternating three bland and ready-to-send-to-the-cleaners ties to give the appearance that he was wearing a different outfit each day (but we kept count and weren't fooled one bit). Every day he wore the same pair of never-shined, badly scuffed shoes. He always wore the same half-smile.

"How is your day going, Miss Miller?" he asked my best friend Stephanie one day as we walked down the hall on our way to the lunchroom. (I was pretty sure he had no idea what my name was). The two of us were so scared we ducked into the girls' bathroom instead of going to lunch, afraid that perhaps Stephanie had done something wrong and was going to be hauled off to the principal's office for what the other kids described as a "come to Jesus meeting." I was terrified that Mr. Pierson might be waiting outside the bathroom door and because Stephanie refused to come out, I knew that if I did, I'd be sacrificed in her place. Lunch or no lunch, we stayed in the bathroom the entire lunch period.

Mr. Pierson's strict style was not limited to students; he wasn't very social with the teachers either. Teachers greeted him politely and offered up obligatory pleasantries, but didn't go out of their way to be in his presence.

This demeanor seemed to set the tone that was pervasive throughout the school. How different this felt from the wonder years of Newark #7, where cooperation with your peers was expected, and students helped each other instead of competing against each other, as was the case in this new school. But I was hopeful that I could adjust, even if Mr. Pierson couldn't. He was going to night school to get his doctoral degree. The only doctors we had ever heard of were M.D.'s, not Ph.D.'s. We students felt he was leaving because he didn't like us, although we thought he would make a good physician. At recess one day, third-grader Claude James got hit in the head by a flying baseball bat and was knocked unconscious. Mr. Pierson held Claude's nose and mouth and blew life back into his body so there was, at least, the consolation of knowing that we were in the hands of someone who could keep us alive.

Regardless of the situation, Mr. Pierson not only commanded respect but had a way of coercing it. We both respected and feared him.

When our regular music teacher began to show signs of being pregnant, she disappeared and a new music teacher by the name of Miss Thomas was assigned to the school. On her first day, she hung up a poster in our room with the words: EXCELLENCE IS LOVE IN ACTION. Because she was the music instructor for the four schools in our county, she arrived at our school, usually late, every Wednesday after lunch.

I thought Miss Thomas was wonderful. Aside from being a good music teacher, she was a pleasure for the senses. A delightful woman, she was always smiling, always joyful. She was beautiful, feminine, and she smelled as good as she looked. Her white and graceful teeth overlapped just enough to add a touch of appeal and intrigue to her smile. She wore her long dark hair in big loose curls and dressed in colorful stylish clothes. Just looking at this woman was music.

Mr. Pierson thought so, too. It wasn't long before he took to visiting our music classroom. If a note needed to be delivered to a student in her class, he delivered it personally rather than having a student messenger deliver it, as was custom. We could tell he was making time with her and it wasn't too long before she noticed—and approved.

By Christmastime she made a special effort to arrive to class on time, and soon thereafter, arrived at the school early enough to have lunch in the cafeteria with Mr. Pierson. By Easter, Mr. Pierson and Miss Thomas carried their lunch trays to his office, where they ate with the door closed. Some of us children hovered near the office door, just close enough to see if we could overhear their conversations. We didn't hear anything but chatter and laughter.

The following fall on the first day of the new school year, we students arrived and were filled with enthusiasm at seeing our friends. To our amazement, there, standing outside the building, greeting all the students, was a very different Mr. Pierson. This man looked more like a male model in the made-to-order catalogs than the Mr. Pierson we had known the previous school year.

"Good morning, Bettie, nice to see you today," he said, looking directly at me. I hoped he hadn't noticed my obvious stare.

"Good morning," I said meekly.

"Good morning, Jack, welcome back," he said to my friend and classmate.

He called every student by name as he welcomed them back. We all drooled with delight. We also took note of the fact that though Mr. Pierson was as tall as ever, he was even more handsome. His brown eyes twinkled, and his gleaming white straight teeth were displayed in a generous smile. His thick black hair was in the latest style, every strand immaculately in place. He wore a white starched shirt with a stiff collar, a bright and colorful (and clean) tie and stone cuff links. His fashionable dress slacks were the same as those on display in the store window at Spangler's Clothing for Men. New and recently shined black wing-tip shoes with little black tassels complemented a black leather belt. But perhaps the biggest change was that the paddling stick that hung on the wall outside the principal's office had been replaced with a poster reading: EXCELLENCE IS LOVE IN ACTION!

We also checked immediately: The poster in Miss Thomas' room was gone! And, she had a diamond engagement ring on her finger! But that wasn't all. Mr. Pierson laughed more, was playful, and whistled all the time. He sat with us in the cafeteria at lunchtime, as did Miss Thomas on the days she came to our school. He walked around and talked with students on the playground, occasionally stopping to push us high on the swings or to take a turn at bat. And he no longer spent long periods of time in his office. For the first time, he substituted when a teacher was absent, and what's more, he liked it. And he liked us students, too! It was wonderful. And school was beginning to feel like fun!

One day when he was substituting for Mrs. Fisher, he engaged us in a lively discussion about his new favorite topic: Excellence is love in action.

"What is excellence?" he asked. Too young to really understand what excellence was, let alone to recognize it in action, we sat quietly. Mr. Pierson tried again, "What is love?" The girls giggled and the boys frowned. He looked over the sea of empty faces and realized not one of us knew the answer. He tried again, "What is a friend?" Now he was on to something. We felt like we knew the answer to this question, so when he asked us to name some of our friends, we all raised our hands and nominated our classmates.

"Yes," Mr. Pierson said, "classmates are friends." But soon he realized we were naming mostly those kids who held power over the rest us because they could select, or reject, fellow students on the playground or in the classroom.

"Which adults are good friends?" he asked. "And how can you tell? How can we recognize friendship?" Becky

Faulkner raised her hand and said in her Future Teacher of America voice, "My mom and dad are good friends." That seemed like a dumb answer to us so we all laughed, but it appeared to be the answer Mr. Pierson was looking for.

"Very good, Becky," he praised. "How do you know they are good friends?" And so the discussion went.

Mr. Pierson then proceeded to give example after example of what our parents had done within the community that not only showed us what friendship and love meant in action, but also let us see that our parents knew and lived it on a daily basis.

"Remember," he said in conclusion, "friendship, when practiced, produces excellence. And someday, children, you will meet someone other than your parents who by virtue of their loving actions, demonstrates excellence, and when you do, you will know it."

We had already met that someone. Miss Thomas was excellence in action. She had come and won our hearts. She had given us excellence, shown us love, and by loving us, brought forth our excellence. And her loving actions had more than a spellbinding effect on her students. It had changed our principal, and he had changed our school. Mr. Pierson's new sense of fashion and his new style of leadership caused our school to come alive. The walls that were once stark were now virtually a mosaic of student works. Teachers buzzed with vitality. Mr. Pierson was right. It was easy to know when you were in the presence of excellence and friendship and, when practiced, both produced excellence.

Miss Thomas and Mr. Pierson were married on the first day of summer. We students were all invited to their wedding and every last one of us attended. In a long white dress, our dark-haired Cinderella stood next to Mr. Pierson, surrounded by the entire school of children, all looking adoringly at these "excellent" adults.

If there was any piece of our hearts these two youthful, beautiful and loving professionals had not won over, it was clinched when Mr. Pierson hung their wedding photo, with schoolchildren included, up for all to see. There, where once hung the dreaded paddling stick, hung the poster with the words EXCELLENCE IS LOVE IN ACTION and next to it, the photo of love in action. Not one single child in the picture was looking toward the camera. Nor was Mr. Pierson.

Bettie B. Youngs, Ph.D., Ed.D.
1976 Iowa Teacher of the Year

The Poems

My stomach was doing flip-flops as my sixth-grade teacher, Mrs. Cloe, approached my desk. She was returning our graded poems, and I was excited to see my mark. I liked to write, and I had worked extra hard on my collection of poems, lying on my bed at home every night for a month, carefully crafting my phrases to make each poem sing and dance and flow.

Mrs. Cloe was a smart and energetic teacher who walked as she talked, and to me she seemed to sort of float around the room. I had a crush on her. I wanted her to notice me, and since I was terribly shy and did not like to raise my hand, I hoped I could impress her with my poetry.

Mrs. Cloe came down my aisle and set my poems on my desk. I had bound the poems in the form of a book using two pieces of cardboard covered with a soft blue fabric. I remember hearing the whispers and giggles of my classmates as they shared their marks with each other. Their poems were just sheets of paper held together with staples or paper clips, not book-bound like mine. I was sure to get an A, maybe even an A-plus. Mrs. Cloe liked to write comments next to our marks, and I was eager to see what she thought of my poems and of me.

My heart pounded as I opened the cover to see my grade. And there it was at the top of the page—an F. No words, no explanation, just the letter F, in red ink. A wave of heat surged through my body. I could barely breathe. I mustered the courage to approach Mrs. Cloe at her desk after class. "Those poems weren't yours," she said sternly. "They were too good. You must have copied them." What she said shocked me. I did not know what to say. I think I muttered, "No, I didn't," and I ran from the room and hurried home.

I told my parents what Mrs. Cloe said, and my mother got very upset and said she would talk with Mrs. Cloe. "No, no," I said. "Don't say anything. Don't make it worse. Don't embarrass me." My mother agreed not to get involved, but that night as she spoke to her friends on the telephone about the incident, I remember she kept repeating the same phrase over and over again: "How can Mrs. Cloe prove such a thing? I mean, how can Mrs. Cloe prove such a thing?"

The next day after class I went to Mrs. Cloe again with my poems and said, "My mom wants to know, how can you prove such a thing?" Mrs. Cloe replied, "Prove to me that you didn't copy the poems." I considered Mrs. Cloe's words. I felt her glaring straight at me, but I was so nervous that I couldn't look in her eyes. I just stared at a blue button on her blouse. I could not think of anything to say. Mrs. Cloe broke the silence. "Okay, here's what," she announced. "I'll raise your grade to a C. But I don't want to hear any more about this."

I walked home more upset than the day before. I felt cheated. I even left the poems on Mrs. Cloe's desk. I did not want them anymore. That grade C stood for "crummy." That C stood for "Cloe." I hated Mrs. Cloe. Then suddenly another thought struck me. It was this very thought that made me become a professional writer. *If Mrs. Cloe thinks my poems were copied,* I said to myself, *then they must be very good poems. I must a be a very good writer. I must be an excellent writer!* I suddenly felt this powerful sense of ability—like I could do anything. My parents had always believed in me and told me I could be anything I wanted to be, and I guess it made me believe in myself somewhat, but this was different to me. This was the first time someone who was not in my family was telling me I had a talent. Mrs. Cloe did not intend it that way, of course. But that is how I took it. And from that moment on, that C stood for confidence.

Later in my life, when I became a children's author, I still thought about Mrs. Cloe. I had long since forgiven her and considered what had happened a blessing. She had been my secret inspiration, even though she had no idea what she had done. Since many of my books were in elementary schools, I sometimes hoped that she was still a teacher and that she noticed my name on a cover and remembered the incident.

A few years ago, Mrs. Cloe died. A friend from my hometown in Northern California sent me her obituary. I read about her upcoming memorial service and decided to attend. I drove to the service with my wife, and on the way she asked me if I were going to say a few words to the congregation about being a former student. My wife knew of my incident with Mrs. Cloe, of course, and the profound impact that it had on my life. "I'm not saying a word," I said. "I'm just going to see some childhood friends and pay my respects."

At the service, we listened to many people share their memories of Mrs. Cloe. Several of her former students spoke. Despite the unfortunate incident with me, Mrs. Cloe really was a wonderful teacher. Near the end of the service, a man stepped to the lectern. It was Mr. Cloe. He quietly thanked everyone for coming, and then put on his reading glasses and opened a thin blue book and began reading.

Hold—we must hold
onto things not by our fingertips
but with a grip
For life is precious
do not let it slip—hold
We must hold all its joy
Hold
before we take flight
into that dark good night

I sat stunned. That was my poem. I remembered those words. It seemed so long ago, but I was sure of it. Now I recognized the book in Mr. Cloe's hands. It was that soft blue fabric I had used for a cover. I could hardly believe it.

After the service I asked Mr. Cloe if I could see the book he had read from. He had a glint in his eyes as he handed me the blue book. He was greeted by others, so I turned away and leafed through the pages with my wife. There were two dozen or so poems, and a few of them I remembered. I noticed that the red F had been wiped away. I gave the book back to Mr. Cloe. "These are nice poems," I said, smiling. I did not tell him that the poems were mine. "Yes," Mr. Cloe said. "These were Judy's favorite poems. She pulled them out to read from time to time. She kept them in her nightstand drawer next to the bed."

Jeff Savage

Positive Reinforcement

Act as if what you do makes a difference, because it does.

Source Unknown

Several years ago I served as an assistant principal in a large public high school of fourteen hundred students. I found many aspects of my responsibilities both enjoyable and rewarding, however, there was little joy or satisfaction in supervising the three lunch periods each day. Making sure students were diligent in picking up their lunch trays, not smearing mashed potatoes on one another, or sticking peas on the ceiling or on their neighbor were not high on my list of "professional" things to do.

Days prior to vacation periods were particularly bad times in the cafeteria. It was on one of these days that I observed a student spill his milk. What a mess. It was all down the front of him, on the table, on the bench and on the floor. I quickly diverted my attention elsewhere and watched him out of the corner of my eye with my superior peripheral vision. I knew this guy would try to escape, leaving someone else (like me) to clean up the mess. Well,

I had this guy's number and as soon as he stepped one foot outside of the cafeteria, he was going to get his. I would make him clean up everyone else's mess for the day so he could see how much fun it could be.

I slyly watched as he began his escape. To my surprise he approached the snack bar upon which I was leaning and gathered several napkins and returned to the scene of the crime. After wiping up the table, he got on his hands and knees and wiped up the bench and then the floor. Making his way to the exit, he deposited the soggy mess in the proper receptacle and left the cafeteria.

After regaining my composure, I quickly followed the young man out into the hallway. I asked him his name, thanked him for his consideration and commended him for being so conscientious. He replied, "No problem," and went on his way. The thought crossed my mind to contact his home, and I determined to do it later that day.

It was a little after 5:00 P.M. when I opened my car door to go home. It suddenly occurred to me that I had forgotten to contact the parents. My first thought was to call the next day, but then I thought better of it and went back to my office. After pulling his enrollment card, I went to my phone and dialed the number listed. After a few rings a lady answered.

"Hi. This is Rich Kornoelje calling from the high school."

I heard a hard swallow (or maybe it was a gulp) on the other end and realized that the only time I ever contacted parents was when there was trouble or bad news. I quickly said, "Your son showed me something today that really demonstrated some good upbringing. . . ." I then went on to relay the story.

At first there was silence. Then I could hear a few sniffles, followed by some sobs. After gaining her composure, the mom said, "You will never in your entire lifetime realize what your phone call has meant to me. My husband left me several years ago, and I have had to raise this young man by myself, and it is so hard. I know how he behaves at home with me, but I always wonder about his behavior away from home. You will never know how much your phone call has done for me."

That phone call was a life-changing experience for me. Since that time many years ago, I have purposed to make at least one positive contact with parents per week and urge—not require—my teachers to do the same. We strive to make contact with the parents of a student who is not often praised for his or her actions. The parents are happy, the student does well with positive reinforcement, the teacher is blessed and everybody wins.

Rich Kornoelje

So Little Meant So Much

My plan was to slip out of the conference before the keynote speech to avoid rushing to the airport. The wind-up luncheon featured Sandra McBrayer, the 1994 National Teacher. I can't remember why I remained seated while she took her place at the podium, but I will never forget the story she told.

Sandra discarded her prepared speech and talked straight from her heart. She told us about a bright, enthusiastic young man she had taught in high school. He was constantly frightened and was the target of repeated severe beatings when several students learned he was gay. One day after school he went home, where he lived with his father, and told him what was happening at school. His father, mortified with his son's sexuality, replied with a beating even more brutal than any he had received at school and worse than others he had previously received from his father. At that point, he felt that the street was the only safe place left for him. Life there gave him his next dose of brutality as he was forced to earn sustenance money as a young prostitute.

One late night, after an especially abusive encounter, the young man's spirit was finally broken, and he felt he could not go on. He remembered one person who had showed him kindness. He reached out to his former teacher, Sandra McBrayer. She told him to stay by the pay phone and she would be there as soon as she could. Within twenty minutes she found a slumped, quivering, bone-thin figure waiting for her, his hollow eyes swollen, but still holding a glimmer of trust and a trace of the smile she used to see. She told him to get in her car but wondered where she would take this young man. He had nowhere to sleep. Tonight, she knew that in order to survive, he needed much more than a homeless shelter could offer him. Going against "the rules," she decided to take him to her own house to give him warmth, something to eat, and mostly, some hope.

Sandra sat the frail, shaking young man in her kitchen and made soup. After hours of talking together, he seemed to calm down somewhat. He looked shyly at Sandra and surprised her with a request—a bath. Sandra got the bath ready, even adding bubbles, and then went back into the kitchen to clean up, wondering if perhaps she had overstepped her bounds as a teacher. Sure she had, she decided, yet she would do the same thing all over again, if necessary.

Suddenly, she heard sobbing that seemed to come from the depths of the young man's soul. When he came back into the kitchen a little later, Sandra gently asked him why he had been crying in the bathroom. The young man looked at her and said, "I'm sorry you heard me. I couldn't help it. I was so happy I couldn't stop crying. It was a dream I've had since I was a little boy. This was the first bath I ever had. I've always wanted to sit in a bathtub with bubbles."

I drove to the airport inspired to never give up encouraging other teachers. We may be the only people to ever have a positive influence on a child's life.

Beth Teolis

An Ordinary Woman

The newsroom where I work is small, so even though I was at my desk, concentrating on finishing my story ahead of deadline, I could see our intern frantically waving from across the room. She had the phone to her ear, but she stood up to signal me. When I leaned over her desk, I saw that she was taking down the information for an obituary. The form is standard. She had done many of them, so I knew she didn't need my help. But when I saw what she had written under the column for survivors I knew why she had called me over. The deceased woman was survived by 57 children and 428 grandchildren!

I took the phone and introduced myself as a feature writer for the paper. The well-spoken woman on the other end identified herself as the dean of one of the local colleges. She told me that her mother, Mavis Burlington, had died that morning at age ninety-eight. She wanted to get the notice in the paper quickly so that as many of Mavis's relatives could attend the funeral as possible.

I had to ask the obvious question, "How is it that she had fifty-seven children? I know a good story possibility when I hear it. But I was wrong. Mavis's story wasn't just good—it was great!"

The woman told me that Mavis was the daughter of former slaves and grew up on a small farm in the deep South. Her immediate family was large and poor. But Mavis had a special gift—she could read. Whether she was taught by her parents, a mentor, or if she had some formal schooling is unclear. But there was nothing that Mavis Burlington couldn't read. And there was no one that Mavis wouldn't try to teach to read.

Throughout Mavis's long life, Mavis taught people—anyone—to read. Her students were children, adults, friends and friends of friends. Total strangers who heard of Mavis by word of mouth would bring their children to her for a reading lesson. Of course, in this way, they didn't remain strangers for long.

The woman on the phone, the college dean, told me her story: She had grown up in the Cabrini projects of Chicago, an area plagued by violence, drugs and poverty. Her mother had heard about Mavis from one of the teachers at the local Catholic elementary school, Saint Joesph's. The teacher wasn't sure if Mavis was still teaching, as she was already in her seventies by then, but the teacher told her mother that Mavis was worth a try.

"Mavis lived on the south side of Chicago then," said the women. "My mother and I had to take three different buses to get there. But we did it three times a week. At first, Mavis gave me coloring books, then picture books. At seven years old, I liked that. After awhile, I graduated to chapter books. I don't know where Mavis got all those books. She wasn't rich. Her apartment was bare like those of most of the folks we knew. She just had a couch, a table, one lamp and hundreds of books everywhere!"

In my mind I was conjuring a picture of a warm, lovely lady, someone who changed the life of each person she taught. I felt sure that if I were to investigate, I would find other students of Mavis's who had gone on to distinguished careers as doctors, lawyers and teachers. I wanted to find people who had found their way out of their desperation by learning to read with Mavis. I imagined a beautiful, wrinkled lady, holding the hands of a recalcitrant child, encouraging him, telling him, "Ignorance is worse than poverty." I told the woman what I was thinking. She was quiet for a long minute.

Then she said, "That's not Mavis's story. . . ." She paused. "I'm going to bring someone in to talk to you, someone else Mavis taught. Is that all right?"

It was better than all right, and we made an appointment for that afternoon.

When they first walked in the door, they made an odd couple. The woman was older, in her mid-thirties, I guessed and dressed well. The young man with her was about seventeen. He wore the uniform of a local fast food restaurant. They sat down in the chairs I had provided near my desk.

"Tell her about Mavis, Jason," the woman said. He did.

"She taught me to read. No one else ever tried the way she did," he said simply. "I thought I was too stupid to learn. Mavis made me feel that other teachers just hadn't tried hard enough.

"But the thing about Mavis you should know is this," Jason continued. "She wasn't a savior. She didn't try to be. She said that whatever you ended up to be in your life was because of something inside of you. It wasn't something she or anybody else put there. What you did with it was your own business. Mavis had something inside of her—the need to teach. And she didn't think she had to be anything to anybody except a teacher."

"You see," said the woman, the college dean, "you might find some doctors or lawyers or teachers among those of us Mavis taught. But you'll find plenty of people who are just working at whatever they can. And you'll find an equal number of us who were pushed so far down by other things that just knowing how to read wasn't enough to raise them up.

"I guess the point is," she continued, "Mavis gave us each a gift, but what we did with that gift was our own doing. She made us feel responsible for ourselves—if we succeeded, we could be proud of our own accomplishment. If we failed, well, it wasn't her fault. She never wanted us to feel that we owed her anything—not thanks or credit or blame."

I was beginning to understand.

Mavis didn't want to be considered any more or less than exactly what she was, a teacher. But for the two people sitting in front of me just then, that had been enough.

Mavis thought of herself as an ordinary person, just like all the people she taught. She did her job because she thought it was important. If her students learned a few extra lessons from her example—things like commitment to work, responsibility and self-respect—well, that was because the ability to see those things was in *them.*

Mavis was just ordinary. But hundreds and hundreds of ordinary people just like her loved her enough to consider themselves her children.

I took down the date, time and place of the funeral, not just for the obituary but because I wanted to attend myself.

On the day of the funeral, I drove to the largest funeral home in our city. But I never got to pay my respects. I couldn't get near the place. The parking lot was full and cars were lined up on every side street in the biggest traffic jam I had ever seen.

I turned my car around. After all, it's only fitting that her "family" gets first priority.

Marsha Arons

9

LEARNING BY TEACHING

Much have I learned from my teachers, more from my colleagues, but most from my students.

Talmud

Master Teacher

Teach your students to use what talents they have; the woods would be silent if no bird sang except those that sing best.

Anonymous

"Hey, Teach. Long time, no see!" A standard greeting from teenager to teacher after summer vacation. For my most unforgettable student, "Long time, no see" was the literal truth, one of Heath Thorson's many "blind" jokes. Left completely sightless at birth from too much incubator oxygen, this teenager maneuvered his way through regular classes in regular schools while those around him wondered at his remarkable courage, his "other" sight.

In the fall of 1986, a fourteen-year-old boy tentatively entered my English classroom. Behind him followed a woman, his aide, carrying a large typewriter-looking contraption. My apprehension blossomed quickly into full-blown anxiety as Mrs. Parker supplied details of my newest student. Heath Thorson was a blind freshman whose parents insisted their son receive the same educational opportunities as sighted students. Translated, this meant regular classes in public school.

My first response was a muted, "That's expecting too much of a regular classroom teacher." After all, I was expecting more than usual myself that fall. At age forty, I was (gasp) pregnant. Full-time teaching plus pregnant at forty seemed quite a sufficient helping on my plate. Now this tall, gangly special-needs student appeared before me. Accommodating special-education students had become a federal law. I had no recourse except to welcome Heath and hope for the best.

Our beginning was awkward. The first few weeks, Mrs. Parker attended class with Heath. Their leaving class early to avoid the hall crowds usually signaled Heath's classmates to close up shop. Also, Heath took copious notes, which meant he tapped away on that cumbersome contraption, a Braille typewriter. Each strike of the keys sounded a discordant kerplunk. Heath's keyboard mastery intrigued and distracted everyone. Before long, though, we adjusted. Eventually, I welcomed the sound; I knew at least one hormonal adolescent in my classroom was tending to the day's lesson.

Heath's routine for each academic course was the same. Mrs. Parker worked tirelessly typing assignments in Braille for him, then transcribing his work to written words for teachers. With great relish, Heath even read aloud parts in classroom plays from his Braille copies.

To his freshmen peers, Heath was, at first, a curiosity. But soon his bright, quick mind and flair for wit began to beckon us all. His comic banter was unstoppable. He fascinated fellow students with his expertise in recognizing voices and in navigating the labyrinth of our school hallways. By the end of his freshman year, Heath was more than tolerated or even accepted—he was popular.

The fall of 1989 arrived, and Heath became a senior. Not

one to leave much to chance or computer whim, I conspired with his counselor to have Heath placed in my senior English class. This time there was nothing tentative in his classroom entrance. The tall, lanky boy had metamorphosed into an even taller, self-assured young man whose unseeing eyes had given way to an all-seeing heart.

Still playful, Heath enjoyed showing off his Alabama driver's license (the "For I.D. Purposes Only" print was quite small) or commandeering the intercom to test his latest jokes.

Heath called his lack of sight an inconvenience; he refused the word "handicap." His blindness was hardly even an inconvenience on graduation night in May 1990. He ascended the ramp in the civic center arena, walked to our principal without hesitation, received his diploma and exited on the other side. He heard the thunderous applause; all Heath missed of his commencement ceremony was seeing his senior class and the entire arena audience rise to their feet to honor him.

Choose your words carefully before arguing with me that special-needs students detract from a regular classroom. I'll counter with the life lessons Heath taught his classmates and me: lessons in patience, determination, courage, humor, love of life and ability. As a twenty-five-year veteran in public education, my memory album overflows with students who, although they've left my classroom and school, are bound in the loving place of my heart. They have provided my continuing education. But in lessons of struggle and victory, Heath Thorson was my master teacher.

Marikay Tillett

Brush Strokes

William liked everything about painting at the easel. He liked the big, smooth sheets of newsprint that felt cool to his touch. He liked the wooden handle of the paintbrush that extended his reach. Even the springy clothespins that fastened the paper to the board, the ones that could "bite" his finger if he didn't move it quickly enough, made William smile. The paintbrush bristles were cut off in a straight line, the better to move the paint around. And oh, the paints! Yellows as bright as lemons, greens and reds that vibrated with intensity.

Other children in William's kindergarten class enjoyed painting, too. But William painted every day that fall and sometimes more than once a day. At first I noticed simple lines and shapes he drew. He crisscrossed the page and seemed to experiment with how fat or thin to paint the lines. He concentrated on how many lines it took to cover a page. Some days he painted several pages orange.

"William, that is a bright color. How does it make you feel?" (I was trained not to ask him what he was painting.) William smiled.

"Count the paintings you did today," I encouraged.

"Four." Together we rolled them up and put a band around them so they could be carried home.

When William mixed greens and reds, the colors muddied, turned brown like the trees outside. Sometime during that fall, shapes emerged—circles, rectangles. I recognized boxes, grass, flowers and cars. He painted quickly, like he was running out of time. It was as if he wanted to get something right by repeating it or see just how many pages he could paint in an afternoon.

Once a month, I had to visit each child's home, and I found that I couldn't wait to see William's grandmother. Since William had done so many paintings, I knew that Sally must have them all taped up on the walls of the simple house where she and William lived. It was a mill house with only a few pieces of furniture. Now Sally could have original art on her walls.

As I parked in front of the house and walked to the door, I wondered which paintings would be hanging. I stepped out of the winter chill into the slightly warm room and looked around. There were no paintings hanging up anywhere. The walls were as bare and dirty as ever. Then I saw them, the stack of fresh paintings that William just finished that day. They were curled in the fireplace, burning slowly. Only the corners of them did I see. William's art had done something important. It had started their fire. It was the much-needed spark to get the flames going and warm the room.

In spite of my shock, I beamed at William and his grandmother. I understood. How could I expect to see paintings on the wall when warmth was what they needed? For the rest of that year, William got as many opportunities to paint at the easel as he wanted. Each day he took home bundles of his work and discarded newspapers as well. Art could still start a flame.

Gail Davis Hopson

A Letter to My Preschoolers

Children: a great way to grow people.

Source Unknown

Someday, when you're as big as me, you may not remember your preschool teachers. But still, I want to help you understand how very much you mean to me.

You have taught me what it's like to be a kid again: I know all of the new children's songs and have become fond of your new favorite, "Hi Ho Silverware!" I've learned to sing and dance again, and I'm an expert on the "hokey-pokey" and the "little tea pot." I know how many blocks you can stack before I have to yell "look out!" as they all come crashing down. I know that "even if play-dough smells good, you still can't eat it," and "even if your hair is sticking out, scissors are for cutting paper." I've learned what hiding in the corner means. I've become best friends with Barney, Raffi and Eric Carle, and at times I even look to them for guidance and support. I know all the names of all the dinosaurs, and that manatees do have ears, but they're on the inside of their bodies. I've learned that bubblegum toothpaste tastes better than mint, and that markers are better than crayons.

I've learned how much fun it is to hug, kiss and rock in the rocking chair after naptime. I've learned that a kiss is usually better than a Band-Aid and works most of the time. I've also learned what it feels like to be loved like only a child can love, and I've learned that it's one of the best feelings in the world. I've learned how fast you grow and how quickly you change, just like the little caterpillar we kept in the jar who quickly became a chrysalis and then, magically, a beautiful butterfly.

But most importantly, I've learned how wonderful children are and how special each one of you is to me. And although you will very vaguely remember who I was, please know that I will always remember you.

Jennifer L. DePaull

You Can't Judge a William by Its Cover

Never have ideas about children and never have ideas for them.

George Orwell

My preschoolers arrived for the first day of school. Six bouncing, bubbling four-year-olds parading a wardrobe of new, primary-colored clothing. Each head of hair was neatly combed or secured with a fancy bow. Number seven arrived a bit late and came with his own personal style. His name was William.

A thin, gray T-shirt stretched across his chest. It looked washed but never bleached, dried but never folded. The faded words from a faraway theme park emblazoned the front, positioned neatly between the stains of what appeared to be a red drink and mustard. William wore the shirt proudly, like a soldier displaying his stripes. His jeans, worn and discolored at the knees, showed the personality of an industrious little boy. Batman beamed heroically below the Velcro fasteners of his mud-caked shoes.

The children continued to sheepishly enter while

William carelessly checked out the art center. Two little girls came through the door with hooded topcoats, while a dark-haired boy carried a new corduroy jacket. Only a thin red parka, unzipped and untied, warmed William.

Weeks passed and William continued to appear each morning amidst scrubbed faces and everybody else's mommy. He came and went escorted by an anonymous day-care person in a schoolhouse-marked van.

I longed to sneak a brush across his ruffled blond hair or even straighten the half-on, half-off jacket he refused to remove. I daydreamed of escaping for an hour with his shirt, dousing it quickly in water and bleach, then returning it to him, still warm from the dryer. Worst of all, I imagined William's parents, uncaring, uninvolved, never attending to their son's needs. I wished for him a day that was special with a shirt that still had creases from the plastic bag or a pair of shoes that squeaked new rubber across the linoleum. I wondered for what William's parents wished.

One day I met William and his mom and dad at the neighborhood market. He sat comfortably in the shopping cart, positioned between the frozen waffles and the gallon of milk.

"There's Miss Mary!" he proudly announced and marveled that his teacher bought groceries at a store. I exchanged handshakes with William's parents and our conversation began. Suddenly, I saw much more than what William had been wearing. I saw the love in his family.

William's mom spoke a quiet hello, adjusting her uniformed blouse as her son continued to resound my name. Shuffling her coupons, she seemed to struggle for conversation. Occasionally, she reached to straighten the scraggly locks of William's hair or brush away the crumbs of his afternoon snack.

I discovered that William's dad worked as a maintenance man for a nearby industrial shop. His days were long, tiring and often unpredictable. He told me how he'd never finished school but was "real glad" William was getting to learn a lot. Dad had arranged to take the next Friday off, one of his three vacation days, to come sit in the classroom and see, as he put it, "how my son is doing." When his boss told him that might not be possible, he proudly "stood tall and insisted it was important, real important." He looked sad when he said his wife wouldn't be able to come with him.

"Her boss won't let her. She wanted to, but there's no one to take her shift—and besides, there's been lots of layoffs, we couldn't take a chance."

"My mom got off early today!" William said. I rejoiced in his pleasure, sensing it was a luxury seldom enjoyed by the tired woman standing before me.

On Friday, William's dad came as promised. He towered over the four-year-olds when he sat in the tiny chair and colored diligently with the markers. He smiled as he surveyed the room. Then his face became serious and he turned toward me and asked "Miss Mary, is William listening to you?" I assured him of William's attentiveness.

"Is he being polite and saying 'yes, ma'am' and 'no, ma'am'? Because that's real important to me and his mom."

With a weathered hand on his son's shoulder, William's dad continued to speak of a love stronger than the weave of any cloth.

"We want him to learn a bunch of things, but most importantly that's why we're sending him to this school. We want him to grow up and do what's right 'cause that's the right thing to do. We want him to be fair to everyone and not just look at what somebody has or the color of his skin."

I stood there, embarrassed with my own prejudice. For

months, I had judged this family by their son's appearance. Before me stood a plain and simple father who didn't need a woolen jacket with an embroidered logo or new denim jeans to show how he cared for his child. He had chosen for his son something not found in a store or reached from a shelf. He had chosen goodness and kindness and respect. He had given him the gift of love and today, the gift of time.

A few days after the visit, William came to me on the playground. Oddly, I didn't notice his shirt or even if his hair was combed. It was a bit chilly, but he ran across the schoolyard as if it was a summer day, arms outstretched, catching each lift of the breeze. His radiant smile spread wide across his face.

"You know, Miss Mary," he said half out of breath. "My daddy and mommy love me a whole bunch!"

"I know, William, I know. I see that love every day when I look into your handsome face." I hugged him and off he ran into the wind.

Mary Chavoustie

PEANUTS
LOOK, CHARLIE BROWN! A LETTER FROM MISS OTHMAR!

ONLY HER NAME ISN'T OTHMAR ANY MORE...IT'S MRS. HAGEMEYER! SHE THANKS ME FOR THE EGG SHELLS I SENT, AND SAYS SHE'LL KEEP THEM FOREVER...
2-15

AND SHE SAYS SHE MISSES ALL THE KIDS IN HER CLASS, BUT YOU KNOW WHO SHE SAYS SHE MISSES MOST? ME!!

Tm. Reg. U. S. Pat Off.—All rights reserved
Copr. 1960 by United Feature Syndicate, Inc.
SCHULZ

Eric

There is no education like adversity.

Benjamin Disraeli

I'd never noticed how tall he was until I stood between him and the objects of his anger. I'd noticed his good looks, his stylish clothes, the gold cross in one ear. I'd noticed his flawlessly smooth skin. How could I not notice his skin? He defined himself by his blackness. I'd noticed his muscular body before, too, but until now I had not been conscious of its power. I knew that he played varsity football, that he was one of the stars, that he carried a weekly progress report and that slipping marks could disqualify him from play. But he was doing well in my class. In fact, he knew more about African history than I did—and occasionally regaled us with stories about his proud ancestral past. He participated avidly in discussions: He was inherently opinionated, always vocal, sometimes loud, often angry. Now and again I cautioned him to temper his passion with logic.

I'd witnessed his anger before, though he'd always kept it leashed. Our discussions analyzing social issues naturally brought out strong emotions, and I'd certainly heard him express his opinions before, sometimes eloquently, always vehemently. This time it wasn't passion but anger that strained at a tether held tight, taut, tense.

We'd been studying the Civil War, focusing on our ancestors—the ones we could all be proud of: Harriet Tubman, Frederick Douglass, William Lloyd Garrison, Harriet Beecher Stowe. We'd discussed how it had been the abolitionists—ordinary people, men and women, black and white—who had made slavery, not secession, the issue of the Civil War. We had compared the issues and methods of protest then to issues and methods of protest now. We'd debated ideology; we'd discussed practicality. Today we'd been watching excerpts from Ken Burn's nine-hour Civil War documentary.

Classroom desks were arranged so that students faced each other, with a wide aisle down the middle of the room. With the exception of two tittering boys in the back corner, the students had been funereally hushed throughout the film. At this moment, the students were riveted to the scene on the television screen: a recalcitrant slave's gruesomely welted back. The awful photo seared our collective conscience. The photo screamed silent pain across the quiet room, hushed, except for the two obnoxiously giggling boys in the two back-row corner desks.

I'd seen his anger before, so I wasn't surprised when it exploded. He erupted like hot lava, challenging the two inattentive boys with his fists. I moved quickly between him and the other two, and noticed for the first time how tall he was. I saw his nostrils flare as he glowered over my head. I saw the veins stand out in his neck. I smelled his body more distinctly than his cologne. Touching his arm lightly, I felt his taut muscles like knotted black walnut. "Please . . ." I soothed, "please sit down." *Please,* I continued in my head, *this is not the way to raise the consciousness of those two boys, not now, not this way.* I don't know how many minutes passed while we stood facing each other. I could feel my heart beating. Or was it his? At that moment, there were no others in the room: only him and me.

Minutes passed. The bell rang. Students exhaled their communally held breath and quietly left the room. The two boys, scared silent by his anger, exited the far door. As he and I stood squarely facing each other, frozen in time by our emotions, I pictured the awful welted back of the Negro slave in the photo, and I sensed the impotent torment of the young black male who stood before me.

I had known his anger before. But until now, until today, I had not known his anguish.

Willanne Ackerman

10

INSIGHTS AND LESSONS

We worry about what a child will be tomorrow, yet we forget that he or she is someone today.

Stacia Tausher

Chuck

Chuck was in my high-school English honors class. He was a writer of great promise. So, when he told me he had been accepted into the journalism program at the University of Missouri, I wasn't surprised.

During his freshman year at college, Chuck stopped by school a few times to keep me posted on his progress. We reminisced about our work together several years before. We had developed public service radio commercials to raise money for twenty-three sick and abandoned Cambodian babies who were being cared for by a nurse friend of mine in Thailand, a place far away yet close to our hearts. Chuck was instrumental by helping to raise several thousand dollars. It was an activity that in some ways transformed our formal relationship into a friendship. Whenever we got together on his visits, my spirits were always buoyed as he was filled with the joy of life.

In his sophomore year, it was discovered Chuck had lung cancer and had only a short while to live. So he left school to come home to be near his loved ones.

I went to see him one day, and in that mysterious way that some seriously ill people have, he reached into a deep place of his rich humanity and made us laugh for most of the afternoon. As I left him and hugged him good-bye, I felt confused and angry. There seemed to be no sense in what was happening.

About six weeks later, Chuck died. It was a great loss for everyone, especially for his family. The youngest of nine children, Chuck was talented and full of promise. More importantly, he was a good and decent person, a just man.

When I went to his funeral, his father asked to speak with me. He took me aside and told me that several weeks before, Chuck had asked him to go over his possessions and memorabilia with him so that he might select a few things to be buried in the coffin with him. He told me how bittersweet the assignment was. How his heart, the heart of a father, nearly burst with love and sadness. In the end, Chuck chose six items, including an essay he had written in my class some years before.

He told me that Chuck had always kept the piece because he liked the message I had written to him at the bottom of the last page. In that little note, I affirmed his talent as a writer and I urged him to be responsible for the gift, to be committed to it as something special. That encouraging postscript would now go with Chuck across the great divide.

I was touched and grateful for the extraordinary gift Chuck gave me that day. His wonderful gesture gave the teacher in me a vital insight, one that would change my life. His taking my reassuring note with him into eternity offered me a tremendous opportunity for impacting students' lives. I felt reenergized with a sense of purpose that was greater than ever.

Whenever I forget my purpose, I think of Chuck, and I am reminded of it once again: Teachers have the power to affect hearts and minds for a long time. Some would even say for eternity.

Gerard T. Brooker, Ed.D.

The Greatest Lesson

My father was dying of cancer, and there was no way that I, a registered nurse, my husband, a surgical resident, or any of our medical and nursing friends, colleagues or professors could save his life. The one thing our family could do was to care for Dad at home until his death, so that he could be with the wife, daughters, son and sons-in-law who loved him so very much.

During the last summer of Dad's life, I was a doctoral student at the Division of Nursing of New York University and was taking a required research course that met twice weekly. Those two classes were my only respite from the pain and grief at home. Yet, when I left for class, I often worried about Dad and the family.

A week before the course ended, Dad's condition became terminal. I knew I had to let the course professor know that I might be absent from the last sessions of the course. After class, I found him in his office. I did not intend to tell him much about my personal situation, as I knew the professor only as one of his students in a large class. However, he closed the door after I entered, sat behind his desk and, looking at me kindly as if he had unlimited time to talk, asked what he could do for me.

Suddenly, I could not find my nurse's calm demeanor or the words I had carefully rehearsed. I simply put my head in my hands and wept. When I could finally stop crying, I told him the truth about my father and asked if he would allow me to make up the last classes.

The professor paused thoughtfully, looked down at his record book and then gently said, "The course ends for you today. You've been an A student; how would this change in a week? Go home to your father and your family. That is where you need to be."

A few days later, as I sat with my father during his last hours, I knew that the professor's kindness had removed an academic burden from my heart and made it possible for me to give all my energy to my father and to my family during the most difficult time of our lives. As head of the course, my professor had the power to help or make things even harder for me. Dad passed away on the morning of the final examination for the course. To this day, I treasure the memory of being able to be at home with him at the time of his death.

Twenty-three years have passed since that terrible summer, and I now am a tenured, associate professor at another university. Over the years, I have had several occasions to remember that professor's example as I worked with students, dealing with tragedy in their own lives. Yes, I did learn about research methods in his class. However, what I learned from him about the impact of a teacher's understanding and compassion remains the greatest lesson I have had in any course.

Carol Toussie Weingarten, Ph.D., R.N.
Previously published in the Nursing Spectrum

Annie Lee's Gift

Christmas had begun its countdown. At this time of the year, Mrs. Stone admitted having only partial control of her students. Even after twenty-five years of teaching, she was amazed how such a lovely holiday could turn her well-disciplined students into spirited, noisy elves.

"Mrs. Stone, I spilled glue down my new pants," whined Chris.

"Mrs. Stone, my paper chain won't fit around the tree," complained Faye.

"Danielle is flicking paint everywhere!" squealed a girl from the sink area.

Where were her organized lessons and normal routine? And where was her peace of mind? They seemed to have taken a long recess. This recess, Mrs. Stone feared, would last until mid-January.

"Teacher?" A child's voice called from the activity table. Stepping over scraps of paper decorating the carpet, Mrs. Stone moved to where a few children were finishing calendars for their parents' Christmas gifts.

"Yes, Annie Lee?"

The little girl tossed back long, shining hair and answered politely. "Uh, if I finish my calendar, could I take it home tonight? My mother wants to see it. She might have to go . . ."

"No, Annie Lee," responded Mrs. Stone automatically. "You may take it home on Friday like everybody else."

Annie Lee started to protest, but the teacher moved quickly from the table, preoccupied with brushing silver glitter from her skirt.

The Little Drummer Boy's pa-rum-pa-pum-pum suddenly vibrated the room. "Lavenia, please turn off the record player!" To the rest of the class, Mrs. Stone announced, "All right, boys and girls, it is time to clean up."

"Awww . . ." The expected groans of disappointment came and went.

At her desk, Mrs. Stone opened the lid to a small wooden chest and "Silent Night" played. A quiet mood settled over the room as they listened to the familiar carol.

"Shay, would you begin our show-and-tell today?" Mrs. Stone asked, closing the music box.

The boy came to the front of the room and said with a slight boast, "I'm getting a red bike for Christmas."

Mrs. Stone closed her eyes. *Here we go again,* she thought. *I want this and I want that.*

Annie Lee was next to share. Her long hair reflected the sunshine coming through the window as she came forward.

"My mother is sick and can't make the cookies for our party on Friday," she said.

Mrs. Stone's eyes narrowed. *Mrs. Brown is never here for Annie Lee,* she thought. *She always has some excuse. She couldn't attend PTA or parent-teacher conference. I wish she'd take her parenting responsibilities more seriously.*

Annie Lee edged close to her teacher's desk and the music box. Her eyes sparkled as she spoke, and one finger tenderly traced the Madonna and child painted on the lid. "When my mother gets well, she's going to buy me a music box exactly like yours, Mrs. Stone."

The teacher smiled and answered, "That's nice, Annie Lee, but it couldn't be *exactly* like mine. You see, this is very old. It was my great-grandmother's music box. Someday, I'll give it to one of my children."

The following day Annie Lee brought a thin strip of red velvet ribbon to her teacher's desk.

"Mother went to the hospital last night but she gave me this ribbon to wrap around the gift I made for her," she said.

"The ribbon is very pretty," said Mrs. Stone. Then she added, "I'm sorry your mother is in the hospital."

"Daddy said I could bring the calendar to the hospital if you . . ."

Mrs. Stone interrupted. "I've already told you that we will wrap them tomorrow and take them home on Friday."

Annie Lee looked disappointed, then her face brightened. "Mother made this for you!" she said happily and laid a red velvet bookmark in front of Mrs. Stone. Then she turned and skipped away. The teacher barely noticed the little girl's hair was dull and tangled and uncombed.

Friday came. The overdecorated Christmas tree stood in the center of the room. Mrs. Stone wore the cranberry red dress she wore every Christmas and Valentine's Day. The children entered the room noisily. But Annie Lee's chair was empty.

Feeling uneasy, Mrs. Stone sat down. She did not want to know the reason Annie Lee was not at school; one more burden to add to her twenty-five years of accumulated frustrations was more than she could bear.

As if in answer to her unspoken question, a student monitor entered the room and handed her a folded note. Trembling, Mrs. Stone read the principal's hastily written note: "I thought you'd want to know. Annie Lee Brown's mother died early this morning."

Somehow Mrs. Stone managed to get through the day. When the party was over and the children had gone home to enjoy their holiday, she stood alone in her classroom and cried. She cried for Annie Lee, Annie Lee's mother, for herself and for the calendar that was intended to bring joy but didn't—and the red velvet bookmark so undeserved.

Mrs. Stone left school very late that night. Stars twinkled in the sky above, lighting the way to Annie Lee's house. In her hands, she carried the precious music box as if it were the wise man's treasure itself. She looked up at the brightest star and prayed the music box would help return Christmas to both their hearts.

Glenda Smithers

Old Miss Mac

A teacher affects eternity; he can never tell where his influence stops.

Henry Adams

Miss Macklewein had a real knack for keeping the kids on their toes. She was a master educator and an ornery woman. This colorful eccentric taught English, and conjugations were her specialty. Miss Macklewein put the fear of God in all of us; we both feared her and liked her, too, for that matter. And for good reason. Consequences were sure and quick. "Old Miss Mac," as the kids secretly called her, was an equal-opportunity teacher; she discriminated against everyone. While some teachers believed in the "don't smile until Christmas" theory of student management, Miss Macklewein simply believed in "Don't *ever* smile." It really worked for her. Nor did Miss Macklewein believe any student when it came to homework; hence she didn't feel the least bit of empathy for any excuse a student might give when any assignment was not completed and turned in on time. When Linda Rund said she didn't have time to do her homework because she had to watch her brothers and sisters while her father took her mother to the hospital to have the new baby, and when Steve Yoder told her he hadn't done his homework because he played in the evening's Junior Varsity football game against the Spencer Mohawks, in Spencer, Iowa, and didn't get home until 11:30, she retorted, "I didn't ask you *why* you didn't have your homework done; I asked *if* it had been completed. I'll see you after school!" Even when a student gave a reason, like "I didn't do it because I didn't know how," it was no use. All excuses went unexcused. This sort of accountability meant we always did our grammar homework. It also stimulated a real buddy system. If anyone from English class asked you if they could copy your completed assignment for Miss Macklewein's class, you forked over your paper—because if a student didn't have his work done, the entire class was assigned additional homework. It was safe to say she ran a tight ship. Old Miss Mac was a work of art—a perfect candidate to illustrate one of those humorous birthday cards where a cranky old woman on the cover doles out a sarcastic comment about getting older. She certainly looked the part. Old Miss Mac's long hair was dyed pitch black. She wore it parted in the middle, with two braids—each going in opposite directions, wrapped around her head. We were sure that she powdered her face with white cornstarch. On each cheek sat two perfect circles of bright red rouge. Her tiny pursed lips were painted vivid red, as were her fingernails. This already imposing image was over-shadowed by her trademark sheer black nylons with the heavy black seams running up the backs of her legs. When she turned her back to the class to demonstrate on the blackboard the obvious simplicity of the elaborate complexity of diagramming, all eyes checked to see just where those seams might be heading off on this day! For some unknown reason the students took a great deal of interest in those seams. Should they be crooked, we would all look at each other and begin a round of uncontrollable laughter, all the while not letting Old Miss Macklewein think that she was the object of our witty humor. It was a huge mistake to be caught laughing; when her eyes fell upon you, you'd better stop immediately, because if Miss Macklewein saw you smirking, she would call you to the board and in front of everybody, make you diagram the exercises in the review section of the book.

Besides being a masterful educator, Miss Macklewein was very effective with her students. For her you got your homework done, you got to class on time and once in class, it was unlikely that you spent your time writing notes to your friends or doing anything else that would break your concentration from the work at hand.

It's surprising how much you can learn when you're paying attention in class! My day of reckoning with Old Miss Mac came unexpectedly as I watched the school bus pull away after delivering thirty-some other kids and me to school one crisp spring morning. It wasn't the sight of the bus that made my heart stop and my stomach seize; it was the realization that I had left my backpack carrying my precious, all-important English homework under my seat in the bus, and the bus was now on its way to the district office. I knew without that homework I was a dead duck, and because it was Friday I would be the scourge of the class, being the one responsible for a hefty homework assignment for everyone over the weekend. Not to mention the hours of conjugation hell I was sure Old Miss Mac would have in store for me after school.

I had no choice. Whatever it took, I had to get that homework assignment back, and fast! I looked at the plastic watch on my wrist and calculated I had exactly nine-and-a-half minutes before the bell rang for English class. My plan of attack formed instantaneously. Run! Without a second thought I sprinted through the schoolyard. If I could cut through the gymnasium, around the girls' locker room, across the basketball courts, down to the baseball diamonds and over to the football field, I could jump the back chain-link fence, hopefully in time to head off the bus, flag down the driver, retrieve my backpack and run back to Old Miss Mac's class—before the bell rang! My race with the bell was on, and I ran as fast as my legs and feet would take me. I became determination in motion.

Unfortunately, my black patent leather Mary Janes weren't quite up to the task. I made it past the gym and girls' locker in record time, but when the terrain changed from the asphalt of the basketball court to the dew-covered grass of the baseball diamond, the smooth leather soles of my Mary Janes sent me tumbling down the hill leading to the dugout. The grass had just been cut and was left in large piles approximately three feet high and about as wide, ready to be collected later in the afternoon after it had dried out a bit. As luck would have it, my crash course placed me headfirst into one of those grass mounds. For a moment everything went GREEN! Now I understood why they waited until the grass dried to collect it. It's because wet grass clings to everything, and I was covered with it. I must have looked like the Loch Ness monster scrambling around on my hands and knees, sputtering as I tried to get the hundreds of blades of grass off me. And then I remembered—the homework, Old Miss Mac, the bus! I leaped to my feet, and once again the race was on. Panicked, I checked my watch; my green collision had cost valuable time. I had five minutes left. *I can still make it!* I said to myself.

As I ran over the fifty-yard line of the football field I saw the bus round the corner, headed for my anticipated point of interception. Waving my arms, running with all my might and yelling to catch the bus driver's attention, I jumped onto the chain-link fence and crawled my way up to the top of it. With my shoe wedged tightly in the chain link I balanced myself on the top of the fence and swung one leg over to the other side. Now straddling the fence, I tried to swing my other leg over, but my Mary Jane was so tightly wedged into the chain link and my position so awkward, I was stuck. Again the vision of Old Miss Mac entered my mind, and a feeling of utter helplessness and doom ran through my body as I heard the rough engine sounds of the school bus pass behind me and continue down the street. Tears of frustration and dread streamed down my cheeks. I had failed, and to make matters worse I was stuck on top of the fence covered with wet grass and mud. All I could do was cry. And then I heard a familiar voice. "Bettie Burres, is that you up there?" I strained to turn my body so I could see who was talking to me from behind. It was Mr. Lewellen, the bus driver. "I just happened to glance up in my rear view mirror and saw you squirming up there. I figured you were after something pretty important. Here, let me help you with your shoe." He gently unbuckled my shoe so I could free my foot and helped me down off the fence. "Is this what you were after?" he said as he handed me my backpack. My arms flew around his waist as I hugged and thanked him. And once again Old Miss Mac's ominous figure entered my mind, and I realized I had ground to cover if I was to have any chance of beating the bell. So with a boost from Mr. Lewellen I was back over the fence, across the football field, through the baseball diamond, up to the basketball courts, around to the girls' locker room, left to the library and down the hallway to the second door on the right. I entered Old Miss Mac's classroom gasping for air, covered with blades of fresh green grass in my hair, and all the way down to my shoes. I looked as if I'd played nine innings. As I slipped into my seat with seconds to spare, I felt an incredible feeling of accomplishment, relief and pride, somehow knowing that day, I'd learned the true meaning behind Rudyard Kipling's words, "We have forty million reasons for failure, but not a single excuse."

I wasn't the only one who learned Old Miss Mac's lesson, nor am I the only one who admired her. Even Donald Kleppe respected her and had learned more from her than any other teacher in his years of schooling, or so he said at the twenty-year class reunion. At first, I was surprised that Donald had been the one selected to do a tribute to Miss Macklewein, because on more than one occasion she had said to him, "I've shown you twice; how much more explanation do you need?" (What she really said was, "Just exactly how dumb can you be?") She expected an answer to the question. Not that Donald could give one. Grammar just wasn't his subject. She called Donald "The Mental Giant." When she needed to get his attention she would say, "Let's ask The Mental Giant." On cue all eyes turned in his direction, waiting for him to notice that a question had been fielded and that a reply—from him—was in order. Eventually he would notice that all had become quiet. With a look of sincerity he invariably asked, "Why is everyone looking at me?" But on second thought, I realized that Donald knew her nature and so, by smiling sweetly and feigning innocence, he skillfully transformed Miss Macklewein's use of him as the butt of the joke into an out for not producing an answer to her question. Donald knew what he was doing.

"Old Miss Mac was a great teacher because she demanded excellence from all of us," Donald said in the speech honoring her. "Could that woman get our attention, or what! Old Miss Mac scared me to death. She had the congeniality of a pit bull." He laughed good-naturedly and then somberly added, "Old Miss Mac was great because she cared so much. What a phenomenal educator.

She was simply the best. So unwavering in her commitment! I learned in her class first, and then again and again throughout my life, that we either make excuses or get the job done."

I looked at the sea of my classmates' faces at the reunion—all faces were smiling.

"To care about your students as much as she did is to love them," Donald continued. "If the old gal was with us tonight—though she probably is—I'd give her a hug and a kiss and tell her what a huge part she played in the successes I've known throughout my life." After a long pause he said, "So, this is to the teacher who made us all wet our pants. I loved her for it! I suspect the rest of you probably feel the same way. Thanks, Miss Macklewein." He paused again and added, "You were a real jewel. You made such a huge difference in my life. Thank you." And to seal his words, he held up his glass, a gesture of toast in her honor. With that, the master of ceremonies cleared his throat, wiped his eyes and stepped down. And the rest of us dabbed at our tears. Clearly, we revered—and adored—this woman, a master educator who taught us to put aside all excuses and simply get the job done. What an important contribution and skill this would be to our lives—and throughout our lives.

Bettie B. Youngs, Ph.D., Ed.D.
1976 Iowa Teacher of the Year

"Sure, maybe I'm an under-achiever. But did you ever stop to think maybe you're an over-demander?"

The Problem Class

There is no more noble profession than teaching. A great teacher is a great artist, but his medium is not canvas, but the human soul.

Anonymous

Several years ago, along with several other faculty members, I helped develop a course to increase the chances of student success in college. Beyond the traditional study tips, orientation, reading, writing, study and test-taking skills, the class was also designed to foster personal growth on many levels. An additional objective of the course was to build a sense of community within the class, as we're a community college with no dorms, fraternities, sororities, basketball teams or other organized sports.

To varying degrees, the class achieved its objectives. Studies we conducted showed that those students who completed the course tended to stay in school and do better in their classes. I had taught the class for several semesters and deeply enjoyed each experience. I learned as much as the students about human nature and how to solve problems.

Then came the class from hell. It started out badly—most of the students didn't want to be there; they couldn't see the need or purpose of the class and felt it was a waste of their time. Factions among the students developed. They argued with one another. They constantly put each other down. In groups of two or three, students banded together and formed mini-cliques. They were reluctant to work together on many of the group projects that were required for the course. It was a teacher's nightmare come true.

After about four or five weeks, I couldn't stand it any longer. Something had to be done. In fifteen years of teaching (at that time), I had never had a class like this, and I wasn't quite sure what to do.

Following much reflection I decided that the real problem was they didn't see each other as equal human beings. They couldn't or wouldn't relate to one another.

My solution was simple.

I had given every student a pack of three-by-five index cards at the beginning of the semester to take notes on (or whatever they chose to do with them). I asked them to get out one card.

"Don't put your name on the card," I instructed. "You have ten minutes in which to complete this assignment," I continued. "On the card you have, I want each of you to tell me this: If there were one thing in your life you could change, what would it be?"

With surprisingly little grumbling, the students began. After the allotted time, I collected the cards. I then shuffled them and passed the cards back to the class, each student getting someone else's card.

I considered myself a part of the class, and during every assignment the class was given, I participated as they would. This being so, I had a card of my own and, in turn, had a student's card.

I then randomly selected students to read the card they held. The first student read from her card. "I wish my four-year-old daughter was not deaf." The one deaf girl in the class (no one beside me knew she was deaf) turned so she could read the other students' lips and had a look of understanding on her face.

The next student read: "I wish that my husband's back was better so he could return to work. We have no money, and our car is going to be repossessed next week. I don't know how I'll get to school if that happens."

"I wish that my mother didn't have breast cancer," read another. And so on. And so on.

I stopped after seven or eight students had read their cards. There were tears streaming down the faces of nearly everyone in the class . . . from what had been read to them and from what they were holding.

Without my having to say so, they had realized that they had far more in common than they had thought. Each of them had problems in their lives. Some small compared to others. They could share that. They could relate.

From that point on, the class changed. They worked together. They formed study groups for other classes. They found friends.

Most of those students came back for their second semester of college. They had another reason to go to college besides education—their friends were there.

But that's not the end of the story. After the end of the class session, I collected those index cards and took them to my office where I read them all. One stood out among all others. It was one that had not been read in class. It was the one that brought the tears to my eyes.

Andrew had muscular dystrophy. Most people with Andrew's particular form of muscular dystrophy barely make it to their teens. Andrew was twenty. He came to class every day without fail. He participated in everything.

He had to work physically hard to do his assignments, but he did them all, and he did them well. He was one of the few in the class who never complained or joined in the sniping. He came in his motorized wheelchair along with Ren, a golden retriever who was his helper dog.

Given his physical condition, Andrew's writing was unmistakable. I read his card and was humbled and moved. His reply to the question of "what would you change in your life" was this, "I would be more understanding of people and would like to be a better person."

Andrew died a couple of years afterward of pneumonia, a complication that probably arose from his MD.

I'll never forget what he'd change in his life. It's now the same thing I'd change in mine.

Donald Arney

Permission to Fail

Experience is the name that everyone gives to his mistakes.

Oscar Wilde

Each of us fails from time to time. If we are wise, we accept these failures as a necessary part of the learning process. But all too often as parents and teachers we deny this same right to our children. We convey either by words or by actions that failure is something to be ashamed of, that nothing but top performance meets with our approval.

When I see a child subject to this kind of pressure, I think of Donnie.

Donnie was my youngest third-grader. He was a shy, nervous perfectionist. His fear of failure kept him from classroom games that other children played with joyous abandon. He seldom answered questions—he might be wrong. Written assignments, especially math, reduced him to nail-biting frustration. He seldom finished his work because he repeatedly checked with me to be sure he hadn't made a mistake.

I tried my best to build his self-confidence. And I

repeatedly asked God for direction. But nothing changed until midterm, when Mary Anne, a student teacher, was assigned to our classroom.

She was young and pretty, and she loved children. My pupils, Donnie included, adored her. But even enthusiastic, loving Mary Anne was baffled by this little boy who feared he might make a mistake.

Then one morning we were working math problems at the chalkboard. Donnie had copied the problems with painstaking neatness and filled in answers for the first row. Pleased with his progress, I left the children with Mary Anne and went for art materials. When I returned, Donnie was in tears. He'd missed the third problem.

My student teacher looked at me in despair. Suddenly her face brightened. From the desk we shared, she got a canister filled with pencils.

"Look, Donnie," she said, kneeling beside him and gently lifting the tear-stained face from his arms. "I've got something to show you." She removed the pencils, one at a time, and placed them on his desk.

"See these pencils, Donnie?" she continued. "They belong to Mrs. Lindstrom and me. See how the erasers are worn? That's because we make mistakes too. Lots of them. But we erase the mistakes and try again. That's what you must learn to do, too."

She kissed him and stood up. "Here," she said, "I'll leave one of these pencils on your desk so you'll remember that everybody makes mistakes, even teachers." Donnie looked up with love in his eyes and just a glimmer of a smile—the first I'd see on his face that year.

The pencil became Donnie's prized possession. That, together with Mary Anne's frequent encouragement and unfailing praise for even Donnie's small successes, gradually persuaded him that it's all right to make mistakes—as long as you erase them and try again.

Aletha Jane Lindstrom

"Can I borrow one of your pencils?
Mine has all the wrong answers in it."

Lasting Lessons from a Fifth-Grade Teacher

Teaching kids to count is fine, but teaching them what counts is best.

Bob Talbert

His name was Ray Rinehart, but naturally we—his fifth-graders—called him "Mr. Rinehart." I was a timid ten-year-old on the first day of class, and the teacher's bullfrog rumble made me tremble in my tennis shoes. A man teacher was a new idea to me, and one I didn't like.

One morning, he said, "Pick your best friend in this class and push your desk right next to his."

Huh? We stared at each other.

A girl raised her hand. "Are you telling us to put our desks beside our best friend's desk?"

"I am. This way, you can help each other."

The room buzzed. Other teachers separated buddies. Obviously, this guy didn't have a clue.

When I complained of my new teacher with his weird

notions, my mother said, comfortingly, "Terry, he's just a man. Just a person, like everyone else."

As it turned out, she was wrong. In my life, he turned out to be a person unlike anyone else.

The very next day, as I fidgeted over my page of mimeographed math problems, Mr. Rinehart stopped at my desk. "Trouble?"

I nodded speechlessly.

"Have you asked your seat-mate for help?" Before I could shake my head, he suggested gently, "Why don't you?"

My friend took one look at my paper and said, "How can you work—or even think—in such a mess?" She scrubbed her eraser across my smeary scribbles and half-erasures. "There!" she said. "Start with a clean page. It'll make a huge difference!" It did—and it never would have occurred to me without my friend's advice. *Huh,* I thought. *Well, what do you know?*

Mr. Rinehart on yard duty was different from any other teacher. He didn't have the invisible "I am a grown-up" chalk line drawn around him. We were able to talk with him as if he were our age—no holds barred. In his turn, he spoke with us as if we were adults, listening to our opinions with interest and offering his with no strings attached.

That's the year I was terrified of nuclear war. Frequent bomb drills found us huddling beneath our school desks. Family friends built an underground bomb shelter. In my house, we had a cardboard box of supplies stashed in the hall closet "just in case." My friends and I spent quite a bit of time discussing "when we're bombed." Where would we be? What would we do?

On the playground one day when Mr. Rinehart wandered up, I asked what he thought.

He, never hesitating to share big ideas, said, "Since life

is uncertain, we should celebrate every moment of it." He looked around the blacktopped playground at the kids playing foursquare and jumping rope and leaping for the tetherball and added, almost to himself, "Be sure to do what you most love." It was obvious to me that he was taking his own advice.

I brought to fifth grade a passionate hatred of physical education class. I couldn't organize my too-long legs into a run, couldn't catch, hit or throw a ball. Throughout the years, I had participated in PE only because I was forced to.

Sycamore School's dark gray basement held the cafeteria and a large room for gymnastics on rainy days. That basement room was where Mr. Rinehart held his PE classes, which were lessons in dancing. PE was PE, I figured, my palms wet at the thought of new forms of torture. "Courage," Mr. Rinehart whispered to me the first day.

We waltzed and learned to polka, but mostly we square-danced. Our teacher managed to call, handle the record player, dance and instruct simultaneously. I was amazed to discover everyone—even the most graceful runner, the most gifted ball-player—was stumbling as much or more than I was. Dancing came relatively easily to me. Winter found us strutting to "Jingle Bell Rock," the music and shuffling of tennis shoes and steamy smell of spaghetti from the kitchen an antidote for the black, frigid wind pressing at the basement half-windows.

When I had Mr. Rinehart for a partner, he counted softly in my ear. At the end of the dance, he'd whisper, "You're a good dancer. Don't forget it." It was so much fun, I forgot it was supposed to be PE.

For a social studies project, we were to pair off and give a report to the class. "Be creative," Mr. Rinehart urged us. "Make it fun."

My friend and I, two bashful and bookish introverts,

chose San Francisco as our topic. We sang and danced to a tune from "Flower Drum Song." It started, "Grant Avenue, San Francisco, California, USA!" We practiced every recess, every lunch hour and after school for weeks—until it was second nature. But, in spite of my familiarity with our routine, stage fright clamped my throat the morning of our performance. I fixed my eyes on Mr. Rinehart, who grinned and nodded from the back of the room, seeming not to notice my voice, high and thin with terror.

"Bravo!" he shouted, clapping thunderously, when we made our final bows. No doubt his applause was for victory over self-consciousness more than the caliber of our talent, but no Broadway star showered with roses could have felt prouder than I did at that moment.

"Were you surprised?" we asked Mr. Rinehart after class that day.

"Not in the least." He shook his head. "You were courageous—as I expected you to be."

"I wasn't brave," I confessed. "I wanted to cry or throw up or run out of the room."

"Yes, but you did it anyway—that's called bravery. It's not about how you feel; it's about how you act."

Wow. His words arrowed into me, striking a rare bull's-eye of total understanding. It was one of my life's most tremendous "Aha!" moments.

When Mom asked over meat loaf that evening, "What did you learn in school today?" I doubt I replied, "The very nature of courage."

But I do know I left Mr. Rinehart's classroom equipped with knowledge no quiz could test: truths about cooperation and joy, respect and bravery. Truths about my own uniqueness that have lasted my lifetime.

Terry Miller Shannon

I Touch the Future

When I was a high-school student almost forty years ago, I had little tolerance for my old female teachers with their thick-soled shoes, bulging stomachs, sagging breasts, gray hair and bifocals. I wondered why they didn't retire and give young teachers whom I could relate to a chance to teach and make learning fun.

Now, more than three-and-a-half decades later and facing retirement, I've become the teacher I used to criticize and laugh at so very long ago. I wear cushiony orthopedic shoes every working day. My stomach, breasts and rear not only protrude—they droop. My gray hair demands brown dye every month. I wear bifocals.

What's forced me to face my own professional mortality is this year's batch of new teachers. I now realize how dated I've become. I still prefer whole-class instruction to groups. My classroom writing models come from literary classics instead of rap lyrics. I still grade papers with a red pen. I'm serious and content-oriented, not "fun." But I like to think that I'm a good mentor, that I grade fairly, and that most students appreciate my stern demeanor and realize it's my way of wanting them to take school as seriously as I believe it should be taken. I also believe that even though I've grown tired and old in their eyes, I still have contributions to make in the classroom and to their lives. I love introducing adolescents to good literature and observing their writing mature throughout the year. I delight in seeing a student's poem printed in a school publication or local newspaper. I enjoy watching an enraptured class stare open-mouthed at a student-made video. I rejoice in reading a composition written by a trusting pupil who admitted feeling abandoned and heartbroken the day no one wanted to sit with him at lunch.

I truly admire those who now begin their careers in education. Teachers are faced with ever-increasing incidents of violence and criticism for our students' high failure dropout rates and low-test scores. Yet these same teachers face huge enrollment of special-needs students, youngsters who have been ignored, abandoned and abused, and still others who speak little or no English. These educators spend their own money on teaching supplies in spite of earning an average of forty-three thousand dollars a year. They are faced with the mandate of incorporating service-learning experiences into their curricula, struggling with block-scheduling, ninety-minute classes, required state tests and pleas for year-round schooling, all the while completing paperwork at home most nights and weekends. To describe the plight of today's teachers, this sign hangs in our faculty lounge:

> *If a doctor, lawyer or dentist had twenty-five people in his office at one time, all of whom had different needs and some of whom didn't want to be there and were causing trouble, and the doctor, lawyer or dentist, without assistance, had to treat them all with professional excellence for ten months, then he might have some conception of the classroom teacher's job.*

I've lived with bell schedules, parent conferences,

starting new school years in September and finishing old ones in June so long that I know no other life. I know that the day I leave teaching, I leave the vitality of youth and won't witness daily the joys of discovery I see in these teens as they experience new beginnings: passing their drivers' tests, falling in love, ordering class rings, making the honor roll, scoring a winning touchdown, attending homecoming and prom, signing each other's yearbooks, or walking proudly across the stage to receive that diploma and wave a last good-bye. Maybe I'm reliving my youth each year through these students, and that's what keeps me from changing the constant in life—teaching.

I read in the paper that of all the professions, teachers are considered the most moral, upright and honest. I also read that, according to the Ad Council, 57 percent of Americans cite teachers as contributing the most to society as opposed to the 25 percent who believe that the medical profession gives the most and only 1 percent who believe lawyers do. Each day I witness the competence of my fellow teachers who are dedicated and excellent role models. They are like candles that light others while consuming themselves. They are ignited by the curiosity of children, they like their subject matter and young people, and they know they make a difference in the lives of their students. Teaching is their mission, their calling and like Christa McAuliffe, they can claim, "I touch the future; I teach."

As I reflect on the lessons I've learned over the past years and anticipate my own retirement, I am both amused and humbled while reading one student's end-of-the-year-evaluation: "You would be a great teacher if only you would update your wardrobe!"

Kathy A. Megyeri

11

THANKS

If you can read this, thank a teacher.

Bumper Sticker

Meeting Josiah

I like to listen. I have learned a great deal from listening carefully. Most people never listen.

Ernest Hemingway

It was the last semester before my student teaching in college, where I was majoring in elementary education with concentration in special education. The year was coming to a close, and the stress and pressure were piling up. On top of a breakup with my boyfriend, an argument with my roommate, trying to balance work and schoolwork, I had to finish thirty hours of teaching in the local public schools. I was beginning to wonder if I was really in the right profession. Then I met Josiah.

I was really not feeling well when I woke up that morning because I had stayed up late the night before finishing lesson plans and other assignments that were nearing deadline. I dragged myself out of bed thinking that I couldn't wait to get home and get back under the covers again. I took a shower and got ready, dreading the fact that I had to go into someone else's classroom to work with students who usually hated being dragged out of class and having to miss out on whatever their friends were doing that day. I ran to my car through the rain and dropped my papers on the ground while I stumbled to unlock the door. Just what I needed!

When I arrived at the school I signed in at the office, asked how to get to the assigned room and ventured down the hall to find it. I was going to be working for the next couple of weeks with students who had learning difficulties and behavioral and emotional problems. A colleague of mine met me in the hall and explained that she had also been placed in this class, so we walked in together. The teacher looked up from the magazine she was reading and said, "So, you're the lucky ones today. Do yourselves a favor and get out of this profession now. You'll thank yourselves for it later."

I just smiled and said, "I love working with these students."

The teacher laughed. "We'll see how much you love it after you meet my class."

Several minutes later, students shuffled in. All boys. The teacher placed them at different spots around the room. One of the boys my colleague and I were assigned to was working at a computer with a friend. The teacher said, "One of you can take him. Josiah isn't here yet—late as usual. He must be in trouble again." My colleague decided to get acquainted with the boy at the computer, and I waited for Josiah. It didn't take long before the door flew open and a raging boy flew in. He was tall for his age, wearing old shoes and equally old clothes. His face was red with anger, and he cursed under his breath. He went straight to his desk and flung his chair back. I looked at the teacher and she said, "Meet Josiah. This is usual for him. I just ignore it, and it usually goes away."

Well, I wasn't going to ignore it. This boy was obviously in need of some attention. I pulled a chair next to his desk and explained that I was a student from the university, and I would be working with him on his math for an hour or so every other day over the next couple of weeks. He sat with his head down, still shaking and not showing any sign of hearing a word I said. I went on to say that I knew he needed a moment to himself so that he could calm down, so I would just sit by him until he was ready to talk, and I'd be ready to listen to whatever he had to say. He sat in silence. I thought to myself, *Great. Just what I need today.* Not knowing what else to do, I spoke again. "Josiah, I know you're feeling hurt about something right now. I came here today to help you with math, but if you need to talk about something else, I'd be glad to do what I can."

He looked up and said, "You're pretty, and you smell good." Well, I wasn't sure what to say to that, but it was a start. While I was looking for the right words, he looked up again and said with a slight stutter, "I'm ready to do math now."

I smiled and gave him an assessment sheet to complete so I could see what level he was on and know where he needed the most help. He got out his pencil and silently started his work. The television and the computer were making an awful lot of noise, and I could tell he was having trouble concentrating. After he had done a few problems, he said, "I'm sorry for not talking to you earlier. It's just that no one has ever offered to listen to what I had to say. They usually just yell at me."

He went on to complete his assessment sheet while I sat watching him. I couldn't believe that such little attention meant so much to him. How could he have made it to the seventh grade with no one asking to listen to his problems? It was nearing time for me to leave, so I told him to finish the problem he was on and that would be enough for today. As I was packing up my things, he looked me straight in the eye and asked, "Are you coming back?"

I told him I'd be back in two days and he said, "Good. I can't wait to see you!" That sure made my day!

The next day flew past, and I was looking forward to working with Josiah again. I asked the teacher if I could work with him outside that day because the room was so distracting.

Josiah seemed in good spirits as he came into the room, until he got to his desk. The teacher had cleaned it out and threw away some papers that were apparently important to him. He went into an instant fit, yelling at the teacher, "You had no right to do that! I hate school and hate being alive! I wish I was dead!"

I gave him a minute and then asked him to come with me. He yelled at me, "I don't want to do your stupid math! No one cares about me. No one cares if I learn."

"I care, Josiah. But you have to help me if you want me to help you. You need to take a minute and calm down." He stood and followed me outside. After we sat down I said, "Josiah, I want you to look at me for a minute. I want you to look at me and really listen to what I have to say."

He looked up. "Josiah, you *are* important and you *are* special. You may not realize it now, but you have special gifts to offer this world. I don't care what anyone says; I know you can do whatever you want to do or be whatever you want to be as long as you make up your mind to do it. Don't ever let anyone tell you any different."

He sat in silence staring. I noticed his red, watery eyes. While I was getting my materials out, he said, "I'm sorry I took my anger out on you. You're the only person who's nice to me, and I didn't mean to hurt your feelings. I'm glad you teach me."

We went on with the lesson, and all went well. He struggled with the first few problems, but as I showed him how to work them out, he soon caught on and was so pleased with himself for successfully completing them he kept asking me to make up some more. The more I made up, the more he asked for, exclaiming, "I never knew I could do this before!"

Josiah continued to work hard on his math and showed improvement every day. He was so proud for learning to do the problems that other students in his grade were doing, and he was eager to work extra problems every day. Finally the last day came for us to work together. He asked me why I couldn't come back anymore, and I explained the best I could.

As I packed my teaching materials he said, "Miss Adams."

"What?" I said, without looking up.

"Miss Adams, I want you to look at me and really listen to what I have to say."

I looked up, and his eyes filled with tears as he took my hand and stuttered, "Thank you so much."

"Oh, I enjoyed it. I had fun!"

"No, I really mean it. Thank you. You were very special to me and helped me very much." With that, he gave me a huge smile and walked out of the library.

I sat there in tears. In the four years I had worked with students of all ages in all different schools, Josiah was the first to ever say "thank you." He gave me the inspiration and courage I needed to go into the teaching profession full force. Today, in my own class for children with special needs, I still quote Josiah, "I want you to look at me and really listen to what I have to say."

Denaé Adams Bowen

Gifts of Love on Valentine's Day

We make a living by what we get, but we make a life by what we give.

Winston Churchill

Like so many teachers, I try hard to make each of my students feel they are special. I am not a mother, so I look at my students as my children. In a short year, I have the opportunity to touch their lives. I may go to a baseball game, a dance recital or baseball card sale. I want to teach each child that he or she is special because of who he or she is. During one year of teaching a fifth-grade class, I was shown how important my actions and lessons were.

It was toward the end of January when I started seeing notes passed around. This was unusual because the students had many opportunities to speak with each other while doing class activities and because the notes were between students who weren't friends. There was not a certain individual initiator of the notes nor was there just one receiver. They were simply circulating on a regular basis.

These notes were passed for a few days before I asked

several students caught with them why they were being passed. I then lectured the whole class on their disrespect to me as I was trying to teach while they passed papers. I didn't read the notes but placed them in the trash can.

After a week or two, I thought I had put an end to the note passing because the activity subsided. As January changed to February, thoughts turned towards Valentine's Day, but there was very little of the usual talk that goes on with this holiday. The art teacher taught them to make big envelopes to hold their valentines and those were taped to the desks. I passed out a class list of names so students could address their valentines. Finally, on the day before the holiday, the students asked if they would be having a party. I asked them if they thought the last hour of the day would be a fair arrangement, and they agreed. Later they pushed for a ninety-minute time period, and I gave them the old line, "We'll see how the rest of the day goes first."

On Valentine's Day, we went through the morning's lessons with no problem. I was surprised at how calm they were, considering what a holiday like Valentine's Day could do to ten-year-olds. Before the students went to lunch, I told them we would celebrate when we came back. They finally showed some excitement.

When I went back to the cafeteria to pick my students up from lunch, they were not there. I could not understand this, but the assistant principal said the music teacher had taken them. I walked around the building to the music department and circled back toward the cafeteria. In the doorway was the music teacher, who was waiting to greet me. The cafeteria had been cleared with the exception of one chair in the middle of the room. My students all stood before me on the stage as the music teacher walked me to the lone chair in the center of the room.

Candi, my shy little one, spoke into the microphone. "We wanted to do something very special for you because you do so many special things for us. We had many ideas but decided you would like this one the very most. We have put together a talent show for you as our present. We hope you enjoy it."

Each student performed for me that day. There was dancing, singing, a Rollerblade routine set to music, a piano piece, a poetry reading—every child did something in that show. I watched in disbelief. They had choreographed an entire variety show on their own. There was a master of ceremonies, props, scenery and equipment. All the notes that had been passed weeks before were plans for after-school meetings to prepare and organize the show. They had asked for the help of the music teacher to help them get permission to use the stage and operate the sound system.

After an hour-long performance to an audience of one beaming, teary-eyed teacher, the show ended with all the students lined up on the stage. Together they said, "We knew the best gift we could give you would be a part of us. Happy Valentine's Day."

I have never felt so much love on Valentine's Day—for the students and for being a teacher.

Jodi O'Meara

A Note in My Mailbox

The note I picked up from my mailbox at school read, "Call Margaret at 555-6167." Both the name and number were unfamiliar to me, but as a high-school automotive instructor, I got calls all the time from people who were looking for someone to fix their cars. During my lunchtime at school that day, I dialed the number.

"I'm calling for a Margaret," I said.

"Yes, this is Margaret," a voice answered.

"This is Ron Wenn. I have a message here that says to call you," I continued, all the while wondering what kind of car trouble this woman had.

"Oh, I'm glad you called. If you'll just give me a few minutes of your time, I have something to tell you that I think you'll be interested in hearing."

"All right," I answered looking at the clock. I only had a few minutes before I needed to be back in class.

"I'm a nurse at St. Luke's Presbyterian Hospital, and yesterday on my way home from work I was driving down 290 when my car started acting up."

"Uh huh," I said looking at the clock again.

"It was late at night, and I was alone. I was so afraid to pull over, but finally my car just quit, so I coasted to the shoulder. I sat there for a few minutes wondering what to do."

I didn't want to sound impatient, but I really needed to get back to class. "Would you like me to take a look at your car, ma'am?" I asked.

"Just let me finish," the woman answered.

I tapped my pencil on the stack of papers in front of me as Margaret continued her story. "Suddenly, two young guys, about twenty years old, pulled up behind me and got out. I didn't know what these guys were going to do. I was so scared.

"They asked me what happened, and they said that from the sound of things that they might be able to get the car running again, so I popped the hood.

"I sat in the car praying that these guys weren't up to no good. A few minutes later, they yelled at me to try to start the car. I couldn't believe it! It started right up! The guys slammed the hood and told me the car would be fine but that I should take it somewhere soon and get it checked out."

"And you'd like me to take a look at it and make sure everything's okay, right?" I asked.

"No, not at all, just listen," the woman went on. "I was so grateful. I thanked them over and over and offered them money, but they wouldn't take it. That's when they told me they were former students of yours."

"What?" I asked in surprise. "Students of mine? Who were they?"

"They wouldn't tell me. They just gave me your name and the school's number and made me promise to call to thank you."

I couldn't believe it. I didn't know what to say. Besides teaching my students about fixing cars, I always tried to teach them things about life—about going the extra mile, being honest and using what you know to help other people. The thing is I never really knew if the students learned any of this.

"Mr. Wenn, are you still there?" Margaret asked.

"I'm still here," I answered.

"Well, I hope you know how grateful I am," Margaret said.

"I hope you know how grateful I am to you, Margaret. Thanks for calling," I said and hung up the phone.

I walked back to class feeling inspired with the knowledge that my students had helped someone because of what I taught them in my classroom. I had just gotten the greatest reward a teacher could ever get.

Ron Wenn and Nancy J. Cavanaugh

"The name of my composition is More Pay for Teachers."

A Humble Gift

It is the last day of the school year, and I stand empty-handed with no gift to give you.

It isn't that I haven't tried to think of something thoughtful and kind—quite the contrary. For months, I have combed catalogs, browsed specialty shops and department stores, inquired in novelty shops, and even searched the Internet, only to realize that no bauble or trinket or card could express the feelings of a mother's grateful heart for a teacher's loving dedication.

How I wish a colorful bundle of fresh wildflowers could reflect the beauty of your way with children—the constant patience and nurturing, the gentle encouragement. A keepsake basket laden with soothing soaps and bath oils would eventually serve only as a common gift were its sturdy, woven walls not filled to overflowing with examples of the individual ways you have touched the lives of your students.

Jewelry would be nice, but what can I afford that would not soon tarnish or fall quickly out of style? You deserve the gems of royalty for your perseverance and creativity, your devotion and talent.

During the past year, I have given you many gifts, mostly intangible ones.

My first gift arrived at the moment the first school bell rang last August, when I placed in you my trust, believing you would teach my child and respect me as a parent. I added to that my constant and fervent prayers that you would be objective and fair, with the ability to set limitations while offering my child a chance to learn self-control and to soar a bit in the process. I sincerely petitioned that your classroom would be a safe haven for my child to grow and learn, lending itself to a crazy, yet somehow perfect, mixture of self-discipline and controlled instruction. I prayed for your health and your happiness and for your ability to be supplied with the tools necessary to complete your task as teacher and educator and mentor. I offered you my time as often as I could, and my support for your endeavors. Occasionally, I even offered you a challenge when I spoke my mind, sometimes standing firm, sometimes backing down with a renewed assurance or a "wait and see" attitude.

I wish with all my heart that I could put a delicate ribbon on a gaily wrapped package and give you a "special something" to express my appreciation and affection. But I have nothing to give you that would surpass the most precious gift I have ever had to offer and which you already so graciously accepted months ago—the one you have held close to your heart, laughed with and probably cried with, applauded and scolded, lifted and encouraged, molded and shaped—my child.

And today, as my child returns to my side for the summer, the gift I humbly give to you is found deep within my heart. . . .

I give you my thanks.

Amanda Krug

Hall of Fame

"From Hall of Shame to Hall of Fame" read a recent headline when I received the honor of being one of only five teachers inducted into the National Teachers Hall of Fame. Who would ever have imagined that an overweight, rebellious high-school dropout in the late 1960s would become teacher of the year? It certainly wasn't something my parents, my teachers or even I would have thought possible.

As many teens today, I was a confused and angry sixteen-year-old with low self-esteem. Not only was I extremely overweight, but as my grades began to plummet, I gave up trying to compete with my older sister, Donna. She was head cheerleader, prom queen and valedictorian—much as I wanted to be but couldn't. It was much easier to get attention by being the class clown, and the only honor I received in high school was being voted "wittiest." Eventually, however, I became more pathetic than funny when I began drinking, hanging out with the wrong crowd and eventually running away from home.

My mom and dad were hard-working middle-class parents who did all they could to provide a good home. They had been at school with my teachers numerous times, had taken me to doctors, counselors and always bailed me out of trouble or jail whenever they could. The last time I ran away, they couldn't find me for weeks as I stayed any place I could find. I soon found out that the freedom for which I had longed was full of empty promises, nowhere to live, no money and much danger. Once again, as the prodigal child, I found my way home to the family that welcomed me back with open arms. This time, however, their unconditional love set much-needed boundaries and I had to agree to their rules as I reluctantly returned to school.

The first day back was as miserable as I had anticipated. I heard all the names as my peers jeered, "Hey Fatso! " or "The jailbird is back!" I probably would have run away again had it not been for a familiar voice from the end of the hall. Mrs. Alma Sitton, who let us fondly call her "Miss Alma," had been one teacher who had always treated me with respect and dignity. However, she was tough on all of us and immersed us in literature, grammar and speaking. We all knew that if we missed one day of Miss Alma's class, she had neat stacks of make-up work ready to distribute. Now that I had been gone for weeks I would never catch up!

Ignoring the taunts of my classmates, I dutifully trudged down the hall as Miss Alma called to me. As expected, she ushered me into her warm familiar classroom, near the table of missed assignments. I said nothing, as I rolled my eyes, bit my tongue and waited for a lecture to accompany the piles of missed homework. But what came next was totally unexpected. Miss Alma turned toward me with her back to the table and did the most paradoxical, most unbelievable thing that a teacher had ever done to me. She quietly closed the door, put her purplish ditto-streaked hands on my shoulders, looked me straight in the eyes, down to my soul, and then put her arms around me! As she hugged me, softly in my ear Miss Alma whispered, "Debbie, God has great plans for your life if you'll let him. And I'm here for you, too." I vaguely remember the piles of papers she began explaining, but I will never forget her loving smile that elicited the same from me. That ten-second gift of hope and encouragement has lasted thirty years. I don't remember the stacks of missed assignments, but it was at that point that Miss Alma became my hero.

It may have been a surprise to my entire hometown that I of all people would become a high-school teacher of English, speech and drama—just as Miss Alma had been. But it was no surprise to me—or Miss Alma. Twenty years later, having lost one hundred pounds, now married and teaching in St. Louis, I was selected as teacher of the year. I was compelled to return to my hometown and thank the one who had so inspired me. Miss Alma, now retired, was serving at her church social—fish and loaves of bread! How appropriate! As I approached her, I was immediately transformed into that same insecure, anxious teenager, unable to speak. Once again I was enveloped in that warm, encouraging hug. "Oh, Debbie! Look at you! You've lost a hundred pounds! And I heard you have become a teacher—I am so proud of you." I wanted to tell her what an inspiration she had been, how much I thanked her for not only saving my life but also for inspiring me to be all that I watched her model. But I was too choked up to say much of anything at the time.

Now that I have traveled throughout the United States as a member of the National Teachers Hall of Fame, speaking to thousands of schools, businesses and churches, I have always included the inspiring story of Miss Alma. But next week will be the highlight of all speaking engagements. I have been invited to speak at Miss Alma's church. I know I will sob as I tell the Miss Alma story and finally have the opportunity to publicly thank her for being such a role model, such an encourager and the very reason I became a teacher. I have learned that kids don't care how much you know until they know how much you care. Above all else, I can't wait to feel her arms around me one more time and to tell her that I have passed on that hug and encouragement to over ten thousand other "Debbies" who also needed to be reminded that "God has great plans for their lives." I am so proud that many of my former students have also become teachers. The greatest compliment I have received is hearing the words, "Mrs. Peppers, you are my Miss Alma." And so her legacy lives on.

Debra Peppers, Ph.D.

A Typical Day

Try not to have a good time. . . . This is education!

Charles Schulz

As a high-school teacher, I have understandably become concerned not just about the future of our profession but the public perception of it as well. I decided recently, therefore, to take advantage of the so-called "spare" time that I have in my work day to take a leisurely stroll around the building and see for myself just what goes on outside my own classroom.

The first door I passed was that of a math teacher who was providing individual attention to a student who was quite obviously having some difficulty. The student's face said it all: frustration, confusion, quiet desperation. The teacher remained upbeat, offering support and encouragement.

"Let's try again, but we'll look at it from a slightly different point of view," she said and proceeded to erase the chalkboard in search of a better solution.

Further down the hall, I came across the doorway of one of our history teachers. As I paused to eavesdrop, I witnessed a large semicircle of enthusiastic students engaged in a lively debate regarding current Canadian events and issues. The teacher chose to take somewhat of a back-seat role, entering the fray only occasionally to pose a rhetorical question or to gently steer the conversation back toward the task at hand. They switched to role-playing and smaller groups of students chose to express the viewpoints of various provinces. The debate grew louder and more intense. The teacher smiled and stepped in to referee.

Passing the gym balcony, I looked down to see a physical education teacher working with a group of boys on a basketball passing drill.

"Pass and cut away!" he shouted. "Set a screen. Hit the open man."

Suddenly, there was a break in the action.

"Hold on, guys," he said. "Do you guys really understand why we're doing this drill?"

A mixture of blank stares and shrugged shoulders provided the answer, so he proceeded to take a deep breath and explain not only the purpose of the drill, but exactly how it fit into the grand scheme of offense and team play. A few nods of understanding and the group returned to its task with renewed vigor.

The next stop on my journey was the open door of a science lab where, again, a flurry of activity was taking place. I watched intently as a group of four students explained and demonstrated the nature and design of a scientific invention they had created. As they took turns regaling their small but attentive audience about the unique features of their project, a teacher was nearby, busy videotaping their entire presentation.

As I was leaving, I heard her say, "Okay, let's move the television over here and see how you did."

Finally, on the way back to my room, I couldn't help but

investigate the low roar coming from down the hall. Music blaring, feet stomping, instructions straining to be heard above the din. Dancers of every shape and size were moving in seemingly random directions, although their various destinations were obviously quite well-rehearsed. Good things were happening here: hard work, sweat, intense concentration. And then, a mistake. One of the dancers offered an explanation, which led to a discussion among several of them. The dance teacher intervened and facilitated a resolution. A half-hearted plea by one of the students for a quick break fell on deaf ears.

"We'll have our break when we get this part right," she called out. A brief pep talk imploring them to push themselves just a little further seemed to create some new energy, and once again the place was hopping. "Now, from the top . . ."

My excursion complete, I returned to my corner of the school and reflected on what I had observed. Nothing surprising really. It was essentially what I had expected to find: goal-setting, problem-solving, teamwork, critical analysis, debate, discussion. In short, learning.

The only thing that you may have found surprising, but I didn't, was that when I began my journey, the regular school day had already ended an hour before.

Brian Totzke

Start Your Engine

A teacher was trying to impress her first-grade pupils that good penmanship was important. "Remember," she said, "if you don't learn to sign your name, you'll have to pay cash for everything when you grow up."

Bits & Pieces

"You will use this accounting stuff someday," Larry Lease told his Shasta College students. "And if you become wealthy," he would quip, "you can show your appreciation by buying me a Porsche."

Happily for Lease, one of those students took the suggestion to heart. On February 16, a decade after leaving the Redding, California, campus, multimillionaire software developer Robert Sullivan, thirty-six, returned to visit a teacher who, he says simply, believed in him. Under the pretext of having forgotten something in his car, Sullivan lured Lease out to the campus parking lot. When they came to a spanking new fifty-one-thousand-dollar Porsche convertible, Sullivan tossed him the keys. "It's yours," he announced.

"You're kidding!" Lease, fifty-five, recalls saying as he backed away in shock from the 217-horsepower sports car. "I felt tears welling up," he adds. "Then I started smiling, and I haven't stopped since."

Sullivan's gesture meant even more to Lease than his former student may have realized. In December 1995, Lease and his wife, Berry, fifty, a newspaper editor, lost their seventeen-year-old son Adam to a car accident. Heartbroken, the once-ebullient Lease cut back on his campus schedule to spend more time with daughter Amanda, eleven, at the family's five-acre Shasta, California, farmhouse. "The last several years have been very difficult," says Betty. "When something so horrible happens out of the blue, it makes you that much happier when something so wonderful happens out of the blue."

Sullivan, too, had waited years for his luck to change. The son of Bert Sullivan, a retired career Marine, and Danny Tweedy, a teacher's aide at a preschool, the high-school dropout left the Army before earning a general equivalency degree. He spent most of the 1980s working in fast-food joints in Redding. One bright spot was the accounting course he took with Lease at Shasta in 1986. Sullivan excelled, even becoming a tutor to other students.

"Larry and I hit it off immediately," he says. Still, friendship with an inspiring teacher wasn't enough to keep Sullivan in school. He spent most of the next year living out of his jalopy. "I was eating cans of tuna, crackers, whatever I could afford," he recalls.

By 1992, though, Sullivan had relocated to the San Francisco Bay Area, taught himself computer software applications and become one of the first employees of what later became Commerce One, an online business software company that went public, ballooning his net worth to nearly forty million dollars. It was more than enough to retire on—which is precisely what Sullivan did. But before moving to a six-bedroom, Tudor-style home on twelve acres in Kentucky with his wife, Karen, formerly a nurse, he had a delivery to make in Redding: one red Porsche. "I just figured it would be a killer gift that Larry could show his friends and have a lot of fun with," said Sullivan. "It makes me feel good to do it."

And it makes Lease proud to drive it. Ever generous, the teacher who used to get around in a 1996 minivan will let just about anyone who asks take the car for a spin. "It's a little scary," confesses Betty. "It's small, powerful, new and expensive—but fun!"

Lease himself, who earns sixty-five thousand dollars a year teaching, might have had a high-flying corporate career. The son of an oil-supply company owner in Long Beach, California, Lease earned an MBA from the California State University campus in his hometown in 1978 and then qualified as a COA. But the former physical education and typing instructor realized that it was teaching he loved, so when he heard about an opening at Shasta, he went for it. Students return the respect. "At the Elks Club last year, a guy bought me a beer and said, 'You were the best teacher I ever had,'" Lease recalls.

The recognition means the world to him. "They don't have to buy you a Porsche—heck, they don't even have to say you're the best," he says, "as long as they got something out of the class."

Christina Cheakalos and Kenneth Baker
People magazine

A Very Special Delivery

While sixth-period charges race toward their lockers, I glance across room 815. Content, I recall the earlier scene of twenty-seven sixth-graders actively engaged in the writing and analysis of poetry. I relish their developing maturity and serious commentary. My mind drifts back to the day's activities, and silently I rejoice for one of my fifth-period students. The honesty with which he shared his struggle to stay out of trouble and remain in school impressed me. I was pleased.

Almost effortlessly, I organize papers and folders, quickly preparing for an afternoon of meetings. I am unaware of the young man standing in the doorway, waiting for my attention. "Are you Ms. Moller?" he inquires. "Yes," I respond, anticipating a message from a colleague. "Here." He hands me a manila folder and walks off. Stapled to the front of the folder is a computer-generated cover with the words, "It's a special delivery for Ms. Moller." Interested, I open the folder. Inside, a forest green piece of construction paper, folded toward the center from the left and right sides, prominently displays a large red heart. In block letters, written on each corner, are the words "Thank you." A small note in the bottom left-hand corner reads, "From Andrew." I shed a tear while opening the card, emotionally preparing to read.

Dear Ms. Moller,

Thank you for helping me when I needed it. Thank you for staying after school to help me with my homework and projects. Because of you, I will go to high school. Thank you for everything you did for me. Thank you for getting me through middle school. One more thing: You are the best teacher!

Sincerely,
Andrew

Overcome, I sit and think of Andrew. *Yes, you are going to high school,* I say to myself. *And for that, I want to thank you.*

I was a first-year teacher when Andrew and I met. Frankly, we had little interaction during that fourth-period English class. It always frustrated me when he did not return homework or come to class prepared. He began most in-class assignments, but rarely completed or turned them in. I commented on his disorganized binder and lectured him about the importance of homework and living up to one's potential. I varied activities, hoping to give him ways to be more successful. Still, Andrew was reluctant to participate and made little progress.

One afternoon, in November of that year, Andrew stood silently behind me. In a quiet yet stern way he said, "I need help with reading. I don't understand." My heart sank, for at that very moment, I felt like a failure. *How could I have not known?*

I suggested that Andrew and I meet during lunch. Although he was reluctant to lose time with his friends, he agreed. Almost daily, Andrew would return to the sixth-grade hallway balancing a lunch tray on top of his discombobulated binder. Together, we created agendas to structure his time. We organized his binder, read together, completed work and got to know each other. I was impressed with his determination and drive. I was intrigued that each small accomplishment delighted him. Formally, I was Andrew's mentor. Informally, he was mine.

Andrew taught me how to teach. He taught me how to be patient, consistent and caring. He taught me that there are many ways to be intelligent. Andrew is why I teach.

On the day I receive my special delivery, I reflect upon the road we had traveled. Following sixth grade, Andrew and I continued to meet on an academic and personal level. Through ice cream and Yahtzee, work and play, we grew. Now he was ready for more. Eighth-grade graduation would be in three months, and indeed, Andrew would be going to high school. The sheer thought of Andrew navigating through the masses of that large building frightened me. Yet, I knew it was time.

Dear Andrew,

Thank you for all that you have given me. You were there to let me help you. Thank you for teaching me how to be a better teacher. If I was "the best teacher," it was only because you were my student. I will forever be proud of what you have achieved.

Fondly,
Ms. Moller

Pauline Moller

What I Learned in Spite of Myself

I was an air-force brat, which is a fine way to learn to adapt to new situations but a rotten way to get to know teachers. I never tried in school, because I always knew we'd be moving again, so why bother to please a teacher?

Then I met Mr. Fogarty.

My family moved for the last time, settling in Cannon Falls, Minnesota, where I finished high school. I was the class clown, but Mr. Fogarty had the nerve to see past my wisecracking surface to the intellect beneath. He had the nerve to expect me to—ugh—learn. Get good grades. Excel.

Naturally, I fought this. I'd been coasting just fine for years. I knew I wouldn't have trouble graduating. I wasn't planning to go to college, so who cared what my G.P.A. was?

I explained this to Mr. Fogarty during our student/teacher conference and left his classroom certain he understood what I required—namely, to be left alone to goof off until graduation.

The next day I discovered he had enrolled me in ISP.

ISP was an independent study program for the super-smart kids. I can't imagine the *strings* Mr. Fogarty must have pulled to get me, with my mediocre G.P.A. and smart-ass attitude, signed up. My jaw dropped when he explained that study hall—precious study hall, formerly used for napping!—would be devoted to working on independent study programs.

"*What* independent study programs?" I shrieked.

He remained unperturbed, although I was standing so close my yelling was blowing his bangs back from his forehead. "Whichever ones you like. Pick any two subjects you want to study."

I was furious at his interference. And a little flattered. Mr. Fogarty thought I was smart enough to be in a class with the likes of Marnie Ammentorp and Kirsten Hammer and Jessica Growette—the really smart kids. The last time a teacher took such an interest in my brain was to ask if I had suffered head trauma as a child, since I napped so much during school hours.

Outwardly, I remained irritated. *I'll fix him,* I thought. *Any two topics? Okey-dokey, pal. You asked for it.*

Mr. Fogarty was a religious man, a devoted father and easily embarrassed. I maliciously decided we would learn anatomy together. It would be torture for him; he'd drop this whole independent study nonsense, and I could go back to reading comics during study hall.

My plan didn't work. He got me a copy of *Gray's Anatomy* and we were off, starting with the names of the bones. All 206 of them. He didn't want to be there. *I* didn't want to be there. But he stuck it out and made *me* stick it out. While we studied metacarpals and metatarsals, he talked about the speech team.

As if it wasn't bad enough that I was memorizing the femur and the coccyx, now he was trying to sign me up for after-school activities. The man was insane!

He needed someone for the storytelling category. I resisted. He persisted. I told him I couldn't memorize a hundred stories in time for the tournament that weekend.

He told me I could memorize a hundred thousand stories if I wanted. "You're not fooling anybody," he said. "I know there's a brain in there. Saturday, 8:00 A.M. Don't be late."

I wasn't late. I was amazed to find myself there, but I wasn't late. I was scared. I was sure I couldn't do the work, but Mr. Fogarty thought I could. And for the first time, I didn't want to disappoint my teacher.

Storytelling is just like it sounds . . . you read a big book of fairy tales (that year's book had 216 stories). Then you draw to find out what story you're supposed to tell. That's why it was important to read every story—if you drew one you hadn't read, you were sunk. You'd be standing in front of an audience and a judge with nothing to say.

I didn't have to worry about that; to my surprise, I'd easily read the stories in time. But I worried about the competition. The other storytellers were all tiny and had bows in their hair and big eyes and wore ruffled dresses. I towered over all my classmates and was darned near as tall as Mr. Fogarty. I was clumsy—always tripping or dropping things or stubbing my toe. I didn't wear bows; my hair was usually skinned back in a ponytail. The other storytellers all looked like Goldilocks; I looked like one of the bears.

"I can't do this," I whispered.

I was wasting my breath; Mr. Fogarty wasn't interested in hearing my protests at this stage. "You'll do great."

"No, I will *not.*"

"Yes," he said cheerfully, giving me a shove toward the stage. "You will."

The key to successful storytelling is to really throw yourself into the story. So I ignored the audience and became Simple Simon, blundering about on the stage as Simon blundered about in his life. I couldn't believe the laughs I was getting.

Mr. Fogarty had been right again; out of fifty storytellers,

I took second place. Team Goldilocks never knew what hit them. After that I took first, second or third place at every tournament. By then I was fast friends with the smart kids; they had decided I was one of them.

Meanwhile, Mr. Fogarty and I were doggedly plowing through *Gray's Anatomy.* I now knew more about bones, cartilage and the nervous system than I ever wanted to know. And Mr. Fogarty told me I had to pick my second independent study program.

I groaned; would the madness never end? I'd accidentally gotten an A in biology thanks to my stupid independent study; I was fast losing my reputation as a slacker. And now I had to pick another topic?

I argued, but we both knew who was going to win this one—the same person who'd been winning all of them. So I picked writing, half expecting him to tell me I shouldn't, or couldn't.

He assigned me essays. He assigned me short stories. He made me read O'Henry, Jackson, Bradbury, Chaucer. After I was saturated with words, he asked me to write. My first short story was about a little boy who kills his mother. I was incredibly proud of the gruesome thing and, although Mr. Fogarty was probably appalled, he encouraged me to send it in for publication. I confidently mailed it to *The New Yorker.*

Naturally, they sent me a rejection letter. I'm amazed they didn't set my story on fire and return the ashes. But Mr. Fogarty was as proud as if they'd printed my story on the cover. "A rejection from *The New Yorker,*" he said admiringly, holding the letter as if it was spun gold. "That's really something. Most people will never see something like this." He put my rejection slip up on the bulletin board so everyone could see that I was (sort of) working with *The New Yorker.* Then he told me to write another story.

Mr. Fogarty was my speech coach and teacher all through high school. He made me laugh; he made me furious; he made me try. Today, I've published six books, with four more coming out in the next two years. One of my books has gone into a second printing, and another won a national writing award, but because it was a sensual romance with some—ahem—explicit scenes, I never dared send it to Mr. Fogarty (making him study anatomy was bad enough). But he deserves a crate of books from me; he deserves a million crates. I owe him more than the books I wrote; he taught me to believe in myself, to have the confidence to dare what everyone else told me was impossible. It wasn't just that he expected me to try—he expected me to succeed. And once I started doing that, I found I had a taste for it. All because a teacher wouldn't give up on the smart-ass new kid.

Mr. Fogarty has touched my life in more ways than I could have dreamed, aside from helping me realize my dream of being published. I'm married to a Harvard graduate, a man from a wealthy family who was eating risotto when I was gulping down corn on the cob, the kind of man I once thought beyond my reach. And those smart kids on the speech team? The smart kids became the smart grown-ups and my dearest friends; our children play together.

Most amazing, I've been asked to teach at a writers' colony next summer. I'm nervous—I've never taught. But I'm going to do it anyway. For one thing, Mr. Fogarty would be appalled if he knew I was chickening out. For another, I've got the chance to touch the life of an aspiring writer, encourage her dream, help her be herself. Change her life forever.

Be a teacher.

MaryJanice Davidson

Yours Are the Hands . . .

A teacher
Takes a hand
Opens a mind
Touches a heart
Shapes the future.

Source Unknown

Yours are the hands that brushed my hair from my eyes when I was in kindergarten. You reassured me, comforted me and made me feel that being away from Mom wasn't so bad after all.

Yours are the hands that clapped to get my attention in first grade. You let me know there was work to be done, as well as time to play in this all-day school. You taught me discipline, fairness and patience, still allowing me to be creative and inventive.

Yours are the hands that showed me how to wrap a May Pole in second grade and make a tissue paper carnation corsage that made my mom cry tears of joy. She still keeps that delicate corsage today.

Yours are the hands that introduced me to geography in

third grade by sharing your stories of travel and adventure. You gave me the desire to learn more about other lands and their people. You made my world bigger.

Yours are the hands that made the numbers come alive in fourth grade. You shared your passion for math and helped me see that math is used in every single part of our lives. You challenged me and made me think harder.

Yours are the hands that showed me technology was a fast train that I should jump aboard in fifth grade. You taught me that the computer was user-friendly and showed me the new age of technology. You showed me my future was indeed going to hold this need.

Yes, throughout my education, yours are the hands that held and patted mine in times of trouble; that wiped the tears when I thought the world was against me; that clapped as loud as my parents when I won the Good Citizen of the Month award; that shook the finger to scold me when I was throwing dirt on the playground; that snapped, waved and directed me in the music presentations of the school plays; that placed the bandage on my scuffed knee; that handed me a "Happy Birthday" ribbon on my special day; and that raised a finger to your lips to ever so quietly remind me that the library was a quiet place.

Yours are the hands that now shake mine, wish me luck, and point me onward to the next level of my education. Thank you. Thank you for helping mold my future and caring as you did all these years, for yours are the hands that will touch my life forever.

Julie Sykes

More Chicken Soup?

Many of the stories you have read in this book were submitted by readers like you who had read earlier *Chicken Soup for the Soul* books. We publish at least five or six *Chicken Soup for the Soul* books every year. We invite you to contribute a story to one of these future volumes.

Stories may be up to twelve hundred words and must uplift or inspire. You may submit an original piece, something you have read or your favorite quotation on your refrigerator door.

To obtain a copy of our submission guidelines and a listing of upcoming *Chicken Soup* books, please write, fax or check our Web sites.

Please send your submissions to:

Chicken Soup for the Soul
P.O. Box 30880, Santa Barbara, CA 93130
fax: 805-563-2945
Web sites: *www.chickensoup.com*
www.clubchickensoup.com

Just send a copy of your stories and other pieces to the above address.

We will be sure that both you and the author are credited for your submission.

For information about speaking engagements, other books, audiotapes, workshops and training programs, please contact any of our authors directly.

Supporting Teachers Around the World

In the spirit of supporting teachers around the world in becoming more effective teachers, we are donating a portion of the proceeds from *Chicken Soup for the Teacher's Soul* to the **International Council for Self-Esteem.**

The Council is a nonprofit organization composed of representatives from over sixty countries networking together to share research, expertise, information and resources related to self-esteem. Their purpose is to promote public and personal awareness of the benefits of a healthy sense of self-esteem and personal responsibility, and to establish conditions within families, schools, businesses and governments that foster these qualities. One of its most important functions is to sponsor conferences and trainings on self-esteem for educators. These have been held in the United States, Norway, Greece, Argentina, Slovenia and Malaysia.

If you would like more information on the Council, their activities, services, resources and future conferences, you can contact them at:

International Council for Self-Esteem
234 Montgomery Lane
Port Ludlow, WA 98365
e-mail: *Esteem1@aol.com*
Web site: *www.self-esteem-international.org*

Who Is Jack Canfield?

Jack Canfield is one of America's leading experts in the development of human potential and personal effectiveness. Jack's experience in the field of education includes being a high-school history teacher in Chicago's inner city, the director of teacher training at a job corps center in Iowa, a director of a master's degree program in Amherst, Massachusetts, and a consultant for over five hundred school systems, colleges and universities in the United States and Canada.

His earlier books for teachers include the bestselling *100 Ways to Enhance Self-Concept in the Classroom* (with Harold Wells), *101 Ways to Develop Student Self-Esteem and Responsibility in the Classroom* (with Frank Siccone), and *Self-Esteem in the Classroom: A Curriculum Guide.* Later (with Mark Victor Hansen) he coauthored *Dare to Win, The Aladdin Factor, The Power of Focus* and the bestselling *Chicken Soup for the Soul* series.

Jack is the author and narrator of several bestselling audio- and videocassette programs, including *Self-Esteem and Peak Performance, How to Build High Self-Esteem, Self-Esteem in the Classroom* and *Chicken Soup for the Soul—Live.* He has been seen on television shows such as *Good Morning America, 20/20* and the *NBC Nightly News,* as well as on his PBS special entitled *Making Your Dreams Come True!* The *Chicken Soup for the Soul* television show can also be seen weekly on ABC.

Jack's speaking clients include education associations in thirty-eight states, twenty state departments of education, and schools of education at over thirty universities. Jack conducts an annual eight-day summer training for teachers, counselors and trainers who want to learn how to build high self-esteem and accelerate the achievement of full human potential in their students.

For more information about Jack's books, tapes and training programs, or to schedule him for a presentation, please contact:

Self-Esteem Seminars
P.O. Box 30880
Santa Barbara, CA 93130
phone: 805-563-2935 • fax: 805-563-2945
To e-mail or visit our
Web site: *www.chickensoup.com*

Who Is Mark Victor Hansen?

Mark Victor Hansen is a professional speaker who in the last twenty years has made over four thousand presentations to more than two million people in thirty-two countries. His presentations cover sales excellence and strategies; personal empowerment and development; and how to triple your income and double your time off.

Mark has spent a lifetime dedicated to his mission of making a profound and positive difference in people's lives. Throughout his career, he has inspired hundreds of thousands of people to create a more powerful and purposeful future for themselves while stimulating the sale of billions of dollars worth of goods and services.

Mark is a prolific writer and has authored *Future Diary, How to Achieve Total Prosperity* and *The Miracle of Tithing.* He is coauthor of the *Chicken Soup for the Soul* series, *Dare to Win* and *The Aladdin Factor* (all with Jack Canfield), and *The Master Motivator* (with Joe Batten).

Mark has also produced a complete library of personal-empowerment audio and videocassette programs that have enabled his listeners to recognize and use their innate abilities in their business and personal lives. His message has made him a popular television and radio personality, with appearances on ABC, NBC, CBS, HBO, PBS and CNN. He has also appeared on the cover of numerous magazines, including *Success, Entrepreneur* and *Changes.*

Mark is a big man with a heart and spirit to match—an inspiration to all who seek to better themselves.

For further information about Mark, write:

MVH & Associates
P.O. Box 7665
Newport Beach, CA 92658
phone: 714-759-9304 or 800-433-2314
fax: 714-722-6912
Web site: *www.chickensoup.com*

Jack Canfield's Teacher Resources

Jack Canfield is available for keynotes, speeches and workshops for educators. His topics include:

Chicken Soup for the Soul
Chicken Soup for the Teacher's Soul
Chicken Soup for the Parent's Soul
How to Build High Self-Esteem
Self-Esteem in the Classroom
Parenting for High Self-Esteem
Self-Esteem and Peak Performance
You Make a Difference!
The Keynote Experience

He has delivered keynotes and workshops for international, national, state and local associations as well as hundreds of school districts, colleges and universities. For more information or to book Jack for an event, call 1-805-481-0327. For more information, go to *www.souperspeakers.com.*

In addition to over fifty *Chicken Soup for the Soul* books, Jack has written three books for educators: *100 Ways to Enhance Self-Concept in the Classroom, 101 Ways to Develop Student Self-Esteem and Responsibility,* and *Self-Esteem in the Classroom: A Curriculum Guide.* For more information on these and other materials, go to *www.jackcanfield.com* or write to Self-Esteem Seminars, P.O. Box 30880, Santa Barbara, CA 93130. Or call 805-563-2935.

Contributors

Several of the stories in this book were taken from previously published sources, such as books, magazines and newspapers. These sources are acknowledged in the permissions section. If you would like to contact any of the contributors for information about their writing, or would like to invite them to speak in your community, look for their contact information included in their biography.

The remainder of the stories were submitted by readers of our previous *Chicken Soup for the Soul* books who responded to our requests for stories. We have also included information about them.

Richard F. Abrahamson, Ph.D., is a Professor of Literature for Children and Adolescents in the College of Education at the University of Houston. An author of more than 150 publications on children's books and reading motivation, Abrahamson is the winner of the Education Press Association Award for Excellence in Educational Journalism. He is a frequent consultant to school districts and keynote speaker at conferences dealing with juvenile literature and reading motivation. He can be reached at the University of Houston, Department of Curriculum & Instruction, 256 Farish Hall, Houston, TX 77204-5027.

Willanne Ackerman wrote this story ten years ago, when she was student teaching at Kennedy High School. Today, she probably wouldn't put herself between two angry young men as she did then, but the move was instinctive. She has never forgotten the lesson she learned regarding the thin line between angst and anger.

Marty Appelbaum is president of the Appelbaum Training Institute, the largest training organization in the United States for those who teach children. Each week this organization provides dozens of seminars on hard-to-handle students. He can be reached at *www.atiseminars.org* or e-mailed at *Martya@ghg.net.*

Herb Appenzeller, Ed.D., has been an athletics director for over forty years. He is an Emeritus Professor in Sport Management from Guilford College and currently an executive-in-residence at Appalachian State University. A member of four sport Halls of Fame, he is also the author/editor of sixteen sport law/sport administration books. He is coeditor of the *From the Gym to the Jury* newsletter.

Don Arney received his Bachelor of Science and Master of Science degrees from Indiana State University in electronics and computer integrated manufacturing. He is Professor and Division Chair of Information Technology at Ivy Tech State College in Indiana. His interests include blues, fishing, people-watching and reading.

Marsha Arons is a freelance writer and video producer. Her stories and articles have appeared in *Good Housekeeping, Reader's Digest, Redbook, Woman's Day* and *Woman's World.* She has contributed to eight books in the *Chicken Soup for the Soul* series. She is married and the mother of four daughters.

Aaron Bacall was a pharmaceutical research chemist, teacher, college professor and now a cartoonist. He has had a lifelong love affair with cartooning. His work has appeared in most major publications including *The New Yorker, Barron's, The Wall Street Journal* and *Reader's Digest.* He has also sold his illustration work to corporations such as Citicorp. He can be reached at *abacall@msn.com.*

Donna Barstow feels blessed to be a cartoonist! Her funny drawings appear in over 180 publications, including *The New Yorker, Los Angeles Times, Reader's Digest, NatureMedicine, Infoworld, Harvard Business Review, Salt Lake Tribune,* six gallery shows and many books, including other *Chicken Soup for the Soul* books. Her favorite topics are relationships, computers, pets and mayhem. You can see more of her work at *www.reuben.org/dbarstow.*

Molly Bernard earned her bachelor's degree from FSU and her master's from Barry University. She has taught students from elementary to college level, has won various teaching awards, and presently teaches American literature and creative writing in South Florida. She also writes poetry and short stories.

Bonnie Block currently trains and consults for childcare providers in Baltimore County Public Schools and at state and national levels. She was Teacher of the Year for Baltimore County and a finalist for the State of Maryland. Bonnie has a passionate commitment to helping individuals achieve success. Reach her at *bbhugs@earthlink.net.*

Denaé Adams Bowen is a teacher for students with learning disabilities in Bethel, Ohio. She enjoys outdoor activities, going to church with her family and especially putting aside housework to spend precious time with her baby girl. Her writing has also been published in *A Second Chicken Soup for the Woman's Soul.*

Suzanne Boyce and her husband, Rick, have worked in education in Missouri since 1978. This story is based on an experience in Rick's school.

Adela Anne Bradlee was born in San Salvador, El Salvador. Her family moved to Palo Alto, California, in order for her father to attend Stanford University. When she married, she moved to Florida and raised two children. She worked as a graphic artist and a freelance writer.

Joan Bramsch is a family woman, writer and educator. Her books are published internationally; her articles in magazines, newspapers and on the Internet. She publishes educational E-Books for Families, and the free "Empowered Parenting Ezine" for readers worldwide. She has a lifetime of wisdom to share. Please contact her at *hijoan@JoanBramsch.com* or visit her Web site at *www.EmpoweredParent.com.*

Gerard T. Brooker, Ed.D., honored by the NEA and with two honorary degrees for international humanitarian work with students, was inducted into the National Teachers Hall of Fame in 1998. He recently completed a book of poems, *A Quiet Conversation,* and can be reached at *teacher_jerry@hotmail.com.*

Les Brown is an internationally recognized speaker and CEO of Les Brown Enterprises, Inc. He is also the author of the highly acclaimed and successful book, *Live Your Dreams,* and the newly released book, *It's Not Over Until You Win.* Les is the former host of *The Les Brown Show,* a nationally syndicated daily television talk show which focused on solutions rather than problems. Les Brown is one of the nation's leading authorities in understanding and stimulating human potential. Utilizing powerful delivery and newly emerging insights, Les's customized presentations teach, inspire and channel audiences to new levels of achievement.

Isabel Bearman Bucher retired from teaching and is having a neverending honeymoon with life. This is her second story for *Chicken Soup for the Soul.* Her first story, "The Melding," appeared in *A Second Chicken Soup for the Woman's Soul.* She has completed a 70,000-word memoir entitled *Nonno's Monkey, An Italian American Memoir,* and continues to write stories of the heart. Many of her students keep her in their lives when they marry, have babies and need help on college exams. She and her husband, Robert, travel, dividing their time between their Taos, New Mexico, Ski Valley cabin and the world doing home exchanges. Isabel's eldest daughter, now a teacher, asks her mother to mentor her, which is a joy and an honor. Please e-mail her at *IBBucher@compuserve.com.*

Leo Buscaglia (1924–98) was a well-loved author and lecturer focusing on the dynamics of human relations, especially the topic of love. His books have been bestsellers from Japan to Turkey, with five at once appearing on The American Best Seller Lists in the 1980s. Visit his Web site at *www.buscaglia.com.*

Michele Wallace Campanelli is a two-time national bestselling author. She was born on the Space Coast of Florida where she resides with her husband, Louis, and pet iguana, Jamison. Michele welcomes fans to e-mail her with comments at *www.michelecampanelli.com.*

Joan Gozzi Campbell, a former fifth-grade teacher, is now a published freelance writer and editor. She also mentors writers in grades 4–12. She enjoys reading, gardening and traveling. She lives in Redding, Connecticut.

Dave Carpenter has been a full-time cartoonist since 1981. His cartoons have appeared in numerous publications, such as *Harvard Business Review, Barrons, The Wall Street Journal, Reader's Digest, USA Weekend, Better Homes & Gardens, Good*

Housekeeping, Saturday Evening Post, as well as numerous other *Chicken Soup for the Soul* books. Dave can be reached at *davecarp@ncn.net.*

Tee Carr, Ed.D., is the author of three books for teachers: *All Eyes Up Here! A Portrait of Effective Teaching, How Come the Wise Men Are in the Dempster Dumpster?* and *School Bells and Inkwells: Favorite School Stories and More!* Tee enjoyed over twenty years as a teacher, principal and university supervisor of student teachers. She and her husband, Jack, both educators, reside in Chattanooga, Tennessee. To order books or reach the author, contact Carr Enterprises, 3 Belvoir Circle, Chattanooga, TN 37412. Call 423-698-5685. E-mail: *drtcarr@aol.com* or fax: 423-698-3182.

Nancy J. Cavanaugh taught third grade for thirteen years and now teaches middle-school language arts. She enjoys writing in her free time, and several of her articles and stories have been published in various magazines. Besides writing, she enjoys reading, working out and traveling. Nancy can be reached at *CavieJean@yahoo.com.*

Mary Chavoustie is a photojournalist who loves life. She enjoys taking readers across Texas and New Mexico with AAA's *Journey* magazines and dabbles with interior design through *Houston House and Home.* Mary's sentimental contributions are included in *Women Forged in Fire, Loving the Children* and *Chicken Soup for the Mother's Soul 2.*

Joan Clayton is a retired teacher of thirty-one years in public schools. Her passion is writing. She and her husband reside in Portales, New Mexico. He is a retired educator, too. His passion is ranching. Joan is a religion columnist for her local newspaper. Her Web site is *www.joanclayton.com.*

James Elwood Conner, Ed.D., AWIP (A Work In Progress), performed in a variety of work roles—ranging from elementary-school teacher, to president of a teacher's college, to master speech writer for a governor—before escaping from a nine-to-five lifestyle. He wants to share his paper, "The Neglected Imperatives in Our Schools." E-mail copies can be obtained *free.* Sorry, no snail mail. He and his wife, Meg, reside at 4505 Leaf Court, Raleigh, NC 27612; e-mail: *jec12624@aol.com.*

Dori Courtney, who teaches in Holly, Michigan, recently received a Masters in the Art of Teaching degree. Her passions include working with and writing for children. Her husband, Mike, and her own children, Erin and Sean, are thrilled that her first published effort is in the *Chicken Soup* series. E-mail her at *MandDCourtney@JUNO.com.*

George Crenshaw is an old pro with a long track record of success. He is an ex-Walt Disney animator, a magazine cartoonist with top sales to top slicks for three decades, the creator of *Nubbin* by King Features, creator of *Gumdrop* by United Features, creator of *The Muffins* by Columbia Features, creator of *Belvedere* by Post Dispatch Features and the president of Post Dispatch Features, Masters Agency, Inc.

MaryJanice Davidson has written several critically acclaimed novels and won the

Sapphire Award for Best Science Fiction Romance. Her first book, *Adventures of the Teen Furies,* recently made the young adult bestseller list. She lives in Minnesota with her husband and children, and occasionally runs into Mr. Fogarty. For more information on MaryJanice's books, visit her Web site at *www.usinternet.com/users/alongi/index.html.* She welcomes e-mails at *alongi@usinternet.com.*

Lola De Julio De Maci received her Master of Arts in education and English in 1995 from California State University. She is an elementary-school teacher and freelance writer. The author of several children's stories, Lola loves writing letters, playing word games and watching sunsets. Please contact her at *LDeMaci@aol.com.*

Jennifer L. DePaull earned her Bachelor's Degree in Elementary Education and her Master's Degree in Reading from the State University of New York College at Cortland. She taught preschool at the SUNY Cortland Child Care Center for five years and is now a Special Education Teacher at Dryden Elementary School in Dryden, New York. Jennifer lives in Cortland, New York, with her husband Mark and daughter Grace. The *Letter to My Preschoolers* was written for an annual Teacher Appreciation Dinner at the SUNY Cortland Child Care Center and read to the children, who played a great role in teaching her how to be a teacher.

Daniel Eckstein, Ph.D., ABPP, is president of Encouraging Leadership, Inc. of Scottsdale. He is also an adjunct professor for the Adler School of Professional Psychology, Toronto, Capella University, Minneapolis and Northern Arizona University, Phoenix. Dr. Eckstein is author or coauthor of twelve books, including *Raising Respectful Kids in a Rude World, Leadership by Encouragement* and *Relationship Repair: 'Fix-It' Activities for Couples and Families.*

Joyce Belle Edelbrock, president of RichWorld, Inc., publishes books and educational/multimedia products. As an author, teacher, photographer, model, lecturer and underwater naturalist on Cousteau expeditions, her works appear in publications worldwide, including *National Geographic* and *Smithsonian.* She has a B.A. in secondary education/communications from Eastern Michigan University and did graduate work at SDSU and UCSD. She is the mother of two adult children. She is the author of *Love Your Beauty,* publisher of *Mastermind Your Way to Millions* by Mark Victor Hansen and Robert G. Allen (forthcoming). Her educational programs include *Images of Goodness for Children, The Goodness Dictionary, Writing Excellence Grades K–12* and *Art Lessons 4 You.* Contact her at *joycebelle@aol.com.*

Eugene Edwards received his Bachelor of Science degree from Brenzu University, Gainesville, Georgia in 1997. Eugene enjoys traveling, reading, fishing, golfing, coaching Little League sports and working with children. Please fax him at 404-508-7550, Attn: Helen Hayes.

Joe Edwards is a retired teacher and jazz pianist. He lives in his little "hermitage" in Springfield, Missouri, with his dog, Daisy, and writes short stories. He also produces unique CDs for the Heartwarmers e-zine group.

Earl W. Engleman has been a full-time freelance cartoonist for more than thirty years. His work appears in many major publications in the United States and throughout the world. He can be reached at 6522 S.W. 60th Court, Ocala, FL 34474 or by phone at 352-237-7574.

Benita Epstein is published in *The New Yorker, Reader's Digest, Better Homes & Gardens, Wall Street Journal* and hundreds of other magazines. She was nominated twice for Best Magazine Cartoonist and once for Best Greeting Card Cartoonist by the National Cartoonist Society. Please e-mail her at *BenitaE@aol.com or www.reuben.org/benitaepstein/.*

James R. Estes is a cartoonist whose work appears in numerous publications. He and his wife, Martha, have a son and two daughters: Robert, Kelley and Paige. James likes to read, watch football and take long walks with Martha. He lives in Texas and belongs to the National Cartoonists Society.

Myrna Flood has been an Alaskan businesswoman for the past twenty-five years. An aspiring writer, she resides in Bend, Oregon. Her story is dedicated to her son, Brandon. Her most recent work is "Mr. Eddy's Button Tree," a heartwarming, true story for children and adults. She can be reached at *myrnf@hotmail.com.*

Frankie Germany, a National Board Certified Teacher, has been teaching for thirty years. She currently teaches seventh-grade reading and math at Neshaba Central Middle School in Philadelphia, Mississippi. Frankie and her husband, Robert, live on a farm in rural Neshaba County, Mississippi. Frankie was a contributor to *A Second Chicken Soup for the Woman's Soul* and has been published in various magazines. Reach her at *RGerm33333@aol.com.*

Seema Renee Gersten, a teacher at Hillel Hebrew Academy in Beverly Hills, is the proud mother of Menachem, Shayna and Zevi. She often leads workshops on Developmentally Appropriate Practices in Early Childhood. Seema can be reached at *sgersten@aol.com.* In January 2001, Kelley's story was relived with Zevi's Congenital Bilateral Clubfoot condition. Fortunately, Zevi's feet were fully corrected nonsurgically with Dr. Ponseti's methods at the University of Iowa Hospital: 319-356-3469 or 319-356-1616.

H. Stephen Glenn, Ph.D., speaks to thousands of parents, teachers, counselors and human-service professionals each year. He has been a featured speaker at the White House, where he was honored by Nancy Reagan as one of the USA's most outstanding family life and prevention professionals. His Web site is *www.CapabilitiesInc.com.*

Steve Goodier is the publisher of the Internet newsletter, "Your Life Support System." He sends his e-zine of hope and encouragement to people in over one hundred nations daily. He left his position as senior minister in a Denver, Colorado, church to write and publish his newsletter and has since written numerous books. Steve and his wife (and best friend), Bev, now work together in their home in Colorado publishing the daily e-zine and inspirational books.

You can only get Steve's books here at *www.LifeSupportSystem.com* or by calling 877-344-0989.

Patricia A. Habada earned a master of education degree and a Ph.D. from the University of Pittsburgh. An educator with more than forty years of experience, she now serves as a curriculum specialist and editor of textbooks and religion materials for young children.

Jonny Hawkins is a nationally known cartoonist from Sherwood, Michigan. Thousands of his cartoons have been published in magazines such as *Reader's Digest, Guideposts, Saturday Evening Post, Harvard Business Review, Boy's Life* and over 250 others. He lives with his wife, Carissa, and their two young sons, Nathaniel and Zachary. He can be reached at 616-432-8071, or at P.O. Box 188, Sherwood, MI 49089, or via e-mail at *cartoonist@anthill.com.*

Gail Davis Hopson writes and tells stories that instruct, entertain, inform and inspire. Presently, she is writing stories to be turned into picture books. As a storyteller, Ms. Hopson is available to perform and conduct workshops for groups of one to one hundred. "William" grew out of a seminar for student teachers on using stories in the classroom. E-mail her at *gghopson@aol.com.*

Linda Kavelin-Popov is cofounder of The Virtues Project™, a multicultural initiative to make the virtues accessible in everyday life. She is coauthor of *The Family Virtues Guide* (Penguin/Putnam, 1997) and *The Virtues Project Educator's Guide* (Jalmar Press, 2000). She is an inspiring international speaker on personal and global transformation. Visit her Web site at *www.virtuesproject.com.*

Rich Kornoelje serves as the principal of Riley Street Middle School in Hudsonville, Michigan. In 2001, he was named the Outstanding Administrator of the Year by his alma mater, Grand Valley State University. He can be reached at *rakornoe@hudsonville.k12.mi.us.*

Amanda Krug is a full-time homemaker and "sometimes" writer. She and her husband, Michael, are raising their "perfect-for-us" children: Abby, Lilli, Evan and Grant, in their beloved Hoosier homeland. Amanda's story is dedicated to her sister, Larietha, whose love and talent for teaching knows no boundaries. Contact Amanda at *krug_family@iquest.net.*

Larry L. Leathers is a retired chemistry teacher and Science Department Chairman from Downers Grove Illinois High School (North) with thirty years tenure. His education includes: B.S. in Chemistry Education, Eastern Illinois University; M.S. in Chemistry, Indiana State University; Doctoral Courses and Research for nine summers financed with National Science Foundation Grants at Montana State, Colorado State, Hope College, Northern Illinois University and Illinois Institute of Tech.

Leon Lewandowski, devoted to his family, teaches in Santa Barbara. He's created a fund that awards student scholarships based on academic improvement. Leon has written three books and is completing his first for children. He's recently finished his sixth screenplay. For information on these and other projects, please reach Leon at *LEWSKI711@aol.com* or write to 866 Winthrop Ct., Santa Barbara, CA 93111.

Carolyn M. Mason is a freelance writer living in Tuscaloosa, Alabama. She is the mother of two daughters, Callie, 15, and Laura, 12. She's an adjunct instructor of journalism at the University of Alabama. Her work has appeared in *USA Today, Trucker's News, Commercial Carrier Journal, Overdrive Magazine, MSN.com* and *Salon.com.* Currently, she writes a column about marathon running for *Health.com.* She recently completed her first book, *Waxed,* a collection of essays about mothering, parenting and mid-life musings. You can contact her at *marathonmadness@hotmail.com.*

Dennis McCarthy has been a *Los Angeles Daily News* columnist since 1984. He has won numerous journalism awards in his career, including being named "Best Columnist in California" twice by the California Newspaper Publishers Association and "Journalist of the Year" by the Los Angeles Press Club. McCarthy's four-day-a-week column stresses the poignant, human-interest stories of the average working people who step out of the shadows to do something that makes their community better and safer for everyone. He is married with four children, one still living at home drawing a modest allowance.

Hanoch McCarty, Ed.D. is a nationally known keynote speaker, seminar presenter, educator and writer. As an educational psychologist, he taught at Cleveland State University for more than twenty years. He has been the featured speaker at national, regional and statewide conferences for school systems, professional associations, corporations and government agencies. To contact him, call 209-745-2212 or visit *www.bestspeaker.com.*

Meladee McCarty is a Program Specialist for the Sacramento County Office of Education. She works to provide educational programs for students with disabilities. Meladee is the coauthor, with her husband, Hanoch McCarty, of *A 4th Course of Chicken Soup for the Soul, Acts of Kindness, A Year of Kindness* and the *Daily Journal of Kindness.* Please contact her at P.O. Box 5, Galt, CA 95632, call 209-745-2212 or fax 209-745-2252.

W. W. Meade started writing at the age of fourteen. His first story was published in *Colliers Magazine* when he was twenty-two. He wrote short fiction for the *Saturday Evening Post, Gentlemen's Quarterly, Good Housekeeping, Ladies' Home Journal* and nonfiction for *Cosmopolitan, Redbook* and *Reader's Digest.* Later he took a position in publishing and became managing editor of *Cosmopolitan* and then managing editor of the *Reader's Digest Condensed Book Club.* His last position in publishing was as president and editor-in-chief of Avon Books, which he continued to do for ten years. Today, Walker is writing nonfiction for *Reader's Digest* as well as many other magazines. His first novel was published in September 2001. Titled *Unspeakable Acts,* it is available from *www.Amazon.com.*

Kathy A. Megyeri, a former high-school English teacher, won a Fulbright, the USIA's Excellence in Teacher Award, and ABC's Education award, "Tribute to

Working Women." She is a previous contributor to *Chicken Soup for the Teenage Soul Letters* and is currently an education consultant in Washington, DC. Her e-mail address is *Megyeri@Juno.com.*

Allison C. Miller received her Bachelor of Science, with honors, from the University of Dayton in 1997 and is working towards her M.A.T. in Biological Sciences at Miami University. She currently teaches fourth grade at St. Ann in Cincinnati, Ohio. Allison enjoys playing and coaching volleyball, frisbee, golf, swimming and reading. Susan and Allison remain close friends, and Jackson is doing well.

Sister Helen P. Mrosla, now deceased, was a member of the Roman Catholic religious order known as Franciscan Sisters of Little Falls, Minnesota. She entered the religious order in 1953. After her period of training, she taught in a number of Catholic schools in Minnesota. She also taught for a period of four years at a public school in Kentucky. Later in her career, she taught at Seattle University. She was also elected vice president of her religious congregation and served in that capacity for a number of years. By way of educational background, she held a Doctorate in Instruction from the University of North Texas, which she acquired in 1983.

Maureen G. Mulvaney, better known as M.G.M., is an international motivational speaker and author of *Any Kid Can Be a Super Star: Practical Parenting Strategies for Real Parents.* M.G.M.'s book is a must for all parents and educators wanting to develop healthy, happy, self-assured, bright, kind-hearted, loving children—in other words, SUPER STAR kids! For information about booking M.G.M. as a speaker for your organization, to purchase her book or to get free "Super Star" insights, visit *www.mgmsuperstar.com,* call 800-485-0065 or write M.G.M. & Associates, 16026 S. 36th St., Phoenix, AZ 85048.

Angela K. Nelson received her Masters of Science in Reading in 1998 from the University of Nebraska at Omaha. She is a remedial reading specialist/mentoring program coordinator for Westside Schools. Angela has devoted her career to at-risk youth. She is an accomplished public speaker and can be reached at *anelson@westside66.org.*

Beatrice O'Brien was a WWII Navy nurse, is a mother of six, and a poet and nonfiction writer. She is the author of *One Track,* a railroad narrative, and volunteers for a veterans' writing project.

Jodi O'Meara was a teacher of a wide range of abilities and ages for nine years before becoming the Exceptional Student Education Curriculum Specialist in Manatee County, Florida. She has dedicated her efforts to individualizing student learning and motivating both students and teachers in this position for the past two years. Jodi resides in Manatee County, Florida, where she enjoys the beaches and triathlons. She can be reached at *Omearaj@fc.manatee.k12.fl.us.*

Linda L. Osmundson, a freelance writer, former teacher and art docent in four art museums—Phoenix, Utah, Denver and Seattle—lives in Ft. Collins,

Colorado, with her husband of thirty-six years. She enjoys crafts, golf, writing, reading and grandparenting. You may reach her at *LLO1413@aol.com.*

Debra Peppers, Ph.D., recently retired from teaching and was inducted into the prestigious National Teachers Hall of Fame. Now a university instructor, author, radio and television host, Debra is also a member of the National Speakers Association and is available for bookings at 314-842-7425, *drpeppers@pepperseed.org* or visit her Web site at *www.pepperseed.org.*

Alice Stolper Peppler has been a teacher, textbook editor and general book editor. She's written educational materials and books on divorce and single parenting, and today has her own business, Alice 'n Ink, which helps new writers get their book manuscripts published. For more information, please check her Web site at *www.apeppler.com.*

Suzanne M. Perry, Ph.D., now the Associate Dean of Teacher Education at Regis University, was also a teacher and principal in Aurora, Colorado. She takes pleasure in quilting, gardening, and especially in spending time with her four children, who she will always love. Please e-mail her at *sperry@regis.edu.*

Stephanie Piro is a cartoonist, designer, mom and cat lover. She is one of King Features cartoon team, Six Chix (she's Saturday!) and she also self-syndicates *Fair Game,* a daily cartoon panel and designs T-shirts and other items for her company, Strip T's. Contact her at *piro@worldpath.net* or *www.stephaniepiro.com.*

Kay Conner Pliszka was a teacher for twenty-eight years. Her extensive work with at-risk teens brought school and community awards from Wisconsin Bell/Ameritech, MCADD, Walkers Point, State Exemplary Educational Grants, and an inclusion in *Who's Who Among American Teachers.* Now a motivational speaker, Kay shares her humorous, turbulent and inspirational experiences from teaching. She may be reached at 1294 Weaton Ct., The Villages, FL 32162 or *K.PLISZKA@prodigy.net.*

Kimberly Ripley is a freelance writer and published author from Portsmouth, New Hampshire. A wife to Roland, and mother of Scott, Judy, Jim, Elizabeth, and Jonathan, she relies on her family's adventures to provide fodder for her writing. Kim is an avid school volunteer and is active within her church. Please contact her at *stealth@fcgnetworks.net.*

Kris Hamm Ross lives in Houston, Texas, and has devoted the past fifteen years as a teacher to helping children discover the power and beauty of the written word. She is a published writer whose favorite subjects include education and the people and everyday events that touch her life. Please e-mail her at *klross@pdq.net.*

Jeff Savage is the award-winning author of over one hundred books for children. He visits schools with dynamic presentations that inspire students to read and write. Jeff lives in the Napa Valley with his wife, Nancy, and young sons, Taylor and Bailey. You can contact Jeff by calling 707-A-BIG-DEAL, or via his Web site at *www.JeffSavage.com.*

John Wayne Schlatter is a freelance contributor to *Chicken Soup for the Soul.* His first book, *Gifts by the Side of the Road,* will be in bookstores by Christmas. Sponsored by Showpath Promotions, he speaks at schools throughout the country on "Creating a Culture of Civility." You can contact him at 607-256-8680.

Terry Miller Shannon writes at her home on the southern Oregon coast. Her humorous rhyming picture book, *Tub Toys* (written with son Tim Warner), will be published in 2003 by Tricycle Press. She can be reached at *tmscs@hotmail.com.*

Robin Lee Shope received her Bachelor of Science with honors at the University of Wisconsin at Whitewater in 1975. She now teaches study skills in Texas. Robin enjoys writing, garagesaling, and e-mailing! She is writing Christian romance/mysteries. You can reach her at *hi2robin@home.com.*

Glenda Smithers lives in Lee's Summit, Missouri. She has two grandsons: Isaiah and Matthew. An elementary teacher for fifteen years in Hickman Mills, Missouri, and director of preschool for eight years in Lone Jack, Missouri, she now depends on public speaking, substitute teaching and summertime travel to spark writing ideas. Smithers is an alumni of Southwest Baptist University and received her Masters in Children's Literature from the University of Missouri at Kansas City. She has been writing since she was seven years old with over three hundred articles, poems, devotions, Sunday school material and plays to her credit. *The Adventures of the Blue Goose* is her latest children's mission book from Beacon Hill Press.

Gloria Cassity Stargel, contributing author to *Guideposts, Decision,* and other publications, urgently needed to know: "Does God still heal today?" The answer? Read her award-winning book *The Healing: One Family's Victorious Struggle with Cancer* ($14.95). Please call 800-888-9529 or visit *www.brightmorning.com* or write to Applied Images, P.O. Box 47, Gainesville, GA 30503.

Melinda Stiles taught English in Wisconsin and Michigan for twenty-one years. She retired and moved to Idaho to write. She has published in *Kalamazoo Gazette, Woven on the Wind* and *Pass/Fail.* She tutors in all subjects and learns with her students. She can be reached at *thel@salmoninternet.com.*

Julie Sykes has worked for the school administrators of Montana for the past nine years. She wrote this story in appreciation for the teachers and staff of Smith Elementary in Helena, Montana, when her two sons, Scott and Jeff, left to go on to middle school.

Beth Teolis, M.Ed., enjoys living her passion of enabling educators to appreciate how significant they can be influencing the lives of their students. Inspired after attending three of Jack Canfield's Self-Esteem Facilitating Seminars, she has authored books and presented workshops for educators and parents so that they may be aware just how important their roles are. Beth is the author of *Ready-to-Use Self-Esteem & Conflict Solving Activities for Grades 4–8* and *Ready-to-Use Conflict Resolution Activities for Elementary Students,* both published by Pearson

Education. To order by phone in the U.S.: 800-288-4745; in Canada: 800-361-6128; and for international orders: 201-767-4900. Beth is president of Life Skills Associates International, a member of the National Speakers' Association, founder of the Canadian Council for Self-Esteem, and a member of the executive board of the International Council for Self-Esteem. Beth is now on a task force to initiate ParentCoaching™ at the Adler Professional Schools so that it will reach all parents. You may contact Beth at *teolis@msn.com.*

Marikay Tillett of Huntsville, Alabama, retired in 2001 after twenty-eight years of high-school English teaching. She is currently a community college instructor and enjoys freelance editing and writing. Her family includes her husband, grown daughter and fourteen-year-old special-needs son. Her e-mail address is *Whatsameta4@aol.com.*

Brian Totzke currently teaches history, civics and sociology at Preston High School in Cambridge, Ontario, Canada. During his nineteen years of teaching, he has also taught economics, law and physical education. He lives in Waterloo, Ontario, with his wife, Sue, also a teacher, and their three boys, Jordan, Zachary and Jacob.

Sue L. Vaughn began teaching on a provisional license in September 1966. She taught in Wise County, Virginia, in a federally funded program for two years. In 1968, she enrolled full-time at East Tennessee State University, receiving a Bachelor of Science degree in 1969. After teaching several more years in Fredericksburg, Virginia, she moved to southwest Florida, where she is currently the Reading Specialist at Mariner High School in Cape Coral.

Joseph Walker writes a nationally syndicated column called "Value Speak." His published books include *How Can You Mend a Broken Spleen?* for Deseret Book Company and *The Mission: Inside the Church of Jesus Christ of Latter-Day Saints* for Warner Books. He and his wife, Anita, are parents of five children.

Karen Wasmer received her Bachelor of Science degree from Illinois State University in Elementary Education. She teaches fourth- and fifth-grade music, beginning band, beginning chorus and she is the gifted teacher in second through tenth grade. She has also taught kindergarten and fourth grade. She and her husband, Kim, are parents of two girls. Kari is at college, majoring in marine biology, and Kate is a nursing major.

Julie Wassom is president of The Julian Group, Inc., a training and consulting firm. She is the author of numerous resources on marketing and sales, including *The Enrollment Building Success Library.* Prior to starting her own company in 1986, Julie taught gifted elementary-school students. A sought-after speaker and business consultant, Julie can be reached at 303-693-2306, 800-748-4334 or *juliewm@ix.netcom.com.*

Carol Toussie Weingarten received her Bachelor of Arts from Barnard College of Columbia University, Master of Science in Nursing from New York Medical College, and Master of Arts and Doctor of Philosophy degrees in Nursing from New York University. An author, educator, speaker and practicing nurse, she is an Associate Professor at Villanova University. Please reach her at *carol.weingarten@villanova.edu.*

Ron Wenn has been teaching high-school industrial arts for nearly thirty years. He has also owned several small businesses including a decorating company, restaurant and bike tour company. He directs invention camps for elementary students and has several patents pending. Contact Ron at *RIDEA@aol.com.*

Marion Bond West has published six books and written for *Guideposts* for twenty-nine years. She is a contributing editor and has contributed to *Daily Guideposts* for twenty-six years. She's an inspirational speaker and also conference teacher for inspirational writing. She was a widow for several years, until marrying a *Guideposts* reader, Gene Acuff. She is the mother of four children and grandmother of six. A number of her stories have been printed in the *Chicken Soup for the Soul* book series. She wishes she could rescue every stray cat and dog in the world. She may be reached at 1330 DaAndra Dr., Watkinsville, GA 30677.

Sharon Wilkins is an educator, author and speaker. Her popular book, *Ready for Kindergarten,* has 157 fun activities to give preschoolers a giant head start in school (Zondervan, 4th printing). Sharon's experiences include: teacher, preschool director, nominee for Walt Disney's Teacher of the Year, writer of numerous articles and national speaker for parents/teachers on "Raising Kinder, More Capable Kids." Contact her at 480-892-6684, on her Web site at *www.sharonwilkins.com,* or by e-mail at *swilk44@aol.com.*

Bettie B. Youngs, Ph.D., Ed.D., a former Teacher of the Year, is the Pulitzer Prize-nominated author of twenty books published in thirty-one languages, including the popular *Taste Berries for Teens* series; *A String of Pearls: Inspirational Short Stories Celebrating the Resiliency of the Human Spirit; Gifts of the Heart;* and *Values from the Heartland* (from which these stories are excerpted). Dr. Youngs speaks to audiences around the world. Contact Dr. Youngs at 3060 Racetrack View Drive, Del Mar, CA 92014. E-mail: *BYoungsInt@aol.com.*

Permissions *(continued from page vi)*

The Girl in the Fifth Row. Reprinted by permission of Felice Foundation. ©1972 Felice Foundation.

The Teacher. Reprinted by permission of Marion Bond West. ©2001 Marion Bond West.

Roses in December. Reprinted by permission of Herbert Thomas Appenzeller. ©1995 Herbert Thomas Appenzeller.

Danny's Gift. Reprinted by permission of Karen Wasmer. ©1999 Karen Wasmer.

A Great Way to Make a Living. Reprinted with permission from *The School Administrator* magazine.

You Never Picked Me Last. Reprinted by permission of Dr. Tee Carr. ©1997 Dr. Tee Carr.

Why Choose Teaching? and *Great Answer.* Reprinted by permission of Bonnie S. Block. ©1996, 1997 Bonnie S. Block.

Teacher at Last. Reprinted by permission of Gloria Cassity Stargel and Eugene Edwards. ©2000 Gloria Cassity Stargel.

Full Circle (pp. 105–108) by Erin Kelley, from *Why I Teach* by Esther Wright, copyright ©1999 by Esther Wright. Used by permission of Prima Publishing, a division of Random House, Inc.

Anna. Reprinted by permission of Isabel Bearman Bucher. ©1996 Isabel Bearman Bucher.

Born a Teacher and *The Sunday School Teacher.* Reprinted by permission of Robin Lee Shope. ©1999, 1997 Robin Lee Shope.

Begin at the Beginning. Reprinted by permission of Lola De Julio De Maci. ©1998 Lola De Julio De Maci.

Once a Teacher, Always . . . Reprinted by permission of Kay Conner Pliszka. ©2000 Kay Conner Pliszka.

Let's Go, Daddy. Reprinted by permission of Marty Appelbaum. ©1995 Marty Appelbaum.

A Friday Night in May. Reprinted by permission of Carolyn M. Mason. ©1997 Carolyn M. Mason.

Love First, Teach Second. Reprinted by permission of Joan Clayton. ©1981 Joan Clayton.

All Things Grow . . . with Love. Reprinted by permission of Joan Bramsch. ©1980 Joan Bramsch.

Sarah. Reprinted by permission of Michele Wallace Campanelli. ©1999 Michele Wallace Campanelli.

A Bear and a Rock. Reprinted by permission of Sharon A. Wilkins. ©1997 Sharon A. Wilkins.

I Will Always Love You. Reprinted by permission of Suzanne M. Perry, Ph.D. ©1999 Suzanne M. Perry, Ph.D.

A Couple of Teachers and *An Ordinary Woman.* Reprinted by permission of Marsha Arons. ©2000 Marsha Arons.

Coo-Coo-Ca-Choo. Reprinted by permission of Joseph Walker. ©1999 Joseph Walker.

The Bad Word Box. Reprinted by permission of Julie Wassom. ©1995 Julie Wassom.

Need a Hand? Reprinted by permission of Suzanne Boyce. ©1997 Suzanne Boyce.

That's Just Roscoe. Reprinted by permission of Sue L. Vaughn. ©2001 Sue L. Vaughn.

Mother and Child. Reprinted by permission of Patricia A. Habada. ©1991 Patricia A. Habada. Appeared in the *Adventist Review,* December 19, 1991, pp. 12–13.

Promises to Keep. Reprinted by permission of Kris Hamm Ross. ©1997 Kris Hamm Ross.

Goals and Dreams—A Winning Team and *Gifts of Love on Valentine's Day.* Reprinted by permission of Jodi O'Meara. ©1999 Jodi O'Meara.

You Elevated My Spirit. Reprinted by permission of Adela Anne Bradlee. ©1992 Adela Anne Bradlee.

We Never Know. Reprinted by permission of Larry L. Leathers. ©2000 Larry L. Leathers.

The Reader. Reprinted by permission of Leon Lewandowski. ©2000 Leon Lewandowski.

Sergei. Reprinted by permission of Molly Bernard. ©1995 Molly Bernard.

A Tribute to Many Uncrowned Kings and Queens. Reprinted by permission of Daniel Eckstein, Ph.D. ©1997 Daniel Eckstein, Ph.D.

Every Student Can Learn. Reprinted by permission of Meladee D. McCarty. ©1988 Meladee D. McCarty.

Awakening. Reprinted by permission of Beatrice O'Brien. ©1999 Beatrice O'Brien.

Easter in Jackson. Reprinted by permission of Allison C. Miller. ©1998 Allison C. Miller.

Changing the World—One Clip at a Time. Reprinted by permission of Steve Goodier. ©2001 Steve Goodier.

All the Good Things. Reprinted by permission of the Franciscan Sisters of Little Falls, Minnesota. This article originally appeared in *Proteus: A Journal of Ideas,* Spring 1991, Shippensburg University, Shippensburg, PA 17257-2299.

Miss Hardy. Reprinted by permission of H. Stephen Glenn, Ph.D. ©1990 H. Stephen Glenn, Ph.D.

To Beth's First-Grade Teacher. Reprinted by permission of Richard F. Abrahamson, Ph.D. ©1984 Richard F. Abrahamson, Ph.D.

The Magic Pebbles and *I Am a Teacher.* Reprinted by permission of John Wayne Schlatter. ©1992 John Wayne Schlatter.

Mr. Washington. Reprinted with permission from *Mentors, Masters and Mrs. MacGregor: Stories of Teachers Making a Difference* by Jane Bluestein, Ph.D., Health Communications, Inc., ©1995.

The Royal Knights of Harlem. From *Revolution from Within* by Gloria Steinem. Copyright ©1992 by Gloria Steinem. By permission of Little, Brown and Company, (Inc.).

How Could I Miss? I'm a Teacher. Reprinted by permission of Hanoch McCarty, Ed.D. ©1997 Hanoch McCarty, Ed.D.

A Gift from Brandon. Reprinted by permission of Myrna Flood. ©1997 Myrna Flood.

Standing by Mr. Donato. Reprinted by permission of Dennis McCarthy. ©1997 Dennis McCarthy. Appeared in *The Daily News,* April 9, 1997.

One of My Early Teaching Jobs. Reprinted by permission of Angela K. Nelson. ©1997 Angela K. Nelson.

The Big Kid. Reprinted by permission of Joyce Belle Edelbrock. ©2001 Joyce Belle Edelbrock.

Only a Shadow in His Past. Reprinted by permission of Melinda Stiles. ©2001 Melinda Stiles. Originally appreared in *Pass/Fail,* Issue August, 2001. Published by Kleidon Publishing Co.

Let a Miracle Happen and *Permission to Fail.* Reprinted by permission of Tim Lindstrom. ©1979, 1991 Aletha Lindstrom.

Special Needs. Reprinted by permission of Frankie S. Germany. ©1996 Frankie S. Germany.

Moment in the Sun. Reprinted by permission of Joseph Lee Edwards. ©1999 Joseph Lee Edwards.

The Substitute's Surprise. Reprinted by permission of Linda L. Osmundson. ©1999 Linda L. Osmundson.

Miracle in the Gym. Reprinted by permission of Kimberly Ripley. ©2001 Kimberly Ripley.

Benjamin. Reprinted by permission of Dorothy R. Courtney. ©2001 Dorothy R. Courtney.

The Virtue of Excellence. "The Virtue of Excellence—July 16" (adapted), from *Sacred Moments* by Linda Kavelin-Popov, copyright ©1996 by Linda Kavelin-Popov. Used by permission of Dutton, a division of Penguin Putnam Inc.

In Case of Darkness. Reprinted by permission of W. W. Meade. ©2001 W. W. Meade.

Perils of a Preschool Husband (pp. 119–123) by Roy Freeman, from *Why I Teach* by Esther Wright, ©1999 by Esther Wright. Used by permission of Prima Publishing, a division of Random House, Inc.

Excellence Is Love in Action and *Old Miss Mac* by Bettie B. Youngs. Reprinted with permission by publisher Health Communications, Inc., Deerfield Beach, Florida, from *Values from the Heartland* by Bettie B. Youngs, Ph.D., Ed.D. ©1995 Bettie B. Youngs, Ph.D., Ed.D.

The Poems. Reprinted by permission of Jeffrey E. Savage. ©2000 Jeffrey E. Savage.

Positive Reinforcement. Reprinted by permission of Rich Kornoelje. ©2000 Rich Kornoelje.

So Little Meant So Much. Reprinted by permission of Beth Teolis. ©2000 Beth Teolis.

Master Teacher. Reprinted by permission of Marikay Tillett. ©2000 Marikay Tillett.

Brush Strokes. Reprinted by permission of Gail Davis Hopson. ©1997 Gail Davis Hopson.

A Letter to My Preschoolers. Reprinted by permission of Jennifer L. DePaull. ©1998 Jennifer L. DePaull.

You Can't Judge a William by Its Cover. Reprinted by permission of Mary Chavoustie. ©1999 Mary Chavoustie.

Eric. Reprinted by permission of Willanne Ackerman. ©2000 Willanne Ackerman.

Chuck. Reprinted by permission of Gerard T. Brooker, Ed.D. ©1999 Gerard T. Brooker, Ed.D.

The Greatest Lesson. From *Nursing Spectrum,* issue October 18, 1999; p. 24 (*www.nursingspectrum.com*). Copyright 1999. All rights reserved. Used with permission.

Annie Lee's Gift. Reprinted by permission of Glenda Smithers. ©1983 Glenda Smithers.

The Problem Class. Reprinted by permission of Donald Arney. ©2000 Donald Arney.

Lasting Lessons from a Fifth-Grade Teacher. Reprinted by permission of Terry Miller Shannon. ©1998 Terry Miller Shannon.

I Touch the Future (pp. 87–92) by Kathy Megyeri, from *Why I Teach* by Esther Wright, copyright ©1999 by Esther Wright. Used by permission of Prima Publishing, a division of Random House, Inc.

Meeting Josiah. Reprinted by permission of Denaé Adams Bowen. ©1997 Denaé Adams Bowen.

A Note in My Mailbox. Reprinted by permission of Ron Wenn and Nancy J. Cavanaugh. ©2000 Ron Wenn and Nancy J. Cavanaugh.

A Humble Gift. Reprinted by permission of Amanda J. Krug. ©2000 Amanda J. Krug.

Hall of Fame. Reprinted by permission of Debra Peppers, Ph.D. ©1999 Debra Peppers, Ph.D.

A Typical Day. Reprinted by permission of Brian Totzke. ©1997 Brian Totzke.

Start Your Engine. Christina Cheakalos/*People Weekly.* ©2000 Time, Inc. All Rights Reserved.

A Very Special Delivery (pp. 5–8) by Pauline Moller, from *Why I Teach* by Esther Wright, ©1999 by Esther Wright. Used by permission of Prima Publishing, a division of Random House, Inc.

What I Learned in Spite of Myself. Reprinted by permission of MaryJanice Davidson Alongi. ©2001 MaryJanice Davidson Alongi.

Yours Are the Hands . . . Reprinted by permission of Julie Sykes. ©1996 Julie Sykes.

Also Available

Chicken Soup for the Baseball Fan's Soul
Chicken Soup for the Cat & Dog Lover's Soul
Chicken Soup for the Christian Family Soul
Chicken Soup for the Christian Soul
Chicken Soup for the College Soul
Chicken Soup for the Country Soul
Chicken Soup for the Couple's Soul
Chicken Soup for the Expectant Mother's Soul
Chicken Soup for the Father's Soul
Chicken Soup for the Gardener's Soul
Chicken Soup for the Golden Soul
Chicken Soup for the Golfer's Soul, Vol. I, II
Chicken Soup for the Grandparent's Soul
Chicken Soup for the Jewish Soul
Chicken Soup for the Kid's Soul
Chicken Soup for the Little Souls
Chicken Soup for the Mother's Soul, Vol. I, II
Chicken Soup for the Nurse's Soul
Chicken Soup for the Parent's Soul
Chicken Soup for the Pet Lover's Soul
Chicken Soup for the Preteen Soul
Chicken Soup for the Prisoner's Soul
Chicken Soup for the Single's Soul
Chicken Soup for the Soul, Vol. I-VI
Chicken Soup for the Soul at Work
Chicken Soup for the Soul Christmas Treasury
Chicken Soup for the Soul Cookbook
Chicken Soup for the Soul of America
Chicken Soup for the Soul Personal Journal
Chicken Soup for the Sports Fan's Soul
Chicken Soup for the Surviving Soul
Chicken Soup for the Teacher's Soul
Chicken Soup for the Teenage Soul, Vol. I, II, III
Chicken Soup for the Teenage Soul Journal
Chicken Soup for the Teenage Soul Letters
Chicken Soup for the Teenage Soul on Tough Stuff
Chicken Soup for the Traveler's Soul
Chicken Soup for the Unsinkable Soul
Chicken Soup for the Veteran's Soul
Chicken Soup for the Woman's Soul, Vol. I, II
Chicken Soup for the Writer's Soul
Condensed Chicken Soup for the Soul
Cup of Chicken Soup for the Soul
Sopa de Pollo para el Alma, Vol. I, II, III
Sopa de Pollo para el Alma del Adolescente
Sopa de Pollo para el Alma del Cristiano
Sopa de Pollo para el Alma de la Madre
Sopa de Pollo para el Alma de la Mujer
Sopa de Pollo para el Alma del Trabajador

"If you are a teacher, know a teacher, love a teacher or hold one dear to your heart, *Chicken Soup for the Teacher's Soul* is perfect! Today, that teacher probably faces ever-increasing challenges such as coping with huge enrollments of special-need students, as well as youngsters who have been ignored, abandoned and abused. They no doubt spend their own money on teaching supplies and struggle with increased demands for time. This helping of *Chicken Soup* is needed now more than ever to recall the reasons for entering this profession and why one still loves it."

Kathy Megyeri
high-school English teacher, Kensington, Maryland

"*Chicken Soup for the Teacher's Soul* is must reading for everyone. Children make up 25 percent of the population and 100 percent of our future. Now, through the stories in this book, millions of readers can experience the tremendous responsibility teachers accept and their role in shaping our world. What a wonderful 'classic.'"

Sissy Grapes
teacher and strategic coach,
Performance Dynamics, Inc., Carencro, Louisiana

"Ever since I was very young, I knew that I wanted to be a teacher. As I now realize that dream and start my first teaching job, the stories in *Chicken Soup for the Teacher's Soul* reaffirm that I have made the right career choice. I am full of excitement and inspiration to do all that I can to make positive changes in the lives of my students while impacting the future."

Laura Bacon
first-year teacher, Garden Grove, California

"I am a strong advocate for using *Chicken Soup for the Soul* books in my classroom as teaching tools. Since using the books, my students' writing skills have improved dramatically as well as their attitudes about writing. *Chicken Soup for the Teacher's Soul* has been a long-awaited addition to the series as a way for teachers and students alike to share these motivating stories. I have always said that there is no better way to start the school day than with good old-fashioned *Chicken Soup for the Soul*!"

Barbara Robinson
teacher, Denn John Middle School, Kissimmee, Florida

and demonstrate that what we really teach is who we are. This book will be uplifting and an inspiration to anyone who reads it."

Robert W. Reasoner
superintendent, author, presenter,
president, International Council for Self-Esteem

"We've all been touched by one or more great teachers in our lives. The stories in *Chicken Soup for the Teacher's Soul* reminded me of the gifts that I have received from remarkable teachers. One teacher spent countless hours teaching me to read, while another taught me to think about my values and the important decisions we make every day for the rest of our lives. When you read this book, you can't help but give thanks to the teachers who added to your life and played an important role in who you are today."

Michael Couch
assistant superintendent, secondary education,
Santa Barbara High School District,
1986 Santa Barbara County Teacher of the Year

"What teacher hasn't helped a student at-risk in a special way, hasn't found the courage to invite a parent to pay more attention to the special need of their child, or hasn't felt despair at not reaching a student who is hurting? As teachers read these stories, they will see themselves, feel proud to be a teacher and be inspired to do more. I urge others to eavesdrop on the wonderful experiences of those who educate the next generation. This book will inspire readers' generosity in their support of education, personally and financially."

Dwight W. Allen
eminent professor of educational reform, Old Dominion
University, coauthor with Bill Cosby of
American Schools: The $100 Billion Challenge

"Thank you to *Chicken Soup for the Soul* for writing a much-needed book that celebrates the profession that really can profoundly touch our future—teachers! Each and every priceless story will make you laugh and cry, but most importantly, affirm the limitless power teachers can have on our children's hearts and minds. It is truly a testament to the tremendous responsibility teachers take on and the credit they do deserve."

Michele Borba
author, *Building Moral Intelligence: The Seven Essential Virtues That Teach Kids to Do the Right Thing* and *Esteem Builders*

I am a teacher. *Chicken Soup for the Teacher's Soul* is like a 'Warm Fuzzy File' for educators everywhere. Thank you for creating this wonderful book!"

Camie Worsham-Kelly
teacher, Vieja Valley School, Santa Barbara, California

"What a wonderful and touching group of stories I found in *Chicken Soup for the Teacher's Soul.* Surely, every teacher is overworked and underpaid. We all know that. Yet, every teacher has stories like those in this book where gifts with profound depth are bestowed on teacher and pupil alike. Now, with the help of *Chicken Soup for the Teacher's Soul,* those stories are here to be shared with the world to show the real reason teachers have selected their profession: THEY CARE! Bless you for sharing the joy, excitement, frustration and glory of what teachers do on a daily basis."

Bradley L. Winch, Ph.D., J.D.
CEO and publisher, Jalmar Press/Innerchoice Publishing

"I've often said that teachers are our unsung heroes and heroines. The stories in *Chicken Soup for the Teacher's Soul* really bring that message home, and they serve to warm the hearts of those in one of our most noble professions. It is well done and deeply appreciated."

William J. Cirone
superintendent of schools, Santa Barbara County, California

"*Chicken Soup for the Teacher's Soul* is a moving tribute to the influence and inspiration teachers deliver to students every day."

Jason Dorsey
professional speaker and author, *Graduate to Your Perfect Job*

"These beautiful accounts of real experiences provide insight into the joy of teaching, and why many teach in spite of incredible hardships and little recognition. It is a tribute to all who teach, whether they be parents, mentors or professionals. The stories illustrate the tremendous impact we can have on the lives of others

What People Are Saying About *Chicken Soup for the Teacher's Soul . . .*

"In a time when the stresses of teaching threaten to overwhelm—whether from challenging students, curricular mandates or the pressure for higher test scores—these stories offer comfort, reassurance and validation, reminding us that teachers are, every day, sharing their passion and commitment, and indeed touching lives and hearts of the young people in their care."

Jane Bluestein, Ph.D.
author, *Mentors, Masters and Mrs. MacGregor: Stories of Teachers Making a Difference* and *Creating Emotionally Safe Schools*

"On a daily basis teachers strive to make a difference in the lives of their students, instill hope for their dreams and support for their worthiness. *Chicken Soup for the Teacher's Soul* captures the spirit and heart of these true American heroes, its teachers."

Dr. John Hart and Richard Revheim
coauthors, *The Personally Intelligent Teacher*

"I've been a high-school teacher of English, and as a professor and a consultant, I've worked with teachers, parents and students for my entire career. I must say that *Chicken Soup for the Teacher's Soul* is the single most inspiring and affirming book about educators I've ever seen. The stories get to the heart of the daily business of education: the transaction between teacher and student and the incredible power that teachers have to help children discover their own talents and belief in themselves. This book brings hope and heart with every story!"

Hanoch McCarty, Ed.D.
professor of education, Cleveland State University (retired), author, *Motivating Your Students: Before You Can Teach Them, You Have to Reach Them*

"As teachers we are often isolated in our own little classroom worlds and do not always get the positive feedback we would like. I decided to create a 'Warm Fuzzy File' filled with notes, letters and drawings from adults and children alike. I reflect on this file in those moments when I need something to remind me exactly why